liubov popova

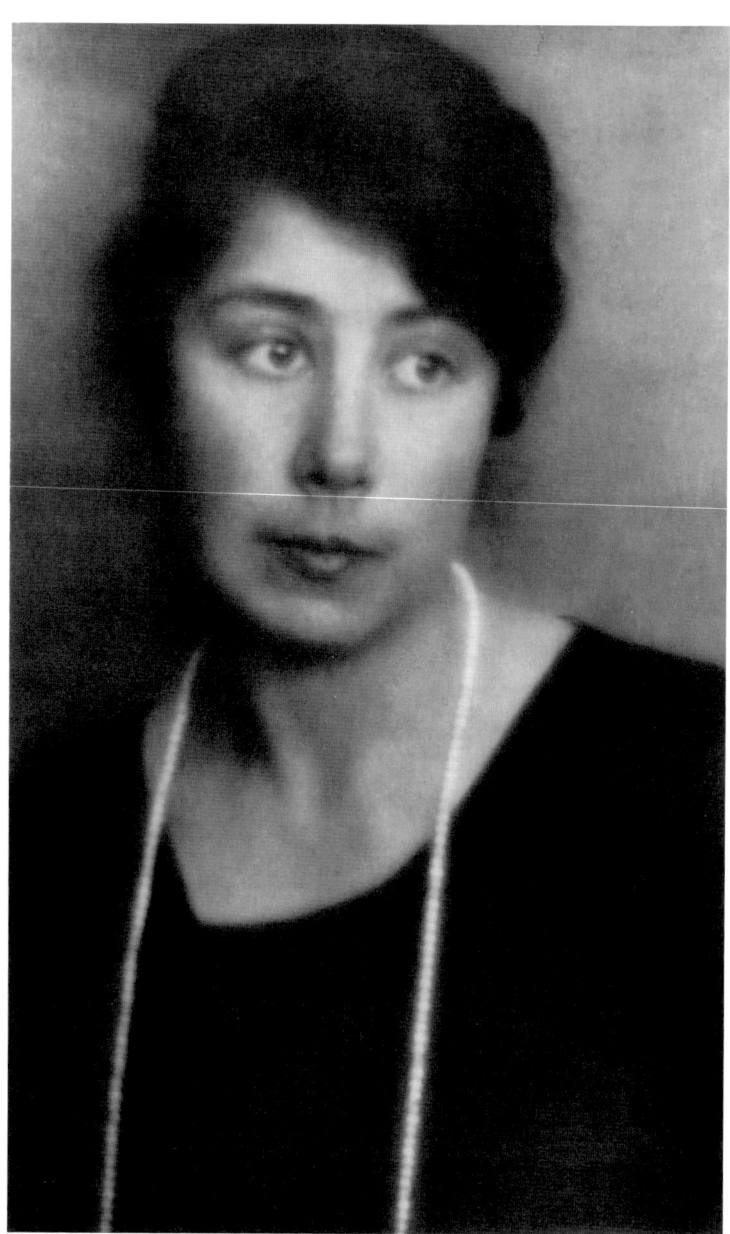

liubov popova

Magdalena Dabrowski

The Museum of Modern Art, New York
Distributed by Harry N. Abrams, Inc., New York

The exhibition and accompanying publication are supported by generous grants from The International Council of The Museum of Modern Art, The Tobin Foundation, The Howard Gilman Foundation, Tambrands Inc., the National Endowment for the Arts, and the New York State Council on the Arts.

Published on the occasion of the exhibition "Liubov Popova," organized by Magdalena Dabrowski, Associate Curator, Department of Drawings, The Museum of Modern Art, New York, in collaboration with the Los Angeles County Museum of Art and the Museum Ludwig, Cologne

Schedule of the Exhibition

The Museum of Modern Art, New York
February 13–April 23, 1991

Los Angeles County Museum of Art
June 19–August 18, 1991

Museum Ludwig, Cologne
October 1–November 30, 1991

Centro de Arte Reina Sofia, Madrid
December 18, 1991–February 16, 1992

Cover: Liubov Popova. *Painterly Architectonic.* 1916. Oil on board, 23½ × 15½" (59.5 × 39.4 cm). Scottish National Gallery of Modern Art, Edinburgh

Frontispiece: Liubov Popova, 1889–1924 (Photographer unknown)

Library of Congress Catalog Card Number 90-633-10
ISBN 0-87070-567-9 (The Museum of Modern Art, clothbound)
ISBN 0-87070-568-7 (The Museum of Modern Art, paperbound)
ISBN 0-8109-6090-7 (Abrams, clothbound)

Edited by Janet R. Wilson
Designed by Emsworth Design Inc.
Production by Tim McDonough and Marc Sapir
Type set by Graphic Technology Inc., New York
Printed by Eastern Press, Inc., New Haven
Bound by Sendor Bindery, New York

Published by The Museum of Modern Art
11 West 53 Street, New York, N.Y. 10019

Clothbound edition distributed in the United States and Canada by Harry N. Abrams, Inc., New York. A Times Mirror Company

Clothbound edition distributed outside the United States and Canada by Thames and Hudson Ltd., London

Printed in the United States of America

contents

foreword

This book has been published on the occasion of the exhibition "Liubov Popova," the first retrospective in the West of this very important but not sufficiently recognized member of the Russian avant-garde of the early twentieth century.
It is hoped that both the book and the exhibition will foster wider appreciation of Popova's work and of her spirit of innovation.

The exhibition has been organized in collaboration with the Los Angeles County Museum of Art and the Museum Ludwig, Cologne. We warmly thank the directors of these institutions, Earl A. Powell, III, in Los Angeles and Siegfried Gohr in Cologne, and our colleagues on their staffs for their active participation in this effort.

The presentation of this exhibition has in large part been made possible through the cooperation of the State Tretyakov Gallery, Moscow; Dimitri Sarabianov, Professor of Art History, Moscow University; the State Russian Museum, Leningrad; and the George Costakis Collection (Art Co. Ltd.). Thanks to their interest and assistance, Popova's works, which have been dispersed since her death in 1924 among Soviet and Western collections, could be brought together here and introduced to a larger public in the West. For the participation of the State Tretyakov Gallery, I want to express our special gratitude to Yuri Korolyov, General Director, and Lydia Iovleva, Deputy Director. For essential loans from the State Russian Museum, we are most grateful to Vladimir Gusev, Director, and Eugenia Petrova, Deputy Director. And for the tremendous generosity of the George Costakis Collection a special debt of gratitude is owed Aliki Costakis.

Generous support for the exhibition has been provided by grants from The International Council of The Museum of Modern Art, The Howard Gilman Foundation, Tambrands Inc., the National Endowment for the Arts, and the New York State Council on the Arts. We deeply appreciate their assistance and encouragement.

This publication has been graciously supported by The Tobin Foundation and The Howard Gilman Foundation. I want to express my very warm gratitude to Robert L. B. Tobin and to Howard Gilman for their interest in this project and for their help in its realization.

This undertaking could not have been accomplished without the exemplary dedication and scholarship of Magdalena Dabrowski, director of the exhibition and author of the main text of this publication. Both the book and exhibition reflect her thorough knowledge of the art of this period, her perceptive eye for its outstanding qualities, and her enthusiastic commitment to communicate her own admiration for these works to a broader public.

Finally, we extend our deep gratitude to all the lenders whose gracious cooperation and involvement have made this exhibition and publication possible.

Richard E. Oldenburg
Director
The Museum of Modern Art

acknowledgments

Since 1962, when Camilla Gray's pioneering book *The Great Experiment: Russian Art 1863–1922* was first published, the art of the Russian avant-garde of the early twentieth century has been the subject of scholarly and public interest in the West. Different aspects of the avant-garde's development have been studied and presented in a number of exhibitions both in Western Europe and in the United States. Yet owing to the limited availability of archival materials and works by specific artists, most of these exhibitions could provide no more than a broad survey; few of these artists, with the exception of Kazimir Malevich, were studied and shown in depth. In 1981, when the Solomon R. Guggenheim Museum in New York presented the exhibition "Art of the Avant-Garde in Russia: Selections from the George Costakis Collection," which familiarized the public with this comprehensive collection of work by the avant-garde artists, it became apparent that the paintings by Liubov Popova stood out on the basis of their quality and originality.

This catalogue and the exhibition it accompanies are the very first attempts in the West to present a synoptic overview of Popova's development, emphasizing her significance as an inventive contributor to the evolution of non-objective art and Constructivism. Despite the importance of her work, the only prior retrospective of Popova's art since the posthumous exhibition in Moscow in 1924–25 was an exhibition drawn from Soviet public and private collections organized by the State Tretyakov Gallery in Moscow in 1989–90 in celebration of the centenary of the artist's birth.

As a committed Constructivist, Popova worked in a broad range of mediums and disciplines, including painting, relief, works on paper, and designs for the theater, textiles, and typography. The works included in The Museum of Modern Art's exhibition were chosen for their beauty as well as their importance to Popova's artistic development. The selection thus highlights the artist's stylistic evolution from the early pre-Cubist phase (1908–12) through the Cubo-Futurist years (1913–15) and the Suprematist and early Constructivist period of her Painterly Architectonics (1916–19) to the later stages of Constructivism (1920–22) and production art (1922–24).

Every exhibition depends on the collaboration, support, and enthusiasm of many people. I would like to express my special thanks to Aliki Costakis, Norman Neubauer, and Angelica Z. Rudenstine of the George Costakis Collection (Art Co. Ltd.) for their unfailing interest throughout the project. Angelica merits particular thanks for her efforts and help at all stages, often under the great pressure of imminent deadlines. I am also grateful to the staff of the State Tretyakov Gallery in Moscow, the State Russian Museum in Leningrad, and the Russian art historian Dimitri Sarabianov for generously lending Popova's works for this exhibition. I am especially indebted to the Tretyakov Gallery's Senior Research Curators Irina Pronina, Oksana Karlova, and Elena Zhukova. In addition, I thank my colleagues Stephanie Barron, Curator of 20th-Century Art at the Los Angeles County Museum of Art; Evelyn Weiss, Chief Curator, Museum Ludwig, Cologne; and Margit Rowell, Curator, Special Projects, Centro de Arte Reina Sofia, Madrid, for their participation in the exhibition.

In The Museum of Modern Art's Department of Drawings my main debt is to Mary Chan, Program Assistant, who patiently, with tireless dedication, took care of all the details of this unusually complex exhibition and catalogue. Her professionalism and support deserve my greatest thanks. Lili Horwitz and Gonzalo Sanchez provided efficient clerical assistance with the manuscript.

Many other people at the Museum contributed to the successful completion of this project, and I am infinitely grateful to all of them. Richard Oldenburg, Director of the Museum, is owed a special debt of gratitude for his enthusiastic support of this undertaking. James Snyder, Deputy Director for Planning and Program Support, skillfully and with great perseverance handled all aspects of the negotiations with our Soviet colleagues. Waldo Rasmussen, Director of the International Program, has played a significant role in raising funds for the exhibition; Elizabeth Streibert, Associate Director, International Program, helped immeasurably with the logistics of international showings. In the Department of Publications I would like to thank Osa Brown, Director; Harriet Bee, Managing Editor; Tim McDonough, Production Manager; and Marc Sapir, Assistant Production Manager, for overseeing aspects of this book and working under impossible deadlines. Janet Wilson, formerly Associate Editor in the department, deserves special thanks for many helpful suggestions that made this book more complete. My gratitude goes also to Michael Hentges, Director of the Graphics department, and Tony Drobinski, the book's designer, for working with great professionalism on a very tight schedule.

Thanks are due also to Richard Palmer, Coordinator of Exhibitions, and Eleni Cocordas, Associate Coordinator, Exhibition Program; to Antoinette King and her staff in the Conservation department, especially Eugena Ordonez, Associate Conservator, who has contributed to the catalogue a very illuminating text on Popova's working methods and materials; to Kate Keller, Chief Fine Arts Photographer, Richard Tooke, Supervisor, and Mikki Carpenter, Archivist, in the Rights and Reproductions department; to Sue Dorn, Deputy Director for Development and Public Affairs, and John Wielk, Manager, Exhibition and Project Funding, in the Department of Development; and to Sarah Tappen, Associate Registrar, for her superb efficiency in coordinating loans. I would also like to extend my special thanks to Margit Rowell and John Elderfield, Director of The Museum of Modern Art's Department of Drawings, for reading my essay and providing valuable criticism. Ingrid Hutton of Leonard Hutton Galleries should be singled out for her assistance and unfailing enthusiasm throughout the project.

Finally, the exhibition never could have been presented without the cooperation of all the lenders listed on page 133, and it is to them that I owe my deepest gratitude.

—M.D.

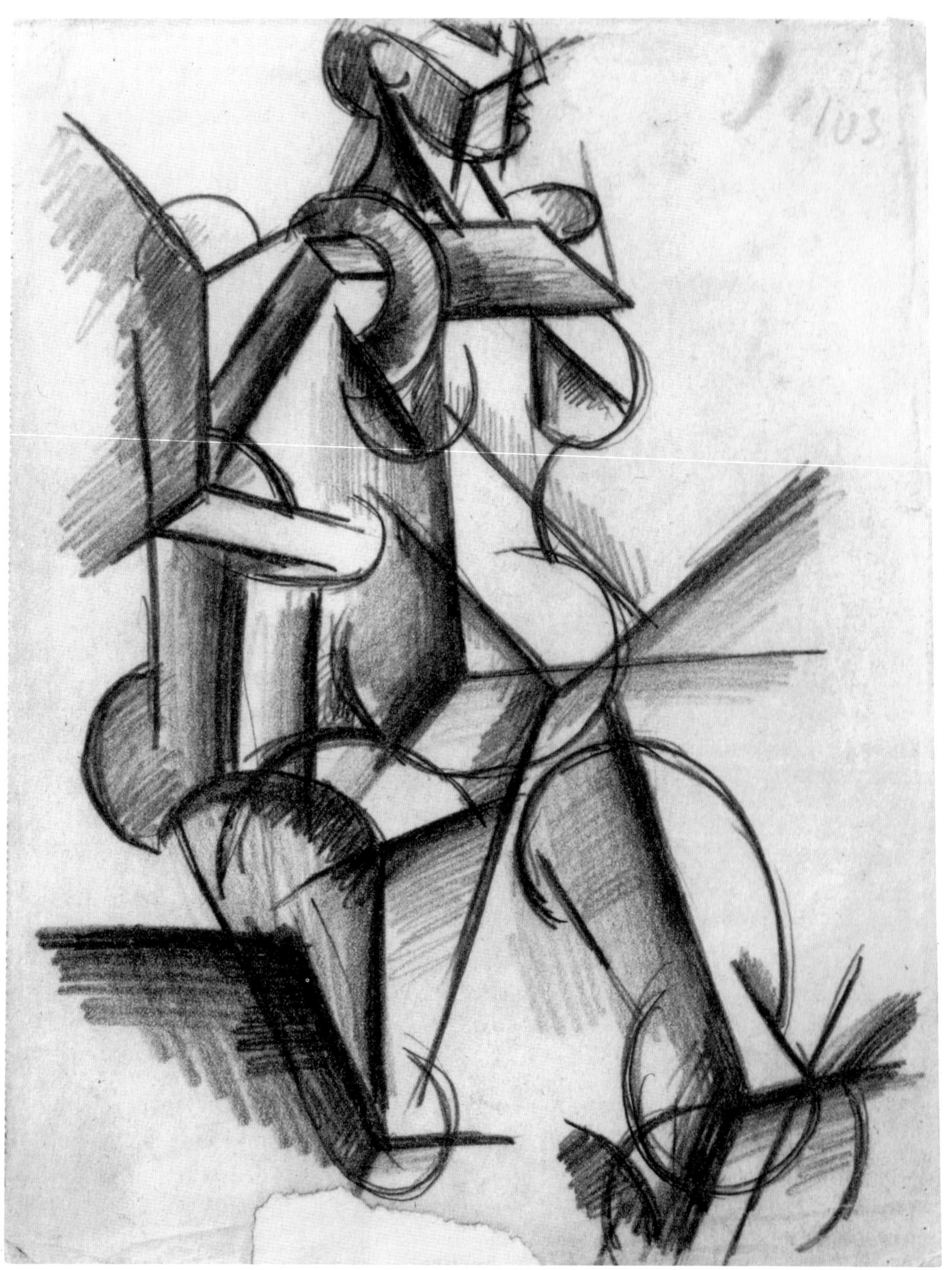

Female Model
1914
Pencil on paper
10½ × 8½″

liubov popova artist-constructor

Magdalena Dabrowski

Although Liubov Popova's mature career spanned only a dozen years, from 1912 to 1924, she produced a sizable body of work that is diverse in style as well as highly innovative. Along with Kazimir Malevich, Vladimir Tatlin, and Alexander Rodchenko, she stands out as one of the four most accomplished artists of the Russian avant-garde in the first quarter of the twentieth century. The work of these artists serves to define important issues in the development of Russian art from figuration to abstraction and, subsequently, from pure art to utilitarian art. Yet in Popova's relentless pursuit of a new visual language compatible with the requirements of modernity and contemporary Russian society, she created a body of work quite different from that of the three other major artists of the period. Unlike Malevich she was not interested in the mystical and spiritual aspects of art; unlike Tatlin she did not work with real materials in real space; and unlike Rodchenko she was not a theoretician.

Popova's evolution follows a path that in many ways was shared by a number of artists of the avant-garde. However, it is essential to remember that throughout all the stylistic changes in her work, Popova's vision always remained rooted in painting. She played a major role in shaping the concepts and ideals of Russian Constructivism during its decade of existence in post-revolutionary Russia. The permutations of her painting after 1919 reflect the transformations of Constructivist concepts, and her oeuvre represents Constructivist painting at its best. Now that many of Popova's works and related documents are available for study, it is possible to evaluate her achievement in a more general art-historical context.[1]

"Artist-Constructor" was the term applied to Popova by her contemporaries in the catalogue of the artist's posthumous exhibition that opened in Moscow in December 1924. In a brief foreword to that catalogue, Popova's artistic path was summarized, and the revolutionary spirit that guided the search for innovative solutions in her work was emphasized:

> A Cubist period (concerned with the problem of form) was succeeded by a Futurist period (concerned with the problem of movement and color), followed by the principle of abstracting parts of objects and then, with a logical inevitability, the abstraction of the object itself. Representation was replaced by the construction of form and line (post-Cubism) and color (Suprematism). In 1917 her revolutionary tendencies came to the fore.... The most productive period of Popova's career took place in the years 1921–24.[2]

In her writings[3] Popova designated the year 1913 as the beginning of her mature independent work. Indeed, her output of the years 1908 to 1912, which included still lifes, landscapes, and studies of trees and human figures, is representative of the then broadly practiced idiom, influenced by Impressionism and Cézanne, that was favored by many Russian artists of the period, including her teachers Stanislav Zhukovski and Konstantin Yuon.

Supplementing these early influences were Popova's numerous trips to historic Russian cities and to Italy between 1909 and 1911. A trip to Kiev in 1909 awakened in her an admiration for ancient Russian art and the religious paintings of the Symbolist artist Mikhail Vrubel. On her first visit to Italy, in 1910, the art of Giotto and Pinturicchio had a particularly strong impact. The summer of 1910 took her to Pskov and Novgorod, where she became acquainted with splendid examples of icon painting. The following year she visited St. Petersburg and admired the collections of the Hermitage; and later that year she traveled to Rostov Veliki, Yaroslavl, and Suzdal. The impressions gained from these journeys remained with Popova and were to serve as formative influences on her work in terms of her perception of form and color. Sensing the necessity to develop a more independent style, Popova took a studio on Antipievski Street in Moscow with the painter Liudmila A. Prudkovskaya in the fall of 1911. Subsequently, in 1912,

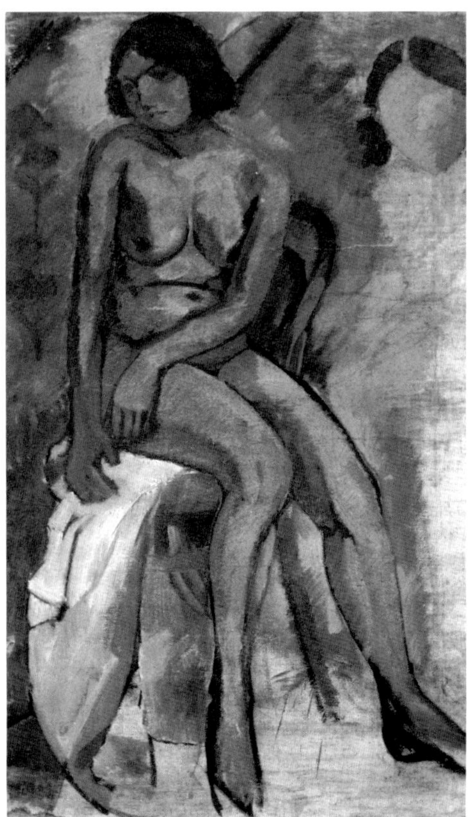

1. Liubov Popova. *Female Model*. c. 1912. Oil on canvas, 49 × 28½" (124.5 × 72.5 cm). Private collection, Moscow

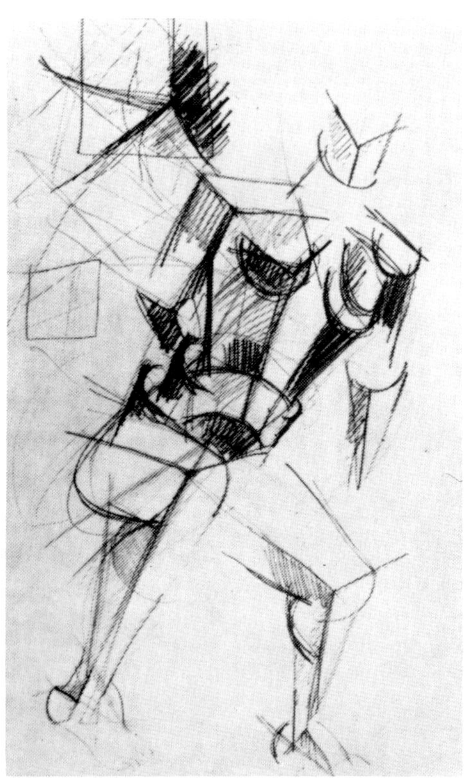

2. Vladimir Tatlin. *Analytical Figure Drawing*. c. 1913–14. Leaf 79 from an album of drawings. Charcoal on paper, 16 × 10¼" (43 × 26 cm). Central State Archive of Literature and Art, Moscow

she joined a collective studio, The Tower, on Kuznetski Most, where she worked alongside such artists as Viktor Bart, Vladimir Tatlin, Anna Troyanovskaya, and Kirill Zdanevich. During this period she also became acquainted with modern French art through visits to the Sergei Shchukin collection in Moscow.[4]

Clearly Popova's artistic independence was triggered by a trip to Paris in the fall of 1912 with her friend Nadezhda Udaltsova. This stay of several months provided Popova with an intensive experience of French Cubism. She had been introduced to Cubism in early 1912 through the works of Picasso and Braque (mostly examples of the years 1908–09) in the Shchukin collection, as well as through her contacts with Russian avant-garde artists, French and Russian art periodicals, and numerous exhibitions that included French Cubist works. She was also certainly aware of the debates on Cubism raging among Russian avant-garde artists, as well as of the controversy over whether to accept or reject Western influences such as Cubism in light of efforts to create a new, purely Russian artistic idiom. Those in favor of rejecting foreign influences, notably the painters Mikhail Larionov and Natalia Goncharova, were opposed by other members of the avant-garde such as David Burliuk and the Jack of Diamonds group, who were strongly interested in modern French art.

Russian interest in Cubism peaked in 1912–13. Besides the debates on Cubism sponsored by the Jack of Diamonds and Union of Youth groups in February and November 1912, an anthology of essays titled *A Slap in the Face of Public Taste,* containing Burliuk's article on Cubism, was published in December of that year, and a number of exhibitions including French Cubist works were presented. In 1912, while Popova was in Paris, the book *Du Cubisme* by Albert Gleizes and Jean Metzinger appeared; it was reviewed in the March 1913 issue of *Soyouz Molodezhy* (*Union of Youth*) and was published that year in Russian translation. All of these events must have stimulated Popova's imagination and curiosity about Cubism. Yet, although certain aspects of Picasso's work of 1910–11 are evident in Popova's work of this period, it is clear that, like most of the other Russian artists, she had been less exposed to the fully developed high Analytic Cubism of Picasso and Braque of 1910–11 than to the slightly modified version of Cubism practiced by such artists as Gleizes, Metzinger, and Henri Le Fauconnier, whose works had often figured prominently in Russian exhibitions of French modern art. In Paris, Popova enrolled at the Académie "La Palette," where she worked under the tutelage of Metzinger and Le Fauconnier. Her understanding of Cubist principles was therefore heavily dependent on the teachings of these artists, particularly Metzinger.

Cubo-Futurism: From Figuration to Abstraction

In comparing Popova's works of 1912 before her stay in Paris with those of 1913, after she had absorbed certain principles of Cubism, one is struck by the difference in quality and the strength of expression. The comparison of *Female Model* (fig. 1) of c. 1912 and *Seated Female Nude* (page 38), one of a group of paintings of c. 1913–14 on this subject, makes manifest the leap that occurred in Popova's work within a reasonably short period of time: from a timid traditionalist to an independent, assured artist. Although it is difficult to attribute specific paintings to Popova's Parisian stay, several of her sketchbooks, containing drawings of trees and human figures done around that time, are still extant[5] and allow us to study her approach to creating form. They reveal a sure hand and tremendous energy of execution.

Among sketches of trees some are very Cézannesque; others show a Neoprimitivist quality defined by heavy black contours and simplified crude drawing, indicative of Popova's contacts with Larionov and Goncharova, the creators and practitioners of Neoprimitivism between 1908 and 1910. A greater number of sketches are of the human figure, which is fragmented and reconstituted in terms of geometric (conical and cylindrical) elements hinged to one another by circular joints. This type of figure construction shows affinities with contemporaneous figure studies by Tatlin (fig. 2), in whose studio Popova often worked during the winter of 1913–14 along with other members of the avant-garde, among them her close friend the architect Alexander Vesnin.

The principles underlying such construction of the figure are derived essentially from Cubism, modified by a certain Futurist inflection. The influence of Metzinger and Umberto Boccioni seems evident during this phase of Popova's development, but it is incorporated into her own expressive idiom. Her three different versions of a seated female nude (pages 37, 38, 39), all executed in 1913–14, bear structural analogies to Metzinger's *Tea Time (Mona Lisa with a Teaspoon)* (fig. 3) of 1911. On the other hand, the title of one of these compositions, *Figure + House + Space* (page 39), perhaps the latest of the three, can almost be read as an *hommage* to Boccioni, whose 1912 work, *Head + House + Light* (fig. 4), was included in the

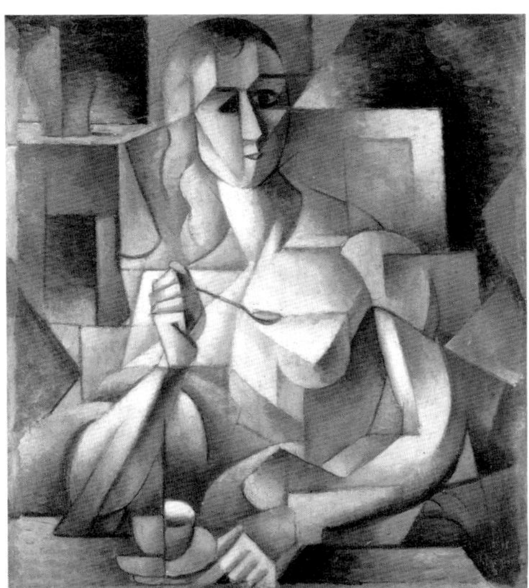

3. Jean Metzinger. *Tea Time (Mona Lisa with a Teaspoon)*. 1911. Oil on cardboard, 29⅞ × 27⅝" (75.9 × 70.2 cm). The Philadelphia Museum of Art, Louise and Walter Arensberg Collection

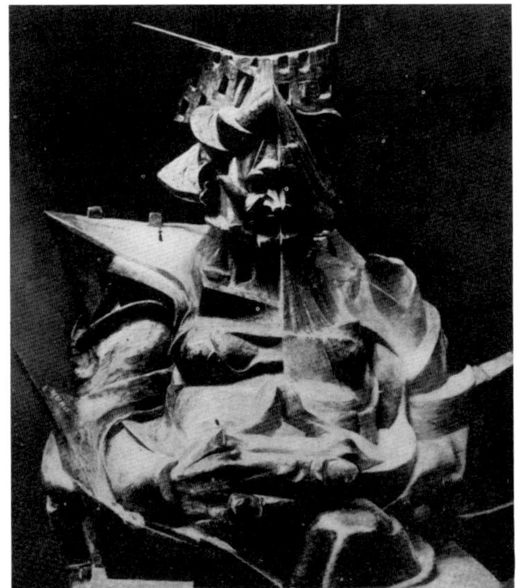

4. Umberto Boccioni. *Head + House + Light*. 1912. Plaster. Destroyed

exhibition of his sculpture held in Paris at the Galerie La Boëtie in 1913.[6]

Popova, who was then still in France, might have seen the exhibition and responded to it in her own work. Moreover, Boccioni's *Technical Manifesto of Futurist Sculpture*, formulated in 1912, was not only included in the catalogue to the La Boëtie exhibition but also translated into Russian in 1914, so that Popova would certainly have been familiar with it. The Italian artist's concern with the relationship between an object and the surrounding space was shared by Popova, who was trying to work out this problem in her own paintings. Boccioni's sculpture *Development of a Bottle in Space*, also included in his 1913 exhibition in Paris,[7] has often been quoted as an inspiration for her work of that period.[8]

An analysis of Popova's work also suggests an affinity with the work of Fernand Léger, whose tubular and conical forms, particularly in his series of paintings of 1913–14, *Contraste des formes*, are similar in structure and geometry to those in Popova's paintings.

Another possible influence on the evolution of the new idiom, composed of nesting cones and cylinders, was the Russian sculptor Alexander Archipenko, then also living in Paris. During Popova's stay in Paris, from the fall of 1912 through the summer of 1913, she visited his studio and was familiar with the three-dimensional work he was then creating. These mixed-medium constructions, such as *Medrano I* (fig. 5), combined wood, glass, and metal, and employed a vocabulary of fragmented conical and cylindrical shapes as well as circular elements emphasizing shoulder, knee, and elbow joints.[9] Popova's figure drawings similarly emphasize fragmentation of the body into geometric components built of planar and three-dimensional sections. A grid is superimposed on the structure of a figure, and in some cases the broad shading strokes intensify a sense of planarity rather than of volume.

At this point Popova's interest is focused on the figure itself and its construction. In the three versions of a seated female nude that mark the beginning of her Cubo-Futurist period, she further explores the relationship of the fragmented figure in space, trying to accommodate the figure to its surroundings. In other, already more fully Cubo-Futurist works of 1914, such as *Cubist Cityscape* (page 42)[10] and *Objects from the Dyer's Shop* (page 43), Popova attempts a much more coherent overall composition; the sections rendered three-dimensionally are fewer and more integrated into the overall structure. The division of figure/ground is almost entirely dissolved. There is also an increased sense of planar composition. It should be noted that Popova's Cubo-Futurism is quite distinct from that of Malevich. Hers shows a much greater Western influence and is devoid of the irrational element that Malevich introduced into his compositions.

In Popova's *Objects from the Dyer's Shop*, the Cubist and Futurist elements are assimilated into a distinctly personal structure. The composition is essentially a still life including objects associated with the dyer's shop, yet the forms are so fragmented, flattened, and dislocated that the initial objects—hat, gloves, a uniform—are barely discernible. Flatness of space is emphasized by the inclusion of lettering, a standard Cubist device (here in the Cyrillic alphabet). In a few instances the vestiges of volumetric forms are still present. But there is nothing Cubist about the overall color scheme, whose brilliance and combination of hues are reminiscent of Russian folk art and icon painting. An effort seems to have been made to incorporate Futurist devices such as lines of force[11] and repetition of forms in sequential order, to accentuate the dynamic quality of the picture.

Although Cubist and Futurist pictorial strategies were well known among Russian artists of the avant-garde (and it should be emphasized that Cubo-Futurism was a purely Russian phenomenon), Popova's interest in Futurist devices was probably intensified by her trip to Italy in the spring of 1914 after her second stay in Paris. Even though she studied mainly ancient monuments and masterpieces of Renaissance art, this direct contact with the birthplace of Futurism must have had a more immediate effect. In a group of still-life paintings of 1914 some are titled *Italian Still Life* (page 44); others have specific Italian references (pages 50, 51). Their compositional structure is quite different from that of *Cubist Cityscape* or *Objects from the Dyer's Shop*. The forms are larger, the space shallower, and the flatness of the picture plane emphasized by the placement of lettering or inscriptions across the picture surface. The inscriptions, primarily in the Latin alphabet and in various languages, contribute to the anecdotal reading of the pictures; some, such as *LACERBA*,[12] are direct references to the incorporated influences.

The series of still lifes marks a continuation of Popova's interest in exploring this genre, along with portraiture, and, in 1916, landscape. These interests, already present since the early phase of her artistic development, would remain until about 1916, when she entered her non-objective phase.

Among the most successful paintings of Popova's mature Cubo-Futurist period are her portraits of 1915, in which she com-

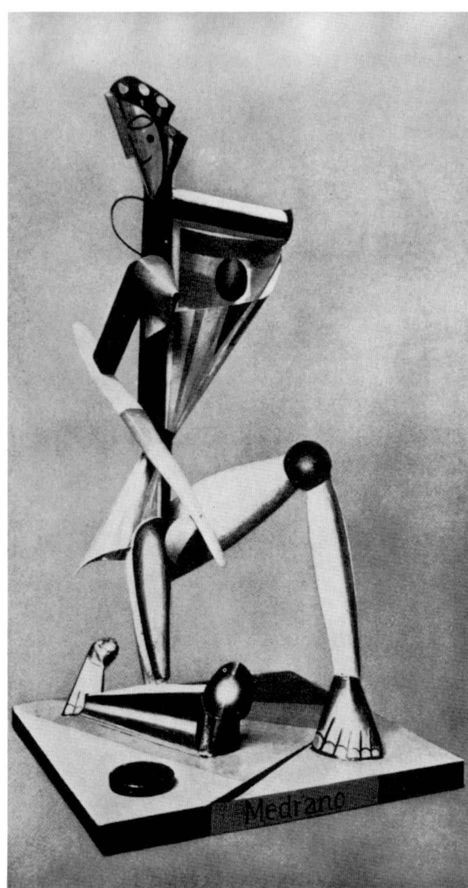

5. Alexander Archipenko. *Medrano I*. 1912. Wood, glass, sheet metal, metal wire, found objects, painted, 38" (96.5 cm) high. Probably destroyed during World War I

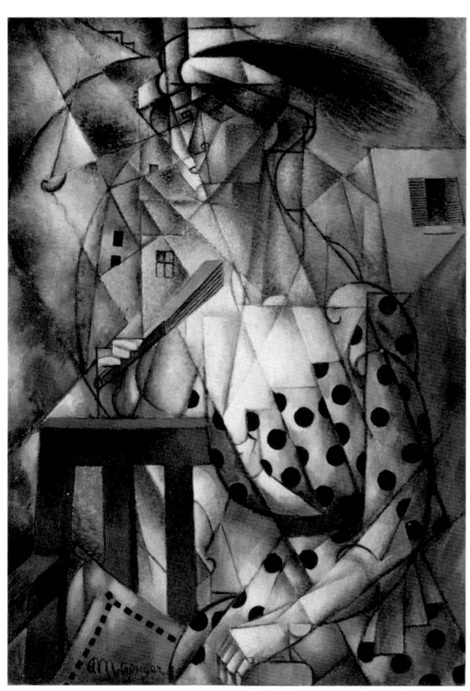

6. Jean Metzinger. *Woman with a Fan*. 1912–13. Oil on canvas, 35¾ × 25¼" (90.7 × 64.2 cm). Solomon R. Guggenheim Museum, New York. Gift of Solomon R. Guggenheim

bines the Cubist and Futurist devices of fragmenting form, including lettering or Western words, and using lines of force. The heightened color she employed was related to the palette of greens and ochres characteristic of the earliest Cubist paintings of Picasso and Braque (1908–09), but the brightness of her color is clearly much more Russian and the final form independent and innovative. The Cubist and Futurist elements, essentially incompatible in nature as representing the static versus the dynamic aspects of the picture, are organized into a harmonious whole.

Popova's experimentation with portraiture produced *The Pianist* (page 47), *Lady with a Guitar* (page 48), *Portrait* (page 51), and *Portrait of a Philosopher* (page 53), among other works. *The Pianist* displays much greater affinities with Cubism than Futurism, in terms both of the color scheme—muted, closely valued grays with touches of ochre and brown—and the compositional structure. Although the picture is painted flatly, certain areas are textured rather heavily, indicating Popova's interest in materials. This is particularly evident at the left side of the picture, which is covered with very Cubist stippling, and the ochre/brown section at the lower right, where the heavy texture creates a comb-like pattern similar to that of the pianist's flowing hair, but here almost incised in paint. Especially heavily textured, with the look of sand or marble dust, is the white plane at top center, curving out directly to the right of the face.

Popova's interest in textural explorations should be viewed in the context of a more general interest in texture, or *faktura*, on the part of Russian avant-garde artists. Although such aspects of the surface had become important in Western European painting, the Russians developed a very specific concept of *faktura*, recognized as a vital element in the construction of a painting. David Burliuk elaborated upon this concept in his article "Faktura," published in the anthology *A Slap in the Face of Public Taste*; it was further articulated in a pamphlet by Vladimir Markov, *Principles of Creation in the Visual Arts: Faktura*, published in 1914.[13] Popova experimented with adding sand or marble dust to paint in order to give the surface an extra dimension. This often contributed to the higher light reflectivity of the surface and in later works emphasized a charged, dynamic composition. This type of texture would later be employed by Popova in her non-objective works, such as *Painterly Architectonic* of 1918 (page 81), and subsequently in the Space-Force Constructions on plywood of 1921 (pages 89, 90, 96, 97).

The year 1915 was very active for Popova creatively and marked the beginning of her serious efforts to exhibit her work. Although she had shown her paintings in 1914 with the Jack of Diamonds group, the exhibitions of 1915 marked an important point in the life of the avant-garde. On March 3, 1915, the exhibition "Tramway V: The First Futurist Exhibition of Paintings" opened in Petrograd, and Popova was represented by six works, among them *Lady with a Guitar*, one of her Cubo-Futurist portraits, probably executed early in the winter of 1915.[14] Here, despite a lingering influence of French Cubism in the coloration as much as in the fragmentation of form and the subject matter itself, the emphasis is on large planar sections throughout the composition, so that the space within which the figure is situated is much more compressed. Depth is only suggested by the perspectival treatment of the hat, circular fragments of the figure's left arm, and vestiges of the three-dimensionally rendered guitar in the lower central section. Popova is clearly grappling with her experiences of Cubism, attempting to infuse them with her own explorations in search of a pictorial language independent of the influence of the French Cubists.

Even if parallels could be drawn to various works by Metzinger, such as the two paintings of 1912 titled *The Yellow Feather*, Popova's interest in a more planar organization of the picture and much greater suppression of the figurative element makes her work quite distinct. The high color of some of the paintings of 1914, such as *Cubist Cityscape* and *Objects from the Dyer's Shop*, is eliminated in favor of a muted palette of grays, which reveals the artist's greater preoccupation with form than with spectral color. The culmination of these explorations can be studied in *Portrait of a Philosopher*, depicting the artist's younger brother Pavel, which was first shown in "The Last Futurist Exhibition of Paintings: 0.10" in Petrograd in December 1915–January 1916.[15] The seated figure of a man in a top hat, holding a copy of the French periodical *Revue Philosophique de la France et de l'Étranger*, can be compared—as Dimitri Sarabianov points out[16]—to Juan Gris's 1912 *Man in a Café* and Metzinger's *Portrait of Albert Gleizes* (1911–12). On the other hand, it might draw its inspiration from Picasso's *Portrait of Ambroise Vollard* (1910), which had been in Moscow since 1913 in the collection of Ivan Morozov. The flowing hair of the sitter is also reminiscent of Picasso's *Portrait of Daniel-Henry Kahnweiler* (1910). Among Russian works, two paintings by Malevich—*Portrait of M. V. Matiushin* (1913), shown in the "Tramway V" exhibition,[17] and *Portrait of Ivan V. Kliun* (1913)—constitute precedents for Cubo-Futurist

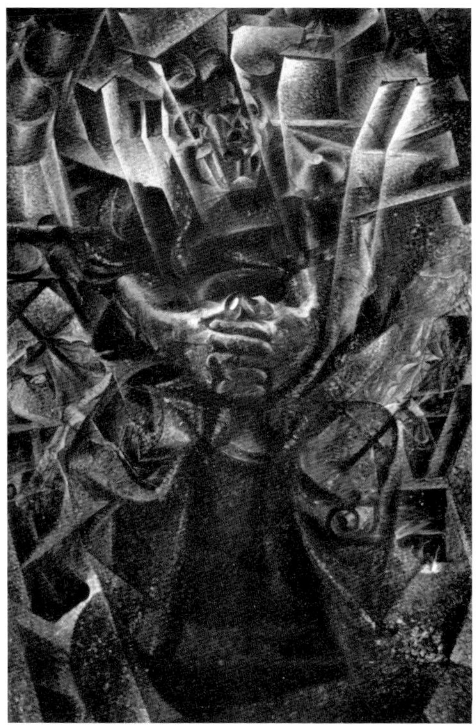

7. Umberto Boccioni. *Materia.* 1912. Oil on canvas, 88½ × 59" (225 × 150 cm). Private collection, Milan

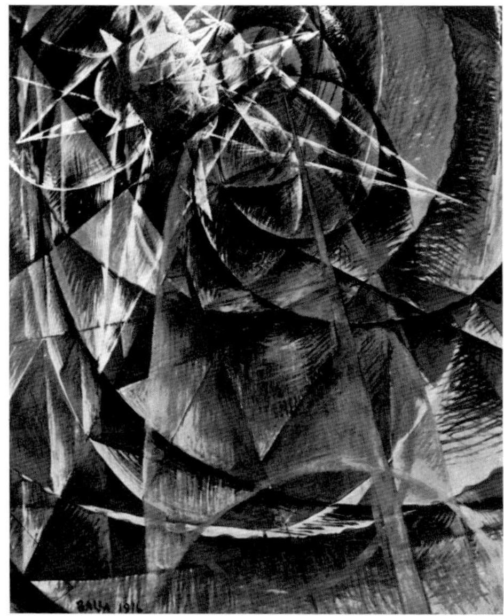

8. Giacomo Balla. *Mercury Passing in Front of the Sun.* 1914. Tempera on paper mounted on canvas, 48⅝ × 39½" (123.5 × 100.5 cm). Private collection, Milan

experimentation with portraiture.

However, departing from the above examples, Popova develops in this portrait her own stylistic principles. She analyzes and reconstitutes the figure as a composite of large overlapping planes often shaded in a darker hue or simply in white. Large sections of recognizable figuration are retained in such areas as the sitter's face, his left hand, and the periodical we assume he is holding. The distinction between background and figure is eliminated; both are created of the same substance—the plane. The relationship of the planar parts becomes very important, and Popova at times makes use of the Cézannesque *passage*—planes situated at different points in space bleeding into one another in such a way that they constitute one continuous pictorial plane. The spatial structure is very tight and the space of the picture very shallow. This impression is further enhanced by the inclusion of the French words *Revue Philos* (an allusion to the sitter's interests and occupation) and fragment *Exp*—the beginning of the word *exposition.* Only the piece of patterned wallpaper in the upper right-hand corner seems to indicate a different point in space, somewhere behind the figure yet brought forward through its color. With *Portrait of a Philosopher* Popova abandons the muted palette and introduces high color in different intensities of deep blue with contrasts of bright yellow and green. She returns here to the color scheme of the earlier pictures of 1914. The bright palette and planar structure of the composition signal pictorial elements that will become principal vehicles of expression in her non-objective works: color and plane.

While working on the portraits, Popova explored another subject equally popular with the Cubists: the still life with musical instruments. Among her six contributions to the "Tramway V" exhibition were *Violin* (page 48) and *Objects* (page 49), the latter essentially a still life with a guitar and bowl of fruit. Because of its inclusion in the "Tramway V" exhibition, this work must have been executed in the winter of 1915, around the time of *Lady with a Guitar.* Other still lifes of 1915 incorporate the same elements: a guitar, a bowl of fruit, a traditional Russian tray (black with a decorated border), and Cyrillic lettering. Here the lettering *TEL 35-0* may refer simply to the artist's or a friend's telephone number. In this group of compositions the forms become larger. Some remain recognizable, such as the bowl of fruit; others, such as the guitar and tray, are indicated by their characteristic shapes. The work repeats the overall blue-gray tonality of *Lady with a Guitar;* the large planar sections throughout the composition unify the pictorial field and create an overall surface composition. The principle of arranging the planes as intersecting elements foreshadows the planar configurations of the Painterly Architectonics.

Popova's search for new formal solutions made 1915 a highly productive and stylistically diverse year. Among her important works of this period are two canvases titled *Traveling Woman* (pages 54, 55). Here she is no longer preoccupied with analyzing the figure in space and recomposing it within the Cubo-Futurist vocabulary. She is now concerned mainly with the flatness of pictorial surface and with finding a way to convey dynamism through the entire compositional arrangement as well as building up all the pictorial elements, that is, both figure and space, from the same formal components.

The two versions differ in color and in the vocabulary of forms used. In one version, in the Norton Simon collection (page 54), the palette consists of deep purplish blues, greens, and yellows that complement and balance one another. The section describing the body of the traveling woman is defined broadly in terms of triangular planes. The composition carries a certain distant analogy to Metzinger's *Woman with a Fan* of 1912–13 (fig. 6). Popova's composition, however, is almost non-figurative; the image of the subject is decoded through the recognition of such Cyrillic words and their fragments as *journaly* (newspapers) and *chliap* (hats), referring possibly to a hatbox. The face under the hat decorated with a feather is dissolved into white triangles, legible as a face only by association with the stated subject of the picture. Still in use are certain Futurist devices for integrating figure and space, not unlike those in Boccioni's painting *Materia* (fig. 7). The dynamic quality of the woman moving against a background that could be associated with a train station is conveyed through the network of diagonal lines defining the sides of triangular planes.[18] The composition exudes great energy through the interplay of form and color.

The *Traveling Woman*[19] in the Costakis collection owes more to Italian Futurism in the way dynamism is projected through lines of force related to the manner of Boccioni and Balla (fig. 8), whose works were certainly familiar to Popova. By making use of multiple diagonals and circular rhythms, she emphasizes her own manner of depicting velocity and light. The overall organization of the picture looks back to the compositional structure of *Objects from the Dyer's Shop* and forward to her planar dynamic arrangements in the Painterly Architectonics of 1916–19. This is particularly evident in the central section, where the two diagonals bordering the fragments of planes come to an apex and create a triangular or pyramidal shape, oriented dynamically upward. The restrained palette of dark blues and purplish burgundies is well balanced and further emphasizes the energy within the composition.

As these paintings indicate, Popova's work of 1915 encompasses a variety of styles. This diversity makes evident her search for a new, personal formal language, and parallels the quest of other members of the Russian artistic and literary avant-garde at that time. Popova's efforts brought results in the non-objective works of 1916, but a year before reaching the point of complete non-objectivity, she explored still another avenue of expression, one more sculptural and three-dimensional—the relief.

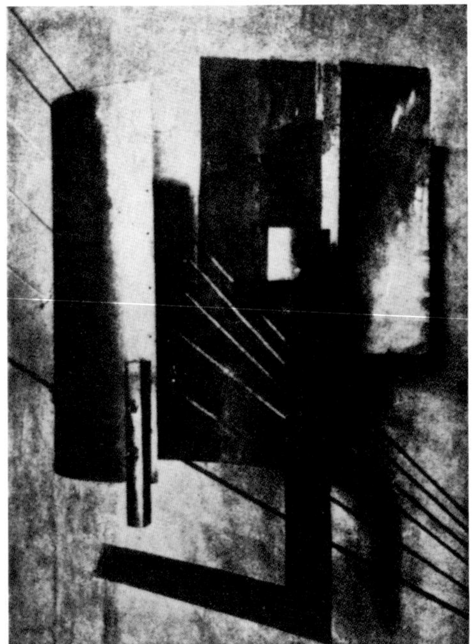

9. Vladimir Tatlin. *Corner Counter-Relief.* 1914–15. Detail of the central section. Wood, iron, metal, cable. State Russian Museum, Leningrad

Three-Dimensional Work: Reliefs

Popova's renewed contact with Tatlin's studio upon her return from France in 1913 added new elements to her stylistic research, namely an interest in real materials and real space. She worked in his studio from 1913 through 1916 in the company of other members of the avant-garde, including Udaltsova and Vesnin. There she saw Tatlin's newly created three-dimensional works—defined by him first as painterly and then as counter-reliefs (fig. 9). These innovative assemblages of planar abstract shapes, made from randomly found ordinary industrial materials (primarily wood, glass, and metal), explored real space as an active component of form. The principle underlying their creation was the "culture of materials," according to which each material dictates the form that best expresses its inherent character.[20] Executed mainly in 1914–15, these works stimulated the development of a new open sculptural idiom defined as "construction" and led to the emergence of Constructivism. Seeing Tatlin's reliefs might have prompted Popova to undertake her own experiments with a three-dimensional medium, as a number of other artists were also doing at the time, among them Vladimir Baranoff-Rossiné, Ivan Kliun, and Ivan Puni.[21]

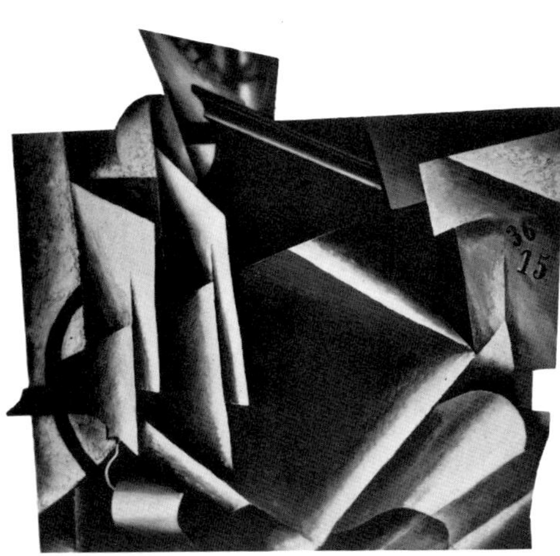

10. Liubov Popova. *Volume-Space Relief.* 1915. Lost

During 1915 Popova created at least three and probably four reliefs: *Portrait of a Lady (Plastic Drawing)* (page 56), *The Jug on the Table (Plastic Painting)* (page 57), and *Volume-Space Relief* (fig. 10). The first two, along with *Vase with Fruit (Plastic Painting),* were exhibited in the "0.10" exhibition.[22] *Volume-Space Relief* was included in Popova's posthumous exhibition and was listed and reproduced in the catalogue under this title, along with the reliefs *Portrait of a Lady* (titled *Relief*) and *The Jug on the Table*.[23] Three reliefs, *Vase with Fruit, Volume-Space Relief,* and *The Jug on the Table,* are clearly visible in one of the installation photographs of the posthumous exhibition (fig. 11). The abstract *Volume-Space Relief* was also illustrated in *Die Kunstismen,* a book published by Hans Arp and El Lissitzky in 1925.[24] Of the four reliefs, only two, *Portrait of a Lady* and *The Jug on the Table,* are extant.

On stylistic grounds, I would suggest that the sequence of their execution proceeds from *Portrait of a Lady* to *The Jug on the Table* to the non-objective relief.[25] *Portrait of a Lady* seems to be a three-dimensional elaboration of the head and shoulders of the sitter in an earlier 1915 painting, *Lady with a Guitar* (page 48). The placement of the figure is frontal, with only some sections of the composition rendered as three-dimensional: the left side of the hat, the eye area defined by a conical form on the right of the relief (at the figure's left eye), and her right shoulder (lower left of the composition). The head is placed against the same wallpaper pattern used in *Study for a Portrait* (page 50) and *Portrait of a Philosopher.* Although the work is conceived as a relief, it operates within the artist's Cubo-Futurist vocabulary. In fact, the protruding elements done in relief can be read as three-dimensional counterparts to the analogous forms clearly visible in the right section of Popova's 1914 Cubo-Futurist painting *Objects from the Dyer's Shop.* Even the brilliant color scheme of *Portrait of a Lady* relates to *Objects from the Dyer's Shop* and *Cubist Cityscape.* Essentially, form is brought to the borderline between figuration and abstraction. Although we can clearly decipher composite parts of a woman in a hat, the shaded planes that define different parts of the face, hat, and shoulders serve also as abstract geometric shapes, anticipating Popova's use of multicolored overlapping planes in her mature non-objective works.

Both in the "0.10" exhibition and on a postcard addressed to her former governess, Adelaida Robertovna Dege, dated October 19, 1915, Popova described *Portrait of a Lady* as "plastic drawing," whereas *The Jug on the Table* was defined as "plastic painting" and reproduced as such on a postcard to Dege dated June 23, 1916.[26]

The artist's distinction between "plastic drawing" and "plastic painting," taken into consideration with the dates on the two postcards, may indicate the sequence of execution. The second relief, *The Jug on the Table,* which stylistically is more sculptural, has a greater number of three-dimensional parts than does *Portrait* and includes a fragment of an actual wooden

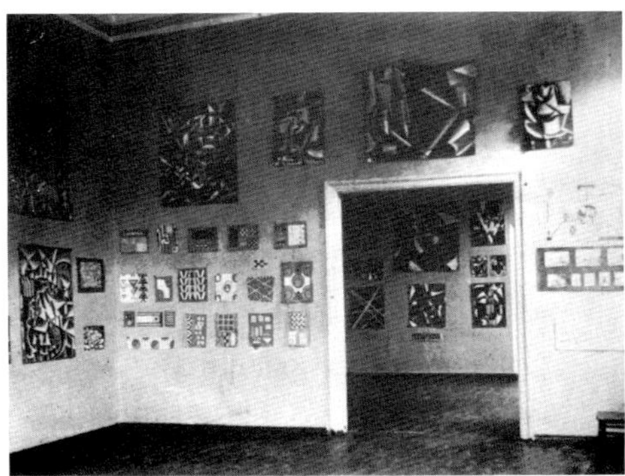

11. Installation view of Popova's posthumous exhibition, Moscow, December 1924

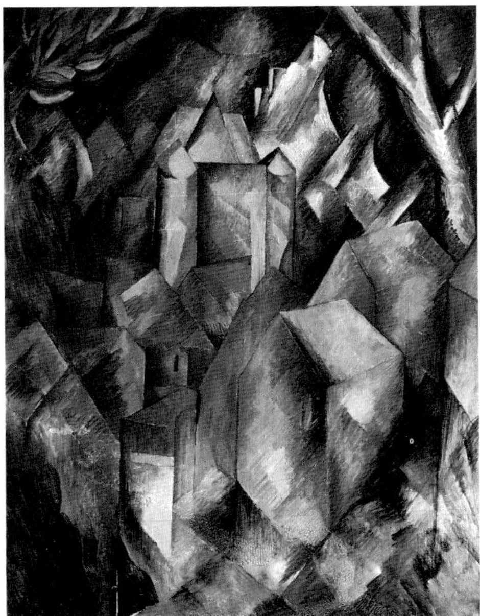

12. Georges Braque. *Castle at La Roche-Guyon*. 1909. Oil on canvas, 25¾ × 21¼" (65 × 54 cm). Pushkin State Museum of Fine Arts, Moscow

table leg. The presence of a section painted in a checkered-cloth pattern and the wooden piece could be considered her *hommage* to Picasso's first collage, *Still Life with Chair Caning* of May 1912. This seems to be the only instance when Popova used real materials as part of a composition. Generally, for her, material is identified as pictorial material, that is, the color and texture of painterly surfaces. In the right-hand section of *The Jug on the Table,* for example, the white/gray and green planes are heavily textured with an admixture of marble dust, creating a thick, crusty surface. In this relief, as in *Portrait of a Lady,* figuration is pushed to the borderline of abstraction; if the title did not clearly define the figurative subject matter, the array of ribbon-like, three-dimensional sections could be perceived as an abstract construction. Certain vestiges of the Cubo-Futurist style remain in the almost modeled quality of the half-shaded three-dimensional parts, but the main issue becomes the relationship of open volume and space.

Another relief, titled *Volume-Space Relief* in the catalogue of the posthumous exhibition, is the most abstract of all the reliefs and is essentially non-referential. Conceived as an arrangement of large, shaded, overlapping planes and ribbon-like sections, it has a compositional structure almost exactly like that of the later Painterly Architectonics. Here the artist's sole preoccupation is with the relationship of geometric form, space, and volume rather than with the descriptive subject matter, as in the other reliefs.

However, Popova's interest in exploring the three-dimensional idiom was limited to these three or possibly four works.[27] Moreover, her three-dimensional works always retained an essentially pictorial format, never really freeing themselves from the relationship to the picture plane in the way that Tatlin's reliefs or those by Puni did.[28] Until the early 1920s Popova remained first and foremost a painter and was interested principally in evolving an idiom resulting from the manipulation of pictorial elements on the surface. Hence her attention was focused on exploring different textural possibilities including the addition of extraneous materials to pigment and building out the surface thickly, away from the picture plane.

An increased emphasis on composition, conceived as the interplay of well-defined planar elements with only vestiges of figurative references, becomes apparent in her 1916 works such as *The Grocery Store* (page 58), *Box Factory,* and *Birsk* (page 59).[29] In these paintings well-articulated, partially shaded planes create a dense overlay of forms, even though one can still detect a certain Cubist parentage. *Box Factory* and *Birsk* in particular are not unlike the structures in Picasso's and Braque's works of 1909, exemplified by the latter's *Castle at La Roche-Guyon,* formerly in the Shchukin collection (fig. 12). Yet Popova's planes are longer and create an essentially vertical scaffolding that indicates a relief-like pictorial space. Such spatial configuration and planar articulation, as well as the larger size of the planes apparent in *The Grocery Store,* can easily be compared with the compositional structure of the lost non-objective relief. Although the titles of all three works still imply a referential subject matter, figuration becomes a vestigial element, and pictorial structure becomes dominant in our perception of the paintings. We begin to read the work in terms of interlocking planes, not as the depiction of a specific subject. In emphasizing the planar definition of parts and the way they organize pictorial space, these works constitute a transitional phase to Popova's entirely non-objective Painterly Architectonics, which she began in 1916.

Early Non-Objective Work: Painterly Architectonics

The catalogue of Popova's posthumous exhibition lists a work of 1915 as *Painterly Architectonic,* although at present it is virtually impossible to identify the work.[30] Also listed are a number of paintings, dating mainly from 1916 to 1918, which are designated by the same title. These were Popova's mature works, her non-objective paintings where the use of the term "architectonic" was possibly applied to emphasize the constructive aspects, the "building up," of such compositions. It is generally assumed on the basis of her exhibited works that Popova began to paint her first non-objective pictures, which she designated as Painterly Architectonics, following a trip to Samarkand and Birsk in the latter part of 1916. Her impressions of Birsk in these pictures still contain vestiges of figuration in a style emanating from Cubo-Futurism. In her subsequent work she made an effort to eliminate all elements related to reality, including the depiction of internal rhythms, and to consolidate expressiveness within colored planes.

It has been pointed out[31] that this type of painting evolved from Popova's interest in architecture, which was stimulated by her close friendship with Alexander Vesnin. According to Vasilii Rakitin,[32] the idea of Painterly Architectonics originated during Popova's trip to Samarkand, where she was stimulated by Islamic architecture and struck by the unusual and complex play of light reflected from different surfaces of the buildings. This enhanced her perception of plastic form, which had already been shaped by her familiarity with ancient Russian icon painting and church architecture. One could, conceivably, see in the planar structure of the Painterly Architectonics an echo of the interplay of architectural planes of brightly sunlit buildings, but I believe that this experience played an auxiliary role in her quest for non-objective form. It is more likely that the architectonic aspect of these works referred to the compositional process of building a solid pictorial structure.

The catalyst in Popova's transition to non-objective painting was Malevich's Suprematism, which he developed in 1915. This new style, taking its name from the Latin word *supremus* (meaning ultimate, absolute), represented one of the earliest Russian attempts at non-objectivity. It was first unveiled to the public in December 1915 at the "0.10" exhibition, where a whole room of Malevich's Suprematist paintings was shown. Austerely composed, with means of expression reduced to the bare minimum of form and color, these works contain arrangements of simple geometric shapes such as squares, rectangles, circles, and cross-like configurations in unmodulated pure colors, organized dynamically against a white ground. The forms float within an infinite, unstructured space symbolized by the whiteness of the flat background, which seems to extend vertically and horizontally beyond the boundaries of the canvas. The philosophical principle underlying Malevich's creation of this style was his search for a new form compatible with the goals and ideas of modern society, unburdened by the traditional canons of bourgeois art based on representation. Suprematism was also an attempt at incorporating into painting the then very popular notion of the fourth dimension, that is, to combine the elements of space and time in a two-dimensional composition and thereby reach, according to Malevich, a higher spiritual plane. This would require the viewer's intellectual involvement in the process of perception of the work of art.[33]

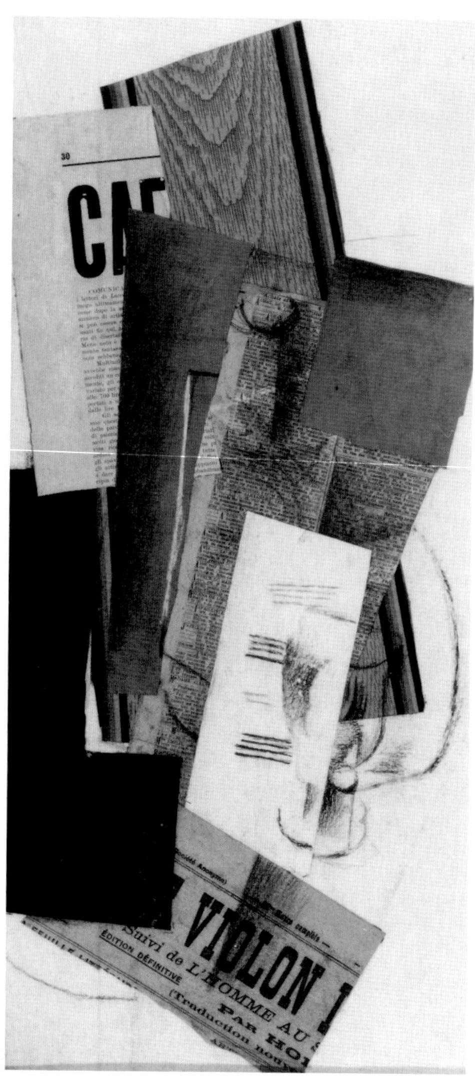

13. Georges Braque. *Glass, Bottle, and Newspaper.* 1914. Pasted paper on paper, 24⅝ × 11¼" (62.5 × 28.5 cm). Private collection

The pictorial radicalism of the Suprematist idiom strongly affected many artists of the avant-garde, among them Popova, Rozanova, Udaltsova, Kliun, Puni, and numerous members of the younger generation. Popova's Painterly Architectonics are in many ways her response to the challenge of Malevich's Suprematism, which helped her to liberate herself from figurative references and to focus on the exploration of pictorial means for their purely non-referential meaning. Yet the intellectual premise of Popova's non-objective works and their pictorial construction differ markedly from Malevich's.

Painterly Architectonics that can be dated to 1916, such as *Painterly Architectonic (Still Life: Instruments)* (page 60) and *Painterly Architectonic with Three Stripes* (page 62), still contain a shadow of Cubism in certain aspects of their composition. *Still Life: Instruments*, by its very title and the use of shapes unequivocally associated with a guitar, is reminiscent of favorite Cubist subjects. The compositional structure indicates Popova's familiarity with the practice of overlapping planar shapes in Synthetic Cubist compositions, particularly characteristic of *papiers collés*, such as Braque's *Glass, Bottle, and Newspaper* (1914; fig. 13). However, Popova's overlapping planes show more regular, deliberately geometric shapes combined so that their interaction creates tension and yet maintains a dynamic equilibrium within the picture. The diagonally placed elements in the upper left, pointed toward the center of the white plane in the very middle of the composition, interact with a vertical plane at the lower right, also pointing toward the white plane. The white rhomboid plane floats in the center and provides a field for dynamic interaction of the other planar forms. This element is counterbalanced by the oval forms that anchor the picture in its verticality. These well-defined floating planes may have developed under the influence of Malevich's Suprematism, yet its influence, as well as that of Cubism, is reworked here into a different pictorial form. The high-key primary colors present in some of her earlier works, of 1914–15, emphasize Popova's gift for daring combinations that result in very bright yet harmonious and visually seductive compositions.

As much as *Painterly Architectonic (Still Life: Instruments)* manifests Popova's interest in the work of Malevich, her *Painterly Architectonic with Three Stripes*, as Margit Rowell has pointed out,[34] can be likened in its compositional organization to the structure of Tatlin's reliefs, also shown at the "0.10" exhibition.[35] Just as Tatlin layered various materials, placing them in different visual planes, so Popova arranges her pictorial elements within the configuration of planes positioned one behind another. Her pictorial planes are painted counterparts of Tatlin's three-dimensional forms.

These two Painterly Architectonics point out the dual influences acting upon Popova at that moment before she firmly established her own independent language. The variety of her production during the years 1916–17 shows her inventiveness and ability to find different expressive solutions. In works such as *Painterly Architectonic* (page 69) her interest in Malevich's Suprematism might be apparent in the use of floating color planes, open space, and saturated, unmodulated colors. Yet her forms are larger, and the composition's strong structural quality results from her extensive use of well-anchored, overlapping geometric shapes. The floating planes are positioned along intersecting diagonal axes, and the interplay of these diagonals gives the composition a great sense of dynamic movement and energy. Although most of the forms are contained within the pictorial field, others are cut off by the edge of the canvas, thus conveying the sense of a composition extending beyond the confines of the picture plane. There is, in fact, a certain architectonic quality about the composition. In their underlying structure of crisscrossing diagonals and interplay of planar elements, the Painterly Architectonics anticipate the purely linear works of the early 1920s, which make similar use of dynamic space and form.

A pronounced Suprematist inflection is evident in *Painterly Architectonic: Black, Red, Gray* (page 64). In its simplicity of means—the use of only three forms and three flat but heavily applied colors and the compact, centralized composition—the work is direct and monumental. The compositional elements move upward from lower right to upper left, but the solid opaque colors, black and red complemented by medium gray, add weight to the floating geometric forms. On the other hand, the large black form fixes the composition to the picture plane, giving it a stabilizing, monumental aspect. It is the contrapuntal use of stabilizing and dynamic devices that creates a canvas bursting with energy. This painting should be seen in the context of Popova's association in the winter of 1916–17 with the Society of Painters Supremus, centered around Malevich.[36] Their plans to publish a Suprematist journal were never realized, but its logo, which is related to this painting and was designed by Popova (page 68), utilizes the form of a large trapezoidal black plane placed centrally within the compositional field.

For all her dependence on the principles of Suprematism, Popova's preoccupations are quite different from those of Malevich. The component elements in her paintings have great physicality; essentially, she is not concerned with the spiritual aspect or cosmic space that dominates Malevich's Suprematism. Her concerns are purely pictorial. The type of composition represented by *Painterly Architectonic: Black, Red, Gray* will evolve into works exemplified by *Pictorial Architectonic,* now in a private collection in Switzerland (page 70) and *Painterly Architectonic* in the collection of The Museum of Modern Art (page 71). In these pictures the artist increases the number of planar elements that build up the composition; she also stretches the composition closer to the edges of the canvas, thus conveying a sense of their extension upward beyond the picture plane. The extraordinary balance of the composition in the Swiss picture is achieved through the very centralized organization of the four composite planes, layered one behind another and poised on the lower right-hand corner of the black trapezoidal plane that just touches the edge of the painting. The Museum of Modern Art painting represents another variation on this type of centralized, layered composition. The composition is horizontal, its center occupied by a large red triangular plane that becomes, by its very placement and the acute angle pointing upward, the major dynamic force within the composition. The main emphasis is on the positioning of planar elements and their interaction.

Popova's works influenced by Suprematism coincide with another group of architectonics that continue the compositional organization of *Painterly Architectonic with Three Stripes* and relate to the structural principles of Synthetic Cubist pictures, particularly *papiers collés,* but also show a very strong "constructive," or architectural, aspect. To this group belong the *Painterly Architectonic* at the State Russian Museum (page 63), *Painterly Architectonic with Yellow Board* (page 63), and a double-sided work, *Painterly Architectonic* and *Painterly Construction* (pages 66, 67), at the State Tretyakov Gallery.

All these abstract compositions, analogous to the relief-like arrangement of parts in the Painterly Architectonics at the Scottish National Gallery of Modern Art (page 65) and at the Tretyakov Gallery (page 66) show Popova's absorption of the principles of construction known to her from Tatlin's reliefs of 1914–15 (fig. 9). Just as these reliefs were assemblages of various commonplace industrial materials whose inherent qualities dictated the forms, so Popova's architectonics are solidly built, almost tangible assemblages of planar elements. The overlapping of the planes, by its very tight structure, creates an ambiguity between the implied three-dimensional, shallow relief-like space and the two-dimensional flatness of the picture surface. The planar components interact dynamically, giving the viewer the impression that these compositions could be translated into actual three-dimensional works whose planar components would interact within real space, and make it an active element of form.

Despite their affinities with the principles of Tatlin's reliefs, Popova's Painterly Architectonics differ greatly in their approach to the medium. Popova is without a doubt looking for a new expressive language, yet her focus remains the painterly medium. Although the preoccupation with materials is obvious in her work, these constitute pictorial attributes—plane, line, color, and texture—counterparts, as it were, of Tatlin's real materials. Popova, like many of her contemporaries, drew on such diverse sources as Cubism, Futurism, Malevich, and Tatlin, extrapolating from these essentially incompatible influences the ideas that allowed her to develop an original, personal vocabulary of form and compositional structure.

Popova's non-objective language of Painterly Architectonics came to full maturity in the works of 1918. Through spatial articulation resulting from the manipulation of form, color, and medium, she was able to achieve an unusually broad expressive range. The interaction of colored planes tightly occupying pictorial space became the principal means of expression. Heavily textured planes, often shaded in feathery brushstrokes that give them a half-dematerialized quality, interact in space, which is conveyed through the materiality of painterly texture. Space as background against which the forms are organized is eliminated. Excellent examples of this type are the *Painterly Architectonic* (page 78) from a private collection and the *Painterly Architectonic* from the Thyssen-Bornemisza collection (page 61). In both works the painting is read as the material construction of color, form, light, and space. The forms vibrate with color and texture, creating a dynamic whole.

Popova's attention to "construction," or the "constructive" aspect of painting, made itself apparent from 1915 with *Portrait of a Philosopher,* but it became her focal interest beginning in 1918. The two Painterly Architectonics in the Costakis collection (pages 82, 83) demonstrate the artist's goal of creating a dynamic construction of diagonally organized, semi-dematerialized planes that interact within pictorial space. The play of light on textured but semi-transparent triangular, trapezoidal, and almost rectangular forms conveys the impression of vibrating space and shimmering light. The composition seems to extend beyond the boundaries of the picture plane in all directions. The color scheme in both works reflects the artist's distinctive color sensibility. In the multicolored work (page 82), dominated by a large acid-green plane in the center which appears to have been pinned down to the picture surface with a black rectangle and a crescent, the hues return almost to the high color of the works of 1914–15. The second architectonic is almost entirely a symphony in blue, ranging from very pale and delicate to almost black. The entire picture is organized around a light center, a large almost white triangle, with blue/gray/black planes vibrating around it. The impression of vibrating light is heightened by a stippled effect, which gives an additional textural aspect. The composition is built on a series of triangular relationships and crisscrossing diagonals, which energize the pictorial field.

In Popova's statement included in the catalogue of "The Tenth State Exhibition: Non-objective Creation and Suprematism," held in Moscow in January 1919, to which she contributed a number of works, she defined her philosophy very succinctly.[37] The statement identified the fundamental sources for the development of painting. She equated painting and architectonics and pointed out five essential elements: painterly space, resulting from the experiments of Cubism; line, considered the basic means of defining form; color, associated with the search conducted by Suprematism; energetics, the focus of Futurism; and texture, an important aspect of surface treatment. All of these elements were integral to a balanced, harmonious work of art. Only by unifying color, line, texture, surface, and construction could one transform the expressive language of painting.

Texture, for Popova, was the content of painterly surfaces, and it indeed played an increasingly vital role in her compositions. Energetics, according to the artist, was expressed "through the direction of volumes and planes and lines or their vestiges, and all colors."[38] Color, in turn, participated in energetics through its weight, which was defined by its intensity; hence, color at its fullest intensity would impart the highest dynamic quality to a picture. Popova explored the dynamic potential of tonal variations within monochromatic and polychromatic color schemes. This principle is well conveyed in her various architectonics, where color is used at its fullest intensity, for example in the blue architectonic in the Costakis collection (page 83). In fact, in all phases of her development, but particularly in her Painterly Architectonics, Popova was a superb colorist. That special ability was recognized by her peers when, in the fall of 1920, she began to teach, together with Vesnin, a course on color at the Vkhutemas (Higher State Artistic and Technical Studios).

Popova's statement on her philosophy of painting should be viewed in the context of the so-called laboratory period of Constructivism and the discussions then originating among members of the avant-garde on the subjects of "composition" and "construction." These discussions were strongly related to the ideological stance of the avant-garde occasioned by the October Revolution of 1917 and reflected a different understanding of the creative principles of art. The new social, economic, and governmental system brought about by the Revolution required that new institutions organize and direct various aspects of life. The Institute of Artistic Culture (Inkhuk),[39] formally established in May 1920, had been assigned the task of evolving a theoretical approach to art within the newly created Communist society and developing a specific program and pedagogical method for teaching art at the post-revolutionary educational and artistic institutions.

Beginning in December 1919, Popova was an active member of the Council of Masters (Soviet Masterov), a predecessor of Inkhuk, and upon the formation of Inkhuk she became one of the forces defining its program, which was initially established by Vasily Kandinsky. The focus of Inkhuk's activities was to establish a scientific basis for the creation of art and to find objective criteria defining artistic creation that would satisfy the search for a completely new language suitable for the unprecedented conditions that now existed. These criteria included such elements as material, surface, *faktura,* color, space, and time (or movement). Form was to be the result of the interaction of these elements and had to be universally understandable. Rejecting the traditional pictorial form of easel painting as outdated, the philosophy of Constructivism postulated that only three-dimensional creations composed of real materials, and using as part of their form the actual space of the viewer, were an acceptable medium of expression in the new order. Popova's definition, presented in the catalogue of "The Tenth State Exhibition," stated that painting is also a "construction" and that painterly constructions were the preparatory stage for real three-dimensional constructions. She very perceptively noted that "construction in painting equals the sum of energy of [the painting's] parts."[40] She tried to enforce this principle in her Painterly Architectonics, consciously combining all of the elements defined as mandatory for the existence of painting.

This understanding of a painting's construction allowed for the reconciliation and harmonious organization of theoretically incompatible elements into one fully expressive composition. Popova believed in a hierarchy of forms and saw the painter's role as choosing those elements which were of greater value for a specific composition. She strongly believed that intelligence and consciousness enabled an artist to select only those elements truly indispensable to a painterly context. Thus non-figurative painting was the main goal of her work at that time. According to her artistic philosophy, "images of 'painterly' and not 'figurative' value are the aim of the present painting."[41] "Painterly values" were those proper and unique to painting itself, which was complete in its own "reality," not in the depiction of reality. Painting thus was to be evaluated not on the basis of its mimetic quality but on the basis of its aesthetic qualities resulting from the interaction of pictorial elements themselves. Color, line, and texture, as already noted, were the essential determinants of form and space, their interaction serving as the conveyor of beauty.

Form and space are built of the same basic elements in the works of 1918–20. It is the difference in texture and modulation of line and colors interacting and creating tension among the composite parts that determines the distinction between form and space and the emotional impact of the work. An excellent example of Popova's belief that dynamism was an all-important organizational agent of the composition and a valid additional factor in conveying beauty is her *Painterly Construction* of 1920 (page 67), the verso of her largest known architectonic, of 1916–17 (page 66), discussed earlier. Here Popova uses an entirely different formal and syntactic code from that in the front panel, which continues the structural principle of assembling planar geometric shapes common to her post-Cubist abstractions. In its organization *Painterly Construction* recalls the system of combining real materials in Tatlin's reliefs. The composition of the recto is solidly structured yet essentially static. The verso, on the other hand, is very dynamic. Two sharply diagonal axes cross the composition from lower right to upper left. Spiraling forms in the central section, semicircular elements in burgundy red and orange, and a heavy black fragment of a crescent at the left center and lower left all contribute to the impression of continuing flux among the pictorial components. This effect is further enhanced through the use of half-dematerialized planes achieved through skillful shading in a different color and change in texture. The picture exudes great energy, heightened by the juxtaposition of vivid colors, and also manifests, in a much stronger way, the artist's emphasis on line as the dominant factor of a composition. In this sense it is a transitional work, situated between the mature Painterly Architectonics exploring the interplay of dense, textured planar forms and the next phase of the artist's work.

Linear Compositions

Throughout the years 1920–21 an increased preoccupation with line rather than plane and color becomes evident in Popova's work. These explorations are related to the Inkhuk discussions on "com-

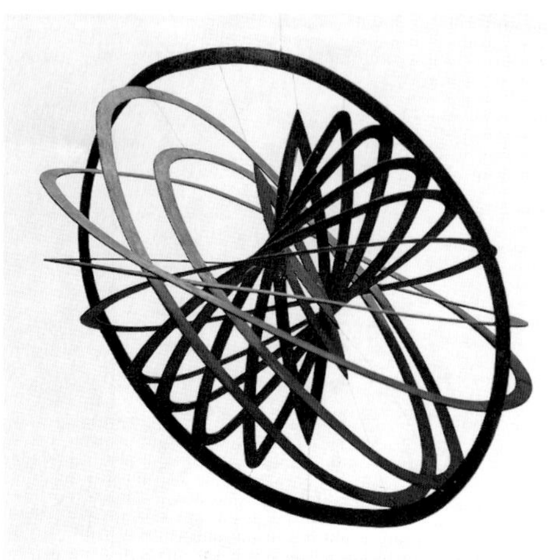

14. Alexander Rodchenko. *Oval Hanging Construction Number 12*. c. 1920. Plywood, open construction partially painted with aluminum paint, and wire, 24 × 33 × 18½" (61 × 83.7 × 47 cm). The Museum of Modern Art, New York. Acquisition made possible through the extraordinary efforts of George and Zinaida Costakis, and through the Nate B. and Frances Spingold, Matthew H. and Erna Futter, and Enid A. Haupt Funds

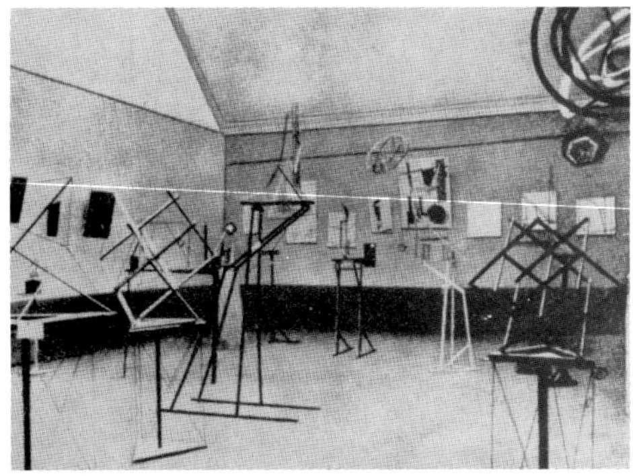

15. Installation view of the third Obmokhu exhibition, Moscow, May 1921

position" and "construction," particularly the attempts to define the latter. Line, as one of the fundamental means of the painter, was able to define abstract components of pictorial space and to convey conceptualized images without violating the two-dimensionality of the pictorial surface. By its sheer existence on the surface, line could elicit the impression of space. Its ability to convey rhythm and depth and to define and be translated into space made line a subject of special investigation for the Constructivists. It was fundamental to their attempts to reduce the means of expression to the bare essentials in order to evolve a concept of "construction." Rodchenko, in particular, emphasized the importance of line, executing many works in the 1920s that are austere, strictly linear compositions. His "hanging constructions" of 1920, composed of homogeneous geometric forms inscribed one inside another, constitute, as it were, three-dimensional transpositions of line into spatial form (fig. 14). His essay on line was intended to be included in a compendium of writings by Inkhuk members on the theme "From Figuration to Abstraction," which was never published.[42] It was the versatility of line that was so attractive to the Constructivists and other artists. For example, in 1919 Kandinsky wrote an extensive essay on the role of line as a means of pictorial expression; it was published in the magazine *Iskusstvo* on February 22, 1919, and was later incorporated into his 1926 publication *Point and Line to Surface*.[43]

In her statement for "The Tenth State Exhibition" Popova had written in 1919: "Line as color and a vestige of transverse plane participates in and determines the force of 'construction.'"[44] In 1920, when she joined Inkhuk along with Rodchenko, Stepanova, and others, the focus of her work became a systematic experimentation with pictorial construction and thus an exploration of the possibilities inherent in line. Her works of that period are composed predominantly of linear elements, sometimes incorporating vestiges of colored planes, but these are no longer well-defined, color-imbued forms. Both form and color are considered superfluous and are reduced to their common symbol—a colored line (since an edge of the colored plane is essentially defined by line). Thus form and color are reduced to a minimum to create the fundamental interpretative means of conveying texture and spatial relations. The varying thickness of line, intensity of color, and medium used result in different textural and spatial possibilities.

The linear compositions executed by Popova within this period are conceived according to two slightly different principles. One group, in two variations, consists mainly of works incorporating only straight lines (pages 98, 99), while the second group combines the straight-line grids and circular or semicircular elements into crisp dynamic structures (pages 88, 89).

Among the works using purely linear elements are a painting in a private collection (page 92) and a number of related drawings, which compositionally seem to be fragments of a larger spatial universe crisscrossed in a zigzag pattern by lines of force. These lines intersect at sharp angles and generate internal space situated between the pivotal points beyond the boundaries of the picture edge at top and bottom. Considered from a structural point of view, these pictorial constructions can be compared with the actual material constructions created contemporaneously by the younger, second generation of Constructivists who belonged to the Society of Young Artists—Obmokhu.[45] In the third Obmokhu exhibition, held in May 1921 in Moscow,[46] members of this group, which included sculptors Karl Ioganson, Konstantin Medunetsky, and the brothers Georgii and Vladimir Stenberg, presented several constructions of diverse materials that were three-dimensional transpositions of linear structures (fig. 15). Their forms, based on straight lines, represented essentially linear drawing in space; they defined space from without and within, making it an active component of form. Popova's pictorial preoccupations paralleled those of the Obmokhu members, all of whom were actively involved in the Inkhuk discussions on "composition" and "construction."

In Popova's case, the dematerialized, fragmented planes of different colors, conveyed through feathery shading, and the variegated colored lines are the structural materials for different parts of the work: the sculptural form, based on line and space, is signaled through the vestiges of colored planes. The tension between various colored lines produces the effect of spiraling movement, enhanced by the dynamic interaction of the supporting triangular areas of color—the shadows, as it were, of the vectors of force. The background, of medium value, provided by an unpainted surface, is perceived as a neutral, all-encompassing, unstructured space, a field for the interaction of linear scaffolding and vestiges of color. The multicolored lines constituting this scaffolding are cut off at random by the edge of the picture, and their rotation seems to occur along the axis joining two points beyond the boundaries of the work. Here again the linear structure that activates the viewer's space and forces him to complete the form mentally can be compared to that achieved by Rodchenko in his hanging constructions of 1920.

In the works described above, Popova creates a secondary structure that supports the linear one. This support structure is formed by the triangular feathery shading that extends along both sides of the colored line, suggesting not only shadows but also imaginary planes or streams of light that are bordered by the firmly drawn colored lines. The fragmentary planes reach out into the space created by the scaffold of zigzagging lines. The dynamism of these compositions is further emphasized by their asymmetry. Here form is not only non-objective but is transformed into the new expression: construction. It exemplifies Popova's conviction, stated in one of her manuscripts of 1921, that "transformation for the sake of painterly or sculptural construction is a revelation of our artistic revolution. . . . What is of importance now is the form or part of a form, line, color, or texture that takes an immediate part in the painterly construction."[47]

Although Popova cannot be considered a theoretician, her observations pointedly describe her objectives and imply a broader comprehension of the goals of art compatible with her country's new identity after the October Revolution. They show her to be a fervent supporter of the idea of a new, non-traditional artistic idiom. Her final definitions of "composition" and "construction," which appeared in the minutes of a meeting held January 21, 1921, described composition as "the regular and tasteful arrangement of materials," and construction as "purpose and necessity," that is, a purposeful combination of such pictorial fundamentals as volume and material, texture, color, and space.[48] The definition of construction was clarified in her notes of March 1921: "Construction is the aim. It is the necessity and expediency of organization."[49] What characterizes Popova's point of view regarding "construction" is her attitude as an artist-painter, not an artist-engineer—the new ideal of post-revolutionary Soviet society—involved with three-dimensional constructions using real industrial materials. Her components of "construction" are essentially the traditional painter's means, even though she interprets them as if they were real materials. This duality between theory and practice, or rather her very personal application of theory in her practice, continued in Popova's work of 1921–22.

Space-Force Constructions

Popova designated most of her works executed within the period 1921–22, whose focal point is dynamic space emphasized by linear structure, as Space Constructions and Space-Force Constructions. One can distinguish several basic series of compositions, each of which includes paintings on plywood and a number of smaller works on paper. Popova used the term for a group of works that were first exhibited in Moscow in September 1921 in the exhibition "5 × 5 = 25" (so-called because each of the five participants—Exter, Popova, Rodchenko, Stepanova, and Vesnin—contributed five works).[50] The exhibition was intended as a final presentation of the traditional medium of painting, signaling "death to easel painting," as the remnant of an elitist, bourgeois culture. Popova called her group of works "experiments in painterly-kinetic constructions," and the individual paintings bore titles such as *Space-Volume, Color-Plane (Surface), Enclosed Space-Construction,* and two called *Space-Force Construction.*[51]

The artist's statement, included in the catalogue, specified that her works "should be considered as a series of preparatory experiments for the concrete material constructions."[52] However, she never tackled concrete materials. As I have already emphasized, she was chiefly a painter, who later, under the pressures of the dominant utilitarian imperative in the Constructivist circle, turned her creative energies to practical ends in typography, textile design, and theatrical design. But even there her primary materials were form, light, color, and space.

Popova's Space-Force Constructions again represent innovative solutions to the handling of form, space, and material. Within a very limited vocabulary of means she was able to create quite diverse energetic, powerful works. For example, *Space-Force Construction* of 1921 (page 96), in oil on plywood, explores to maximum effect the interplay of six straight, diagonally placed lines crossing one another in the central section of the picture. The differing thicknesses of the lines and their varying colors highlight the dynamic effect. Their spatial interaction is enhanced by the multicolored "shadows" extending into the pictorial field and meeting the unpainted plywood plane, which acts as a symbol of space. The pairs of lines are neither parallels nor orthogonals but rather fragments of a web-like structure that seems to continue beyond the boundaries of the picture plane. The illusion of their existence in space increases the longer one contemplates the work. The variations in texture of the "shadows" contribute to the play of light, which further activates the composition. This crust-like effect of the textured planes is particularly visible in another *Space-Force Construction* (page 97), where the palette is limited to white, deep reddish brown, and one touch of black. The thick, crusty reddish-brown

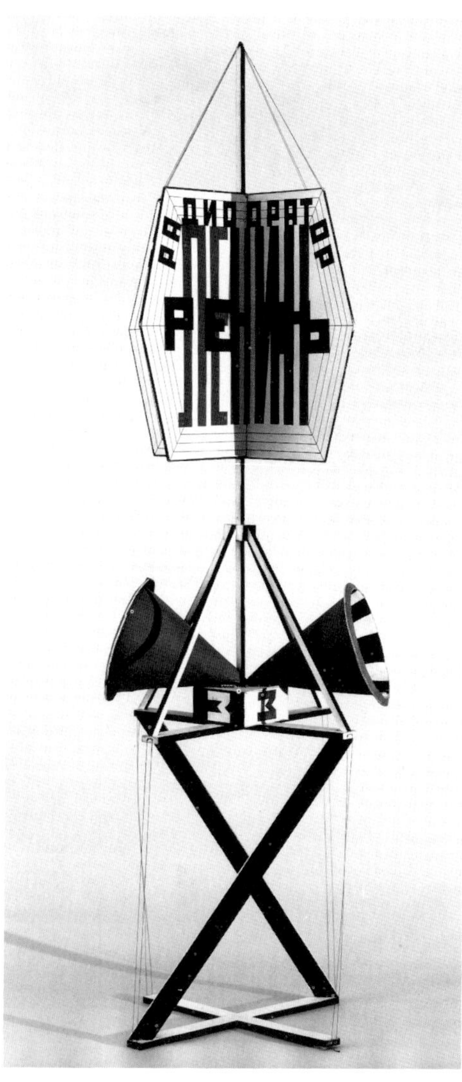

16. Gustav Klucis. Maquette for *Radio-Announcer*. 1922. Construction of painted cardboard, paper, wood, thread, and metal brads, 45¾ × 14½ × 14½" (106.1 × 36.8 × 36.8 cm). The Museum of Modern Art, New York. Sidney and Harriet Janis Collection Fund

pigment is played up against off-white smooth-textured lines crossing the field from lower right to upper left and from lower left to upper right. This creates an almost relief-like surface against the background of unpainted plywood board.

These abstract linear Space-Force Constructions also exist in a more stringent, to a certain degree more static, version, exemplified by a 1921 work in the Costakis collection (page 98). The linear armature of works of this type, with solid verticals cut through at an oblique angle by two other strong bars, creates the impression of representing fragments of industrial structure held together by tensile cables (here further symbolized by thin white lines forming a secondary linear grid). The black feathery "shadows," as in so many other examples already discussed, convey a sense of spatial extension into depth beyond the picture plane. The composition has a layered structure suggesting its existence in space. The two sets of linear elements differing in thickness create tension that energizes the composition. Despite the fact that the linear elements point in different directions and the upright ones are not truly vertical or parallel to one another, the composition shows great stability even within an active field of vision.

This type of work is closely related to a group of other Space-Force Constructions that are composed of more three-dimensional beam-like elements, such as the drawings *Med Vervis* and *Untitled* (1921) in the Costakis collection (page 101). Here the linear armature and thick shading convey almost enclosed three-dimensional form, bringing to mind some of the shapes used contemporaneously by Lissitzky in his architecture and also in early modernist bridge structures. Such linear configurations imply the potential for extending space both vertically and horizontally and explore structural tension among the components.

Analogous concepts in the use of linear tensile structure can be found in the work of other members of the avant-garde, particularly in the propagandistic constructions of Gustav Klucis (fig. 16). The structures of wooden scaffolding held together by the tension of crisscrossing beams and cables reflect in three-dimensional form the concerns obvious in Popova's linear Space-Force Constructions. His wooden beams and tensile cables are counterparts of Popova's differing thicknesses of linear scaffolding. These variations in the thickness of lines and their textural aspect could be considered a transposition of the previously mentioned Tatlinian principle of the "culture of materials," whereby different materials have an inherent potential for specific forms and textures. Popova adapted this postulate by introducing such materials as marble dust into her traditional medium of oil paint, thus enabling her to create new types of texture, more physical and tangible, that added to the materiality of the picture.

The emphasis on the material aspect of the work of art is further evident in another series of Space-Force Constructions, created mostly during 1921, contemporaneously with the purely linear works. Exemplifying this series of paintings are a large square work in oil with marble dust on plywood in the Costakis collection (page 89) and the *Space-Force Construction* in oil with bronze powder at the State Tretyakov Gallery (page 90), both of which have related groups of drawings. All of these works combine straight linear and circular elements, occasionally supplemented by Popova's characteristic feathery shading.

The *Space-Force Construction* in the Costakis collection is rather large in format and, with its textured aspect and thickness of oil and marble dust applied to the plywood support, conveys a sense of great physicality. It is a solid structure whose physical parameters, defined through the use of *passage*, are suggested by the circular paths and different axes of rotational movements. The painting exudes great energy concentrated within the pictorial field but pushing out beyond its boundaries because of the random cutting off of the circular elements. The color scheme of black, red, and white against the natural plywood background enhances the dynamic aspect of the painting. Similar dynamic forces are at work in the Tretyakov's *Space-Force Construction*, but because of the introduction of the aggressive blue color, the final visual effect is much more decorative than in the Costakis picture. In the latter, the austerity of the palette (despite the vivid red) creates the effect of a much more sober and compact dynamic structure.

These Space-Force Constructions closed Popova's experiments with the pictorial medium. Although the break may not have occurred at the exact time of the announcement of the "death to easel painting," it followed shortly thereafter, possibly as a result of the November 1921 schism at Inkhuk when the theoretician Osip Brik officially proclaimed the productivist imperative as the fundamental goal of artistic creation.

Production Art

At the November 24, 1921, session of Inkhuk, Brik called for a definitive rejection of easel painting and declared the necessity for a transition to "real" utilitarian work. Brik's proposal was accepted and signed by twenty-five artists, among them Popova, Rodchenko, Stepanova, the Stenberg brothers, and Vesnin.[53] Thus Russian Constructivism entered a new phase in which functional Constructivism, defined as production art, was to become the absolute and only viable artistic activity.

The relationship between art and industry was part of a much broader debate concerning the nature of proletarian art in Soviet society in the aftermath of the October Revolution. The necessary connection between ideology and technology postulated by members of the group Proletkult (an acronym for Proletarskaya Kultura, or Proletarian Culture) influenced the Constructivists to a certain extent. Their proclamation of "Art into Life," which became the main slogan of the functional Constructivists, called for the artists' total commitment to production and consequently for a fusion of the artistic and the technological.[54] This ideological position rejected the concept of art as expressive of philosophical or aesthetic concerns, viewing it instead as a purposeful material creation. Yet it was different from applied art, which, according to the critic Nikolai Punin, was concerned primarily with decoration. Production art resulted in the creation of "completely artistic objects" and was therefore fundamentally different in nature. The "completely artistic objects" were to be designed by the "artist-constructor," that is, the artist with a knowledge of industrial process and an involvement with actual production. The result was to be an object whose form was dictated primarily by its purpose.

Initially Popova was not among the strongest advocates of production art, but following the lead of Tatlin, Rodchenko, and Stepanova, she gradually revised her attitude, recognizing the need for a closer involvement of artists in industrial production. It was, however, in designing for the theater and executing commissions for various propagandistic projects in celebration of Communist events that many Constructivist artists, Popova among them, found the opportunity to realize their utopian visions of art for the masses. Popova's involvement with the theater began in 1920 when Alexander Tairov commissioned her to design sets and costumes for his production of *Romeo and Juliet,* to be presented at the Kamernyi Theater in Moscow. Although she executed designs for a whole series of costumes, Tairov ultimately chose to use the set and costume designs by Alexandra Exter. Popova's theater designs for Vsevolod Meyerkhold were more successful. In 1922 she designed sets and costumes for his presentation of a play by Fernand Crommelynck, *The Magnanimous Cuckold* (page 106), and in 1923 for *Zemla Dybom (Earth in Turmoil),* an adaptation of Marcel Martinet's verse drama *La Nuit* (page 107).

The sets for the Meyerkhold productions could be considered a concretization of Constructivist ideas, indeed of the concepts that Popova explored so persistently in her later pictorial works. The structure of the sets for *The Magnanimous Cuckold,* based on an interplay of verticals and horizontals and the use of planes and rotating platforms (all executed in wood), complemented by a skillful manipulation of lighting to complete the form and activate the space, displayed basic organizational principles shared with Popova's pictorial works of 1920 and 1921, notably her Space-Force Constructions, which were predicated upon kinetic linear structure. The costumes, composed as combinations of simple geometric shapes, were among the best examples of *prozodezhda* (working clothing—in this case, for actors), designed to allow unrestricted movement and to emphasize the biomechanical rhythms of the actors' movements as devised by Meyerkhold. Popova's sets and costumes made the theatrical production a composite of gesture, movement, music, light, and architecture; the interaction of forms, materials, time, and space resulted in a living, unified work of art. This production marked the culmination of a radical change in stage design, eliminating the idea of sets and costumes as backdrop and illusion and bringing them into the realm of living art. The change can be compared with that which took place in painting when nonobjective art was purged of representation, narrative, and illusion and a painting became a self-referential entity defined uniquely in terms of its own pictorial means.

The set designs for *Earth in Turmoil* were quite different from the schematic, machine-like, kinetic plastic constructions used in *The Magnanimous Cuckold.* Even the same costumes characterized by an ascetic simplicity of *prozodezhda* had a dissimilar effect in another setting. The *Earth in Turmoil* set reflected Popova's changed ideological view of the artist's involvement with the theater and consequently with practical everyday life. Popova proposed the use of real props, such as cranes, machines, and guns, which gave the production the character of an "agit-performance" or a public event for the masses.[55] Conceptually related to the principles used in Constructivist posters, the set wove many realistic elements into an abstractly conceived whole.

Popova's talents were also employed practically, from 1921 to 1924, in the area of typography. Her designs for book, periodical, and music covers made use of such devices as bold lettering arranged asymmetrically and colors juxtaposed to bring out important elements of the titles; different parts of the design created block-like configurations that later came to epitomize Constructivist typography, principally familiar in the West through the work of Lissitzky and Rodchenko.

Popova's activities in the area of textile design were by far the most closely aligned to the ideological tenets promoting production art. During 1923–24 she and Stepanova designed patterns for fabrics for the First State Textile Print Factory (formerly the Emil Tsindel Factory) in Moscow. In her production art she used principles similar to those that had dominated her work as a painter. Her textile designs were based on geometric forms in bright color combinations incorporated into rhythmical, lively patterns (pages 110, 111). The concept underlying her method was based on her conviction, shared and widely publicized by Stepanova, that textile design should relate to the principles of clothing design, and the latter, in turn, should reflect the practical needs of the consumer.[56] Of least importance were the aesthetic considerations, completely subordinated to the functional aspect of design. It was Popova's gift for striking color combinations and her great skill in manipulating forms, however, that gave her designs high aesthetic appeal.

Throughout the period she was involved with production art, Popova continued to teach the future artist-constructors at the Vkhutemas as well as at Gvytm (State Higher Theatrical Studios), and in 1924 she established a special course on "material formation of a spectacle" for the Proletkult in Moscow.

Popova died unexpectedly in 1924 at the age of thirty-five when she was at the height of her creative powers. Although her artistic career was cut short, her contribution was among the most important for the evolution of Constructivist concepts. The sizable body of work that she produced attests to the high quality of her achievement, revealing a versatile, innovative artist who drew on diverse influences, consolidated them, and made them the basis of her own distinctive means of expression.

notes

1. The principal archives of Popova's work are in a private collection, in the department of manuscripts at the State Tretyakov Gallery, and the Central State Archive of Literature and Art (CGALI), all in Moscow. A number of documents from these sources were included in a French translation of the monograph by Natalia A. Adaskina and Dimitri V. Sarabianov, *Lioubov Popova* (Paris: Philippe Sers, 1989), published in English by Harry N. Abrams, New York, in 1990.

2. *L. S. Popova, 1889–1924: Katalog posmertnoy vystavki khuidozhnika konstruktora L.S. Popovoy (Catalogue of the Posthumous Exhibition of the Artist-Constructor L.S. Popova)* (Moscow, 1924), pp. 6–7. Translation by the author.

3. See Adaskina and Sarabianov, *Lioubov Popova,* pp. 13, 42.

4. The renowned Sergei Shchukin collection of modern French art, which included many Impressionist and Post-Impressionist works, as well as numerous paintings by Matisse, Picasso, and Braque, was opened to the public in the spring of 1909 for viewing on Sundays. The catalogue of the collection was published in *Apollon,* a monthly review on art, in 1914.

5. Some of these sketchbooks are in the George Costakis Collection (Art Co. Ltd.) and the State Tretyakov Gallery, Moscow; others are in private collections in Sweden and the United States.

6. See *Exposition de Sculpture Futuriste du Peintre et Sculpteur Futuriste Boccioni du 20 juin au 16 juillet* (Paris: Galerie La Boëtie, 1913), cat. no. 4.

7. For the sculpture *Development of a Bottle in Space;* see ibid., note 6, cat. no. 6.

8. Margit Rowell makes this connection in her essay "New Insights into Soviet Constructivism: Painting, Constructions, Production Art," in *Art of the Avant-Garde in Russia: Selections from the George Costakis Collection* (New York: Solomon R. Guggenheim Museum, 1981), p. 18. The same connection is mentioned in Angelica Z. Rudenstine, ed., *The George Costakis Collection: Russian Avant-Garde Art* (New York: Harry N. Abrams, 1981), p. 352.

9. For an extensive analysis of Archipenko's work, see *Alexander Archipenko: A Centennial Tribute* (Washington, D.C.: National Gallery of Art, 1986).

10. In Adaskina and Sarabianov, *Lioubov Popova,* this painting is identified as *Le Kremlin, Le Tsar-Canon,* 1915 (ill. p. 98, lower left). This identification is based on the listing of works in the catalogue of Popova's posthumous exhibition held in Moscow in December 1924–January 1925. However, this listing does not positively indicate such an attribution. On stylistic grounds, in terms of an overall composition, apparent vestiges of figuration, and three-dimensional treatment of the figurative fragments, as well as in terms of color scheme, this painting seems to be situated between *Seated Woman* (Galerie Gmurzynska, Cologne) and *Objects from the Dyer's Shop.* Furthermore, the vestiges of architecture visible in the center of the composition are more indicative of an Italian Renaissance rather than a Russian influence. The details recall the architecture in the 1914 painting *Florence* by Alexandra Exter, who at that time lived in Paris at the same pensione as Popova and who also traveled to Italy in 1914. Since Popova's trip to Italy took place in 1914, this painting might have been executed after the trip. On this basis and also on stylistic grounds, I would attribute a date of 1914 to the painting. *Objects from the Dyer's Shop* was previously shown under the title *Early Morning.* The title used here is based on the listing in the catalogue to the posthumous exhibition, note 1, cat. no. 24.

11. This phrase, "lines of force," comes from Boccioni's *Technical Manifesto of Futurist Sculpture,* published in 1912 and subsequently included in the catalogue of Boccioni's exhibition at Galerie La Boëtie in Paris in 1913; see above, note 6.

12. The Futurist review *Lacerba* was founded in Florence in 1912 by the Florentine writer Giovanni Papini and the painter-critic Ardengo Soffici. As a biweekly and then a weekly newspaper that appeared until 1916, it was an important *porte-parole* of Futurism that disseminated advanced philosophical writing, political views, and progressive art ideas and illustrations. In 1914 Popova visited Italy, seeing Florence among other places, and might have come into contact with *Lacerba* through Soffici, a good friend of her friend Exter.

13. See D. Burliuk, "Faktura," in *Poshchechina Obshchestvennemu Vkusu* (*A Slap in the Face of Public Taste*), pp. 102–10. Also V. Markov, *Printsipy tvorchestva v plasticheskikh iskusstvakh: Faktura* (*Principles of Creation in the Visual Arts: Faktura*) (St. Petersburg, 1914).

14. The exhibition "Tramway V" opened on March 3, 1915, according to the Gregorian calendar then used in Russia. This would be February 18 by the Western calendar, which runs thirteen days behind the Gregorian calendar. Thus Popova must have painted the work within the first six weeks of 1915. See the exhibition catalogue *Tramway V: The First Futurist Exhibition of Paintings* (Petrograd, 1915), entry no. 45.

15. *The Last Futurist Exhibition of Paintings: 0.10* (Petrograd, 1915), cat. no. 86.

16. Adaskina and Sarabianov, *Lioubov Popova*, p. 66.

17. *Tramway V*, cat. no. 20.

18. A painting titled *Traveling Woman* was included in the "0.10" exhibition in Petrograd (cat. no. 92). A work titled *Traveling Woman* (second version) was later shown in Popova's posthumous exhibition in Moscow in December 1924 (cat. no. 18) and is prominently displayed in one of the installation photographs of that exhibition. This appears to be the Norton Simon picture, but the one in "0.10" might have been either of the two.

19. Although the painting is usually referred to as *Traveling Woman*, and the inclusion of wavy hair in the central section would suggest a female subject, the very center of the apex of the central triangle is occupied by a stiff white bib-like form that suggests a male torso, possibly her companion or attendant. For this reason one wonders whether the more appropriate title might be *The Traveler*.

20. Tatlin first exhibited his reliefs in a brief showing at his studio on Oshozhenka 37 in Moscow on May 10–14, 1914. They were later included in *The Last Futurist Exhibition of Paintings: 0.10*, cat. nos. 132–144m. On the occasion of the opening of this exhibition, Tatlin published a pamphlet, *Vladimir Evgrafovich Tatlin* (December 17, 1915), in which he discussed the philosophy behind his reliefs. This pamphlet is reproduced in H. Berninger and J. A. Cartier, *Pougny: Catalogue de l'oeuvre* (Tübingen: Ernst Wasmuth, 1972), pp. 54–55.

21. For more information on Kliun's and Puni's reliefs, see ibid., note 20.

22. *The Last Futurist Exhibition of Paintings: 0.10*, cat. nos. 95, 96, and 97, respectively.

23. *Liubov Popova*, catalogue of the posthumous exhibition, cat. no. 22, 111.7 (n.p.). The two reliefs were also illustrated as nos. 5 and 6 (n.p.).

24. *Die Kunstismen* (1925), fig. 62, p. 31, where it is incorrectly dated as 1916.

25. Dimitri Sarabianov proposes a different sequence for the first two reliefs, suggesting a progression from *The Jug on the Table* to *Portrait of a Lady* to the non-objective reliefs. See Adaskina and Sarabianov, *Lioubov Popova*, p. 64.

26. Both postcards to Dege are reproduced in Rudenstine, ed., *The George Costakis Collection*, figs. 813–16, p. 366. The works are also listed as such in *The Last Futurist Exhibition of Paintings: 0.10*, nos. 95–96.

27. Sarabianov believes that there were four reliefs and conveyed this in his discussion with the author in Moscow in January 1990 on the occasion of the Popova exhibition held at the State Tretyakov Gallery in Moscow. A still life with fruit bowl recognizable in several of the 1915 paintings might have been the subject of such a relief. In fact, Rudenstine, ed., *The George Costakis Collection*, reproduces another postcard written by Popova to Dege which represents a work called *Still Life*, subtitled "plastic painting" (note 26, fig. 811, p. 365), which could be *Vase with Fruit*, the relief shown in the "0.10" exhibition (cat. no. 97), also visible in the photographs of the posthumous exhibition.

28. See Berninger and Cartier, *Pougny*, note 21.

29. The latter two pictures had been misattributed to 1914–15 until Sarabianov, in the monograph on Popova, situated them in relation to a series of drawings done in conjunction with her trip to Birsk, a city in Bashkiria (Russia), to visit Adelaida Robertovna Dege.

30. Sarabianov, in his essay on Popova in the monograph, suggests a specific painting on the basis of a comparison between the listing in the catalogue and the installation evident in the photographs of the exhibition. However, since the works were presumably dated by the organizers of the exhibition, the accuracy of these determinations is open to discussion. For details, see Adaskina and Sarabianov, *Lioubov Popova*, p. 109.

31. Adaskina and Sarabianov, *Lioubov Popova*, pp. 133–37. See also George Peck and Lilly Wei, "Lioubov Popova: Interpretation of Space," *Art in America* (October 1982), pp. 94–104.

32. Vasilii Rakitin, "Ljubow Popowa," in Krystyna Rubinger, ed., *Women Artists of the Russian Avant-Garde: 1910–1930* (Cologne: Galerie Gmurzynska, 1980), pp. 199–200.

33. To accompany the presentation of his Suprematist paintings, Malevich published a pamphlet, *From Cubism to Suprematism: the New Realism in Painting* (Moscow: Zhuravi, 1915), which explained his philosophy of the new style. English trans. in T. Andersen, ed., *K. S. Malevich: Essays on Art 1915–1928* (Copenhagen: Borgen, 1968), vol. 1, pp. 19–41.

34. Rowell, "New Insights into Soviet Constructivism," pp. 20–22.

35. At "The Last Futurist Exhibition of Paintings: 0.10," Tatlin showed a roomful of reliefs as a counterpoint to Malevich's Suprematist work and also published a pamphlet in which he explained the principles of his reliefs.

36. The Supremus group, which was formed around Malevich in 1916–17, included Rozanova, Udaltsova, Kliun, Vera Pestel, Archipenko, Davydova, Menkov, the poet Alexei Kruchenykh, and the critic Alyagrov (Roman Jakobson).

37. *The Tenth State Exhibition: Non-objective Creation and Suprematism.* (Moscow, 1919), p. 29; reprinted in full in Matsa, *Sovietskoe iskusstvo za 15 let.*, p. 112.

38. Ibid., note 37.

39. "Inkhuk" is the acronym for the Institute Khudozhestvennoy Kultury (Institute of Artistic Culture). For detailed information on Inkhuk's goals and purpose, see Christina Lodder, *Russian Constructivism* (New Haven: Yale University Press, 1983), pp. 78–83; S. Khan-Magomedov. *Rodchenko: The Complete Work* (Cambridge, Mass.: MIT Press, 1987), pp. 55–58. The concept of "construction," including the discussion of Inkhuk, was the subject of the author's Ph.D. dissertation: M. Dabrowski, "The Russian Contribution to Modernism: 'Construction' as Realization of Innovative Aesthetic Concepts of the Russian Avant-Garde," New York University Institute of Fine Arts, 1990.

40. *The Tenth State Exhibition,* note 37.

41. Ibid.

42. The original of the text is in the Rodchenko family archive in Moscow; for excerpts in English translation, see D. Elliot, *Rodchenko* (New York: Pantheon Books, 1979), p. 128; A. B. Nakov, "Alexander Rodchenko. The Line," *Arts Magazine,* 47, no. 7 (May–June 1973), pp. 50–52.

43. V. Kandinsky, "Little Articles on Big Questions: On Point; On Line," *Iskusstvo,* February 22, 1919; later published as *Point and Line to Surface* (1926); reprinted in Vergo Lindsay, *Kandinsky: Complete Writings on Art,* vol. 1 (1982), pp. 425–26.

44. *The Tenth State Exhibition,* note 35.

45. "Obmokhu" is an acronym for Obschchestvo Molodykh Khudozhnikov, or Society of Young Artists, which was organized in 1919 by a group of younger Constructivists from the Vkhutemas.

46. The literature on this subject has created some confusion as to whether this was the second or third Obmokhu exhibition. The problem seems to have originated in the fact that the catalogue of the exhibition defined it as the "second spring exhibition of the Society of Young Artists." However, according to all the documentary materials regarding the activities of Obmokhu, the exhibition of May 1921 was the third in a series of four shows.

47. Manuscript, 1921, private archive, Moscow. Excerpts from the text are reprinted in Rakitin, "Ljubow Popowa," p. 211.

48. Central State Archive of Literature and Art (CGALI), Moscow, fond 681, and private archive, Moscow. Excerpts are quoted in Lodder, *Russian Constructivism,* pp. 88–89, note 80.

49. Quoted in English (from a Russian manuscript in a private archive, Moscow), in Rakitin, "Ljubow Popowa," p. 212.

50. *5 × 5 = 25,* (Moscow, September 1921), n.p., cat. nos. 11–15. [A copy of this handmade catalogue is in the collection of The Museum of Modern Art, New York.]

51. At this time it is not possible to give a positive identification of the works included in the "5 × 5 = 25" exhibition. See *5 × 5 = 25,* note 50.

52. Ibid., note 51.

53. For a listing of all signatories, see Lodder, *Russian Constructivism,* p. 90.

54. This aspect of Constructivism was the subject of an exhibition, "Art into Life," held at Henry Art Gallery, Seattle, Washington, June 4–September 2, 1990, and the Walker Art Center, Minneapolis, Minnesota, October 7–December 30, 1990. The catalogue of the exhibition illuminates in depth different areas of Constructivist art and philosophy.

55. Popova's art of the 1920s and her involvement with the theater are the subject of an essay by Natalia Adaskina in the catalogue of the Popova exhibition held in the Soviet Union in 1989–90. See *L. S. Popova: 1889–1924 Exhibition of Works from the Centennial Exhibition* (Moscow: State Tretyakov Gallery/ARS Publications Limited, 1990), pp. 120–35. This period is also discussed extensively in Adaskina and Sarabianov, *Lioubov Popova,* pp. 190–259.

56. For the philosophy of textile and clothing design, see Lodder, *Russian Constructivism,* ch. 5, pp. 145–55.

plates

In the captions on the following pages, the title or description of the work of art appears in boldface type and is followed by the date, medium, and dimensions. The latter are given in inches, height preceding width. For additional data, see the Catalogue of the Exhibition, beginning on page 126.

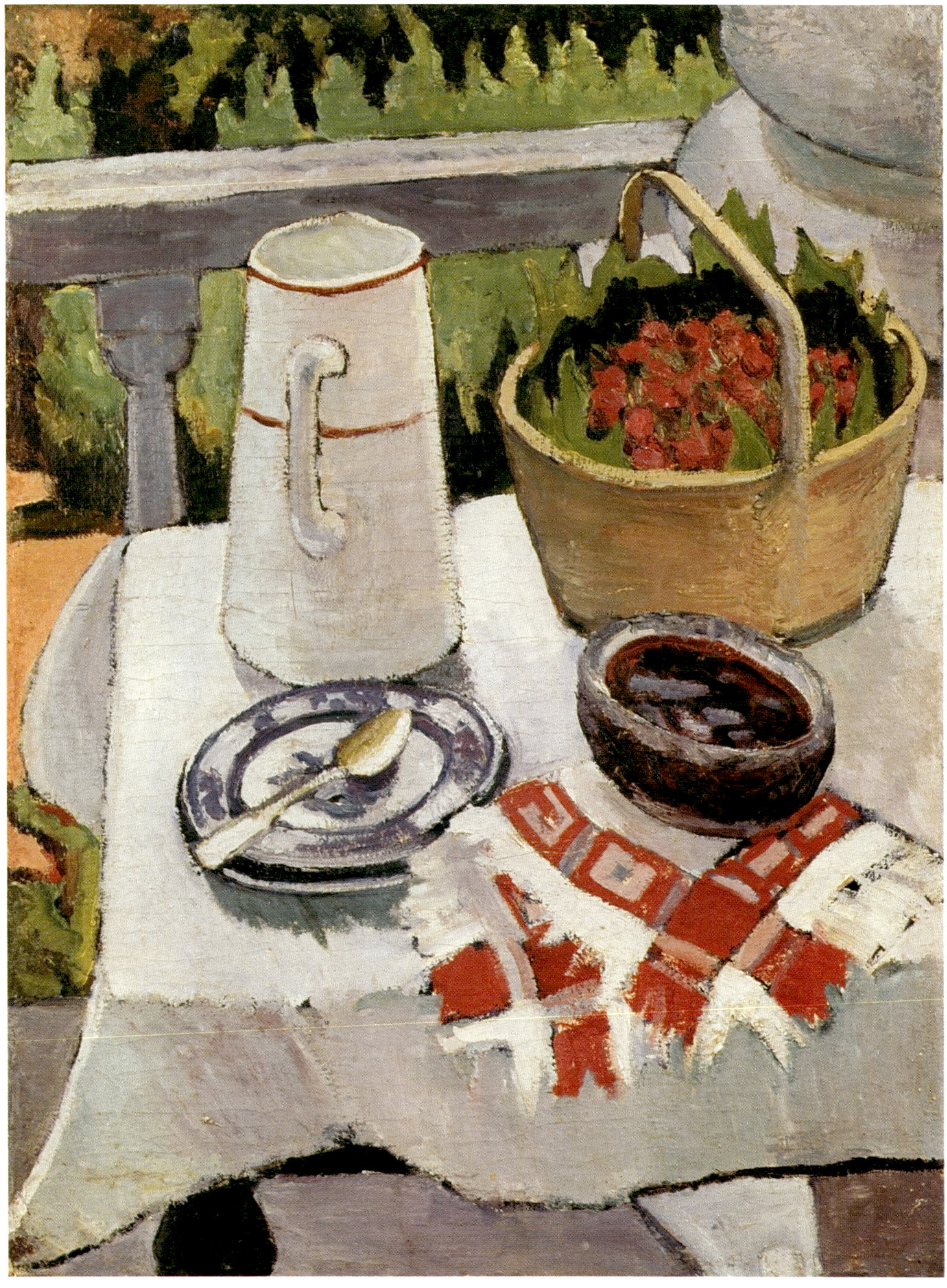

Still Life
1907–08
Oil on canvas
27¾ × 21⅛″

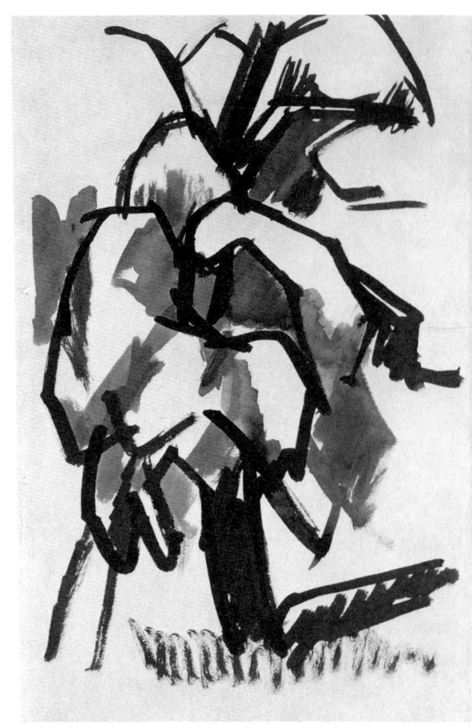

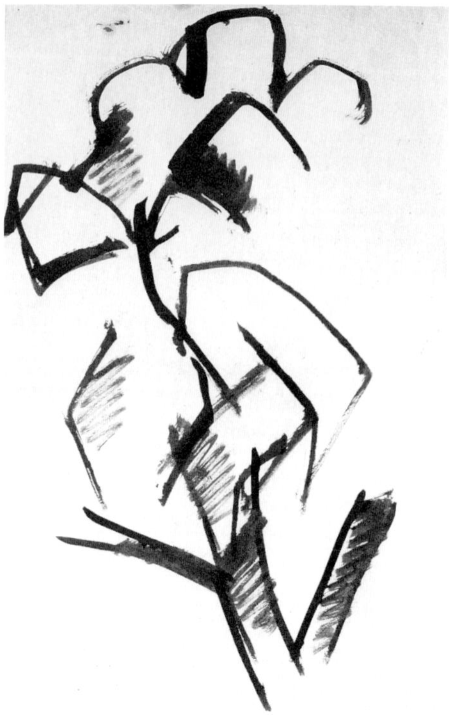

Untitled
c. 1908
Ink and wash
on paper
17⅝ × 13¾″

Untitled
c. 1908
Ink and wash
on paper
14 × 8⅞″

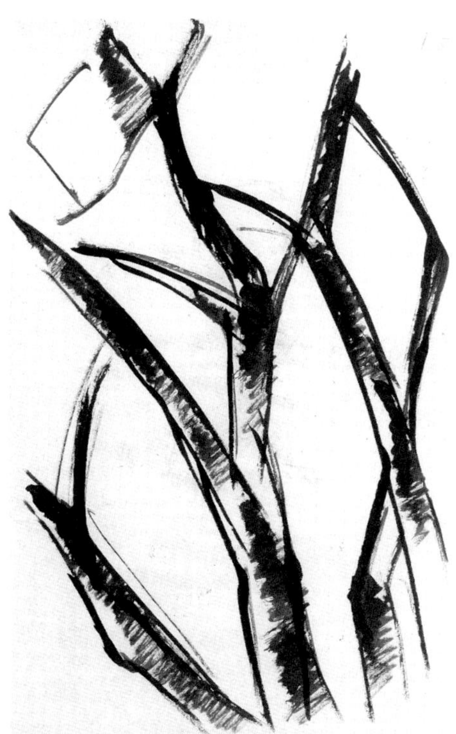

Untitled (Tree)
c. 1911–12
India ink and wash on paper
14 × 8⅞″

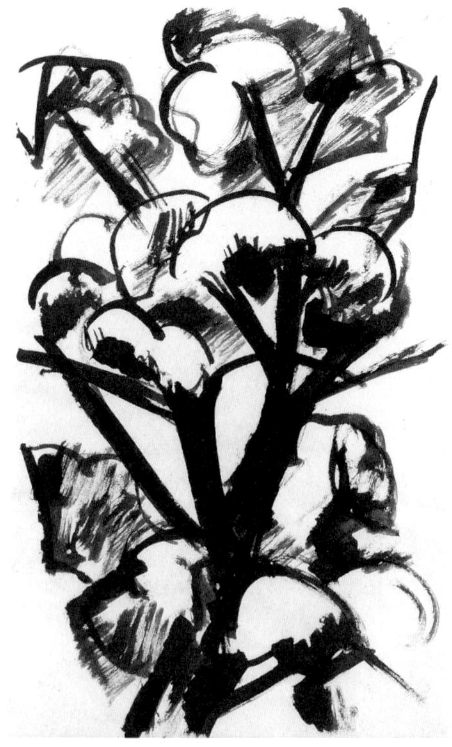

Untitled (Blooming Tree)
c. 1911–12
India ink and wash on paper
14 × 8¾″

Male Model
c. 1910
Oil on canvas
39 × 30″

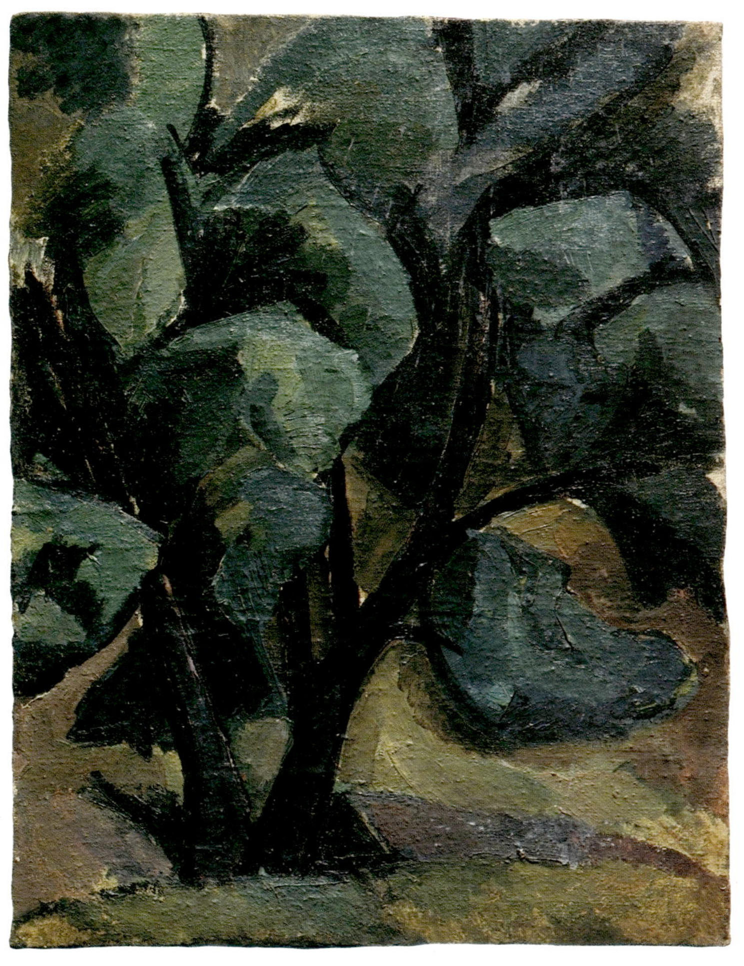

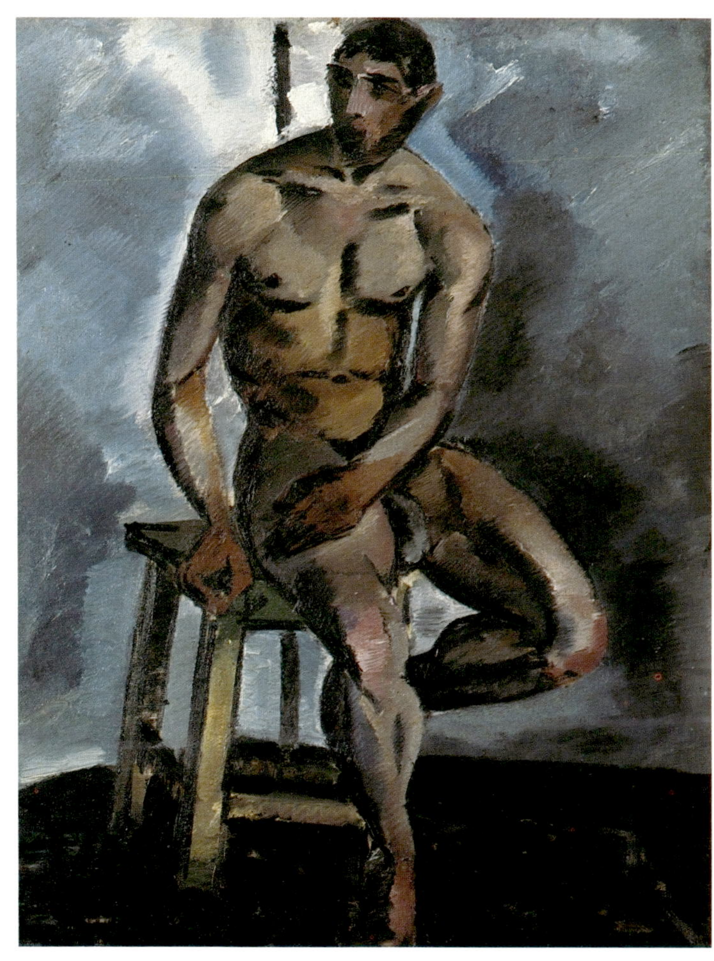

Trees
1911–12
Oil on canvas
23⅞ × 18¾″

Study of a Model
c. 1913
Oil on canvas
41¾ × 27¾"

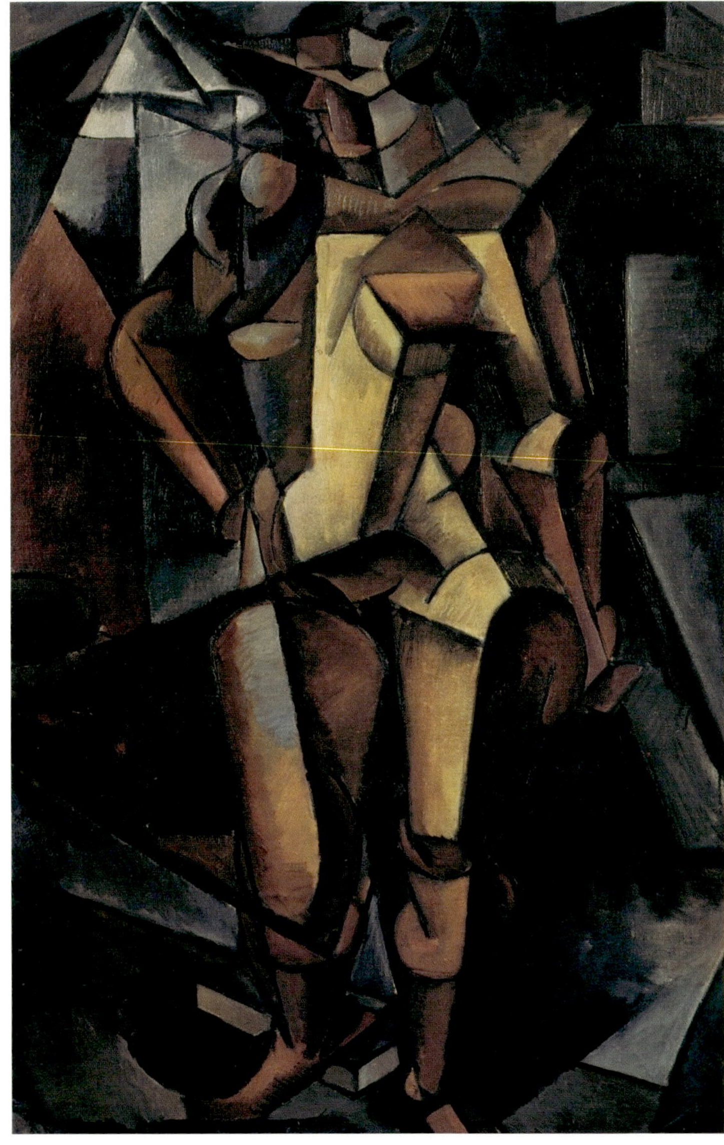

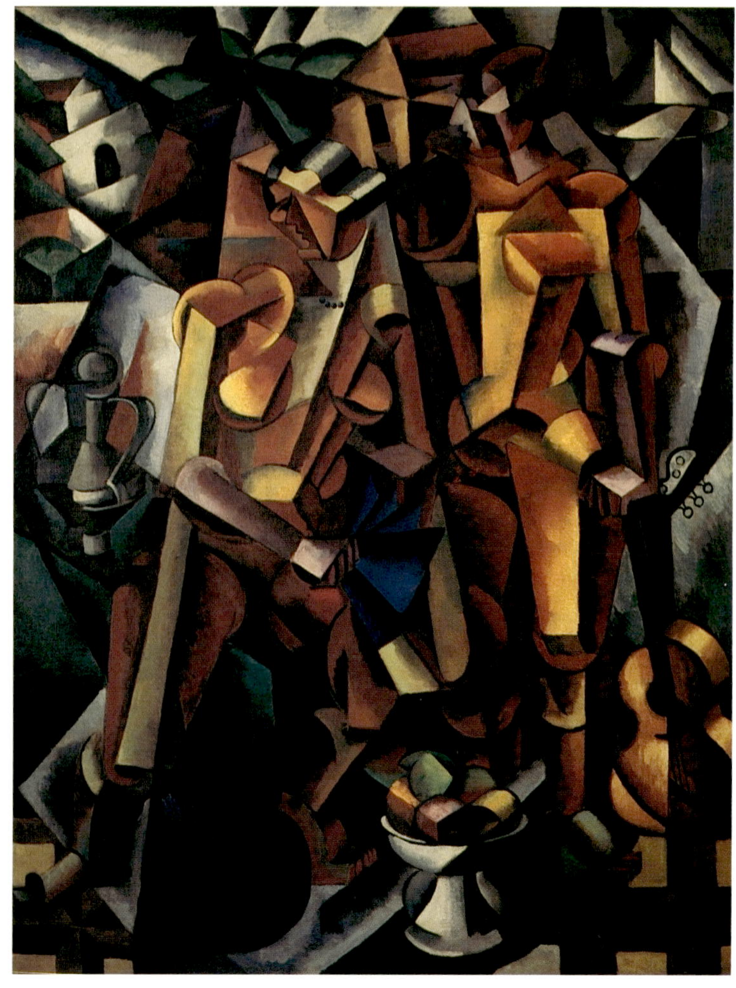

Composition with Figures
1913
Oil on canvas
63⅜ × 48⅜"

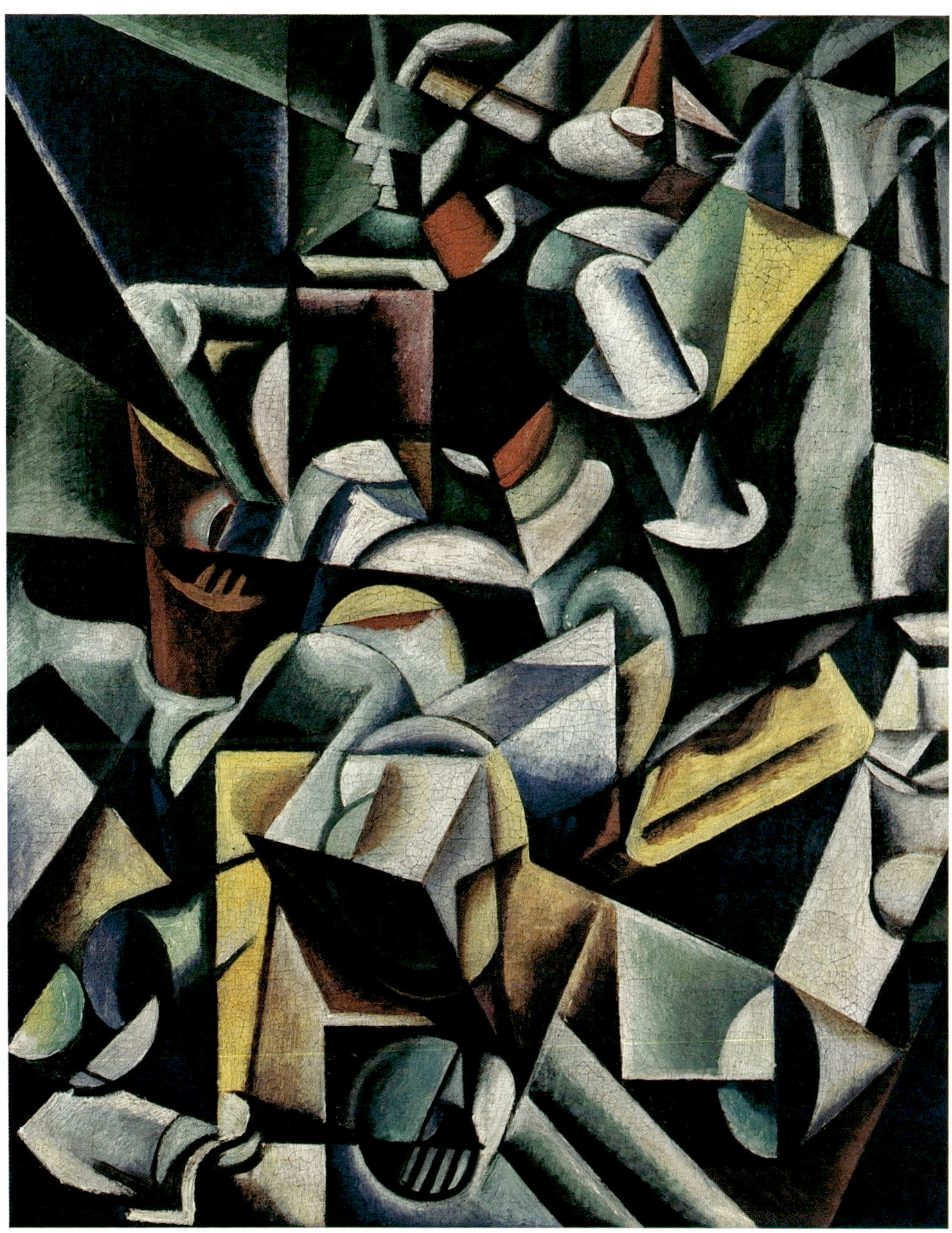

Seated Woman
1913–14
Oil on canvas
24 × 19⅝″

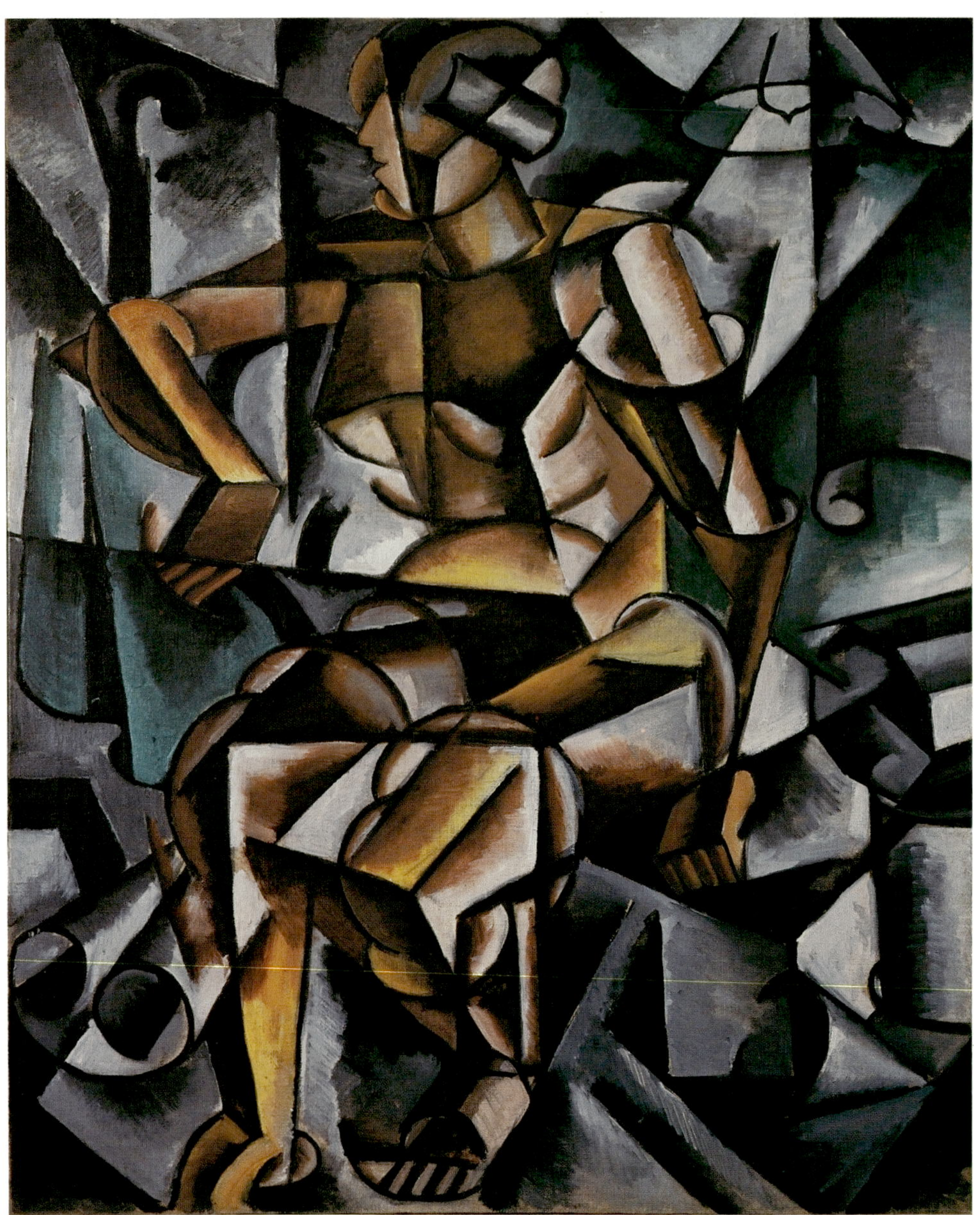

Seated Female Nude
c. 1913–14
Oil on canvas
41¾ × 34¼″

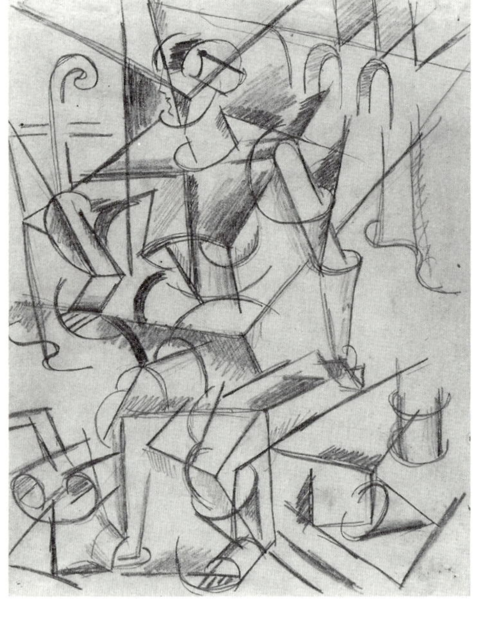

Seated Figure
c. 1913–14
Pencil on paper
10½ × 8¼″

Figure + House + Space
1913–14
Oil on canvas
49¼ × 42⅛″

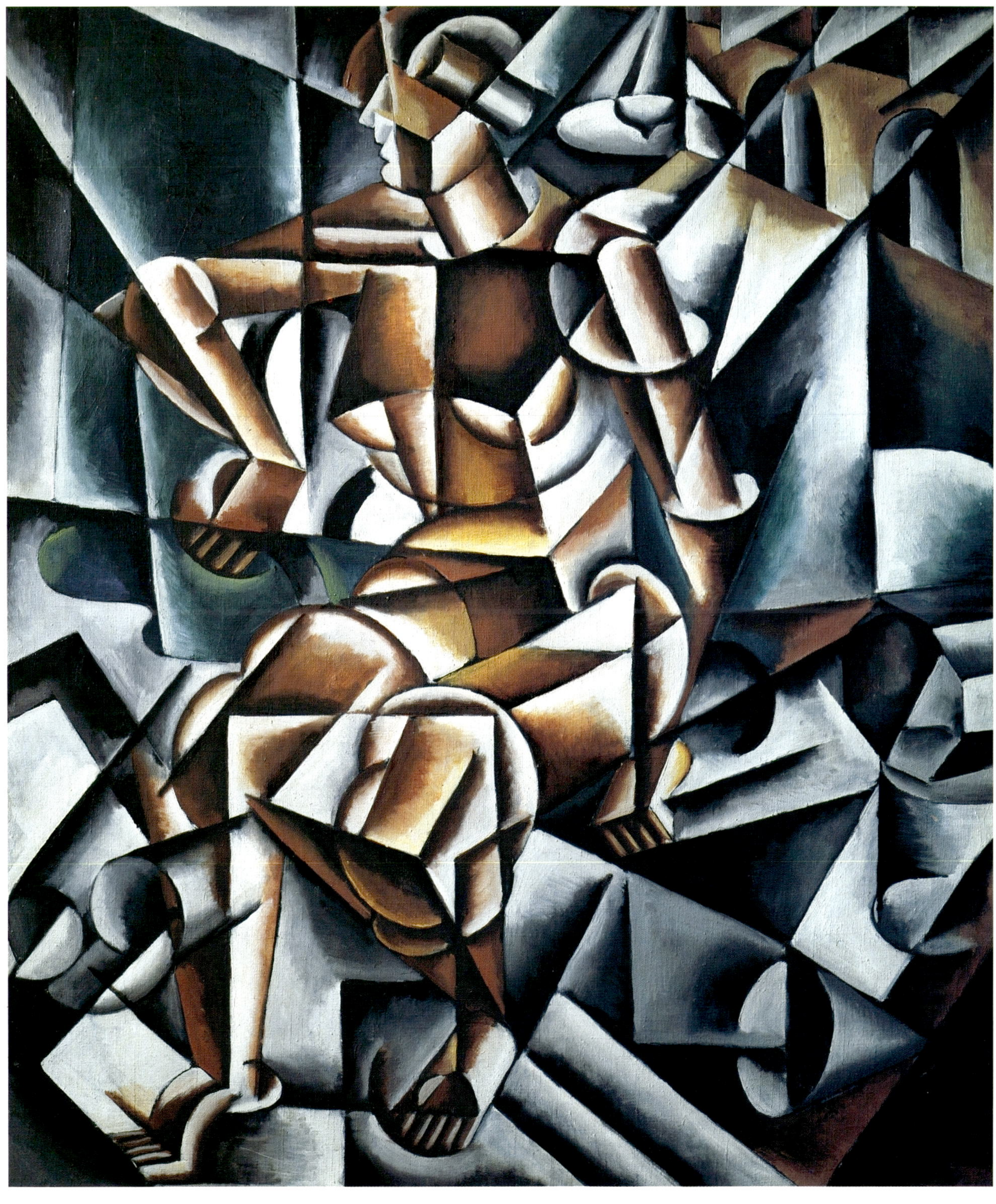

Anatomical Study
c. 1913–14
Pencil on paper
10½ × 8⅛″

Standing Figure
c. 1913–14
Pencil on paper
10½ × 8⅛″

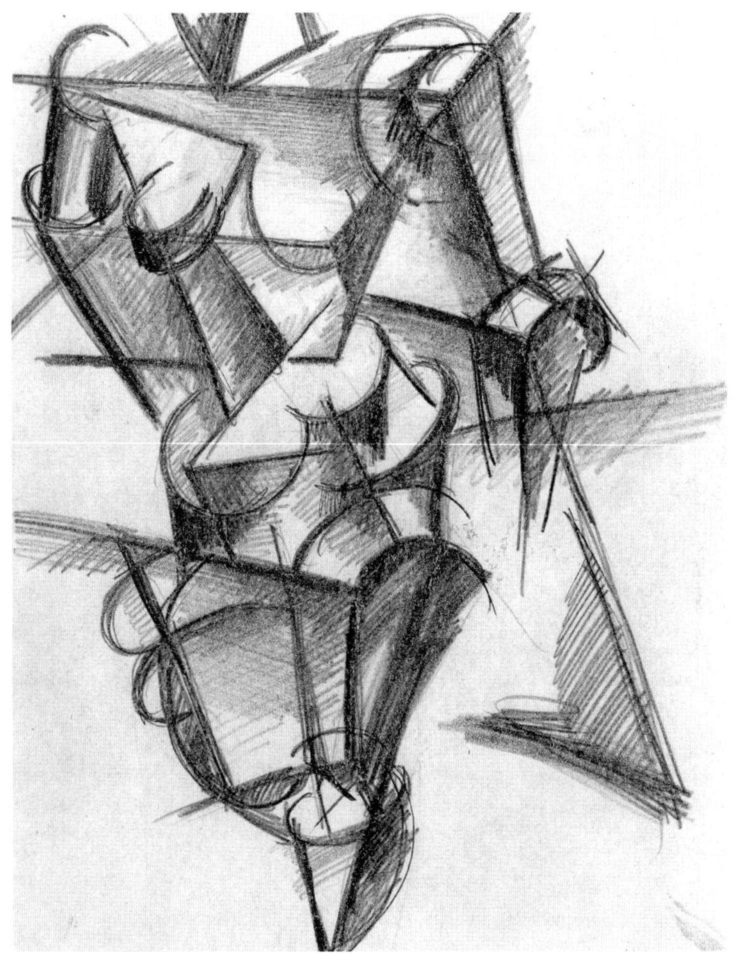

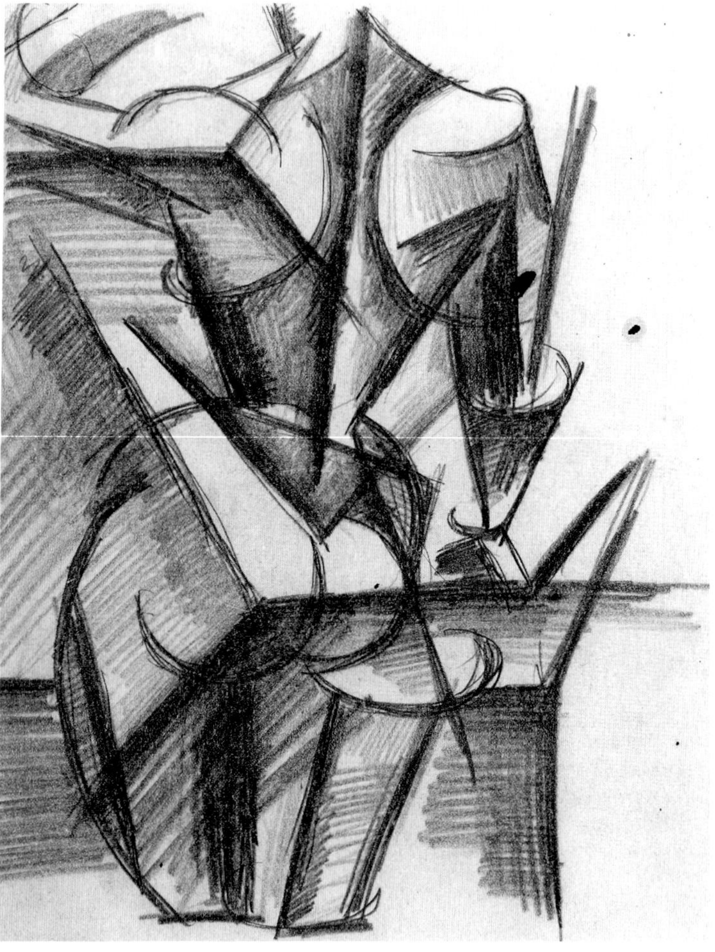

Anatomical Study
c. 1914
Pencil on paper
10½ × 8⅛″

Seated Figure
c. 1914
Pencil on paper
8½ × 6⅝″

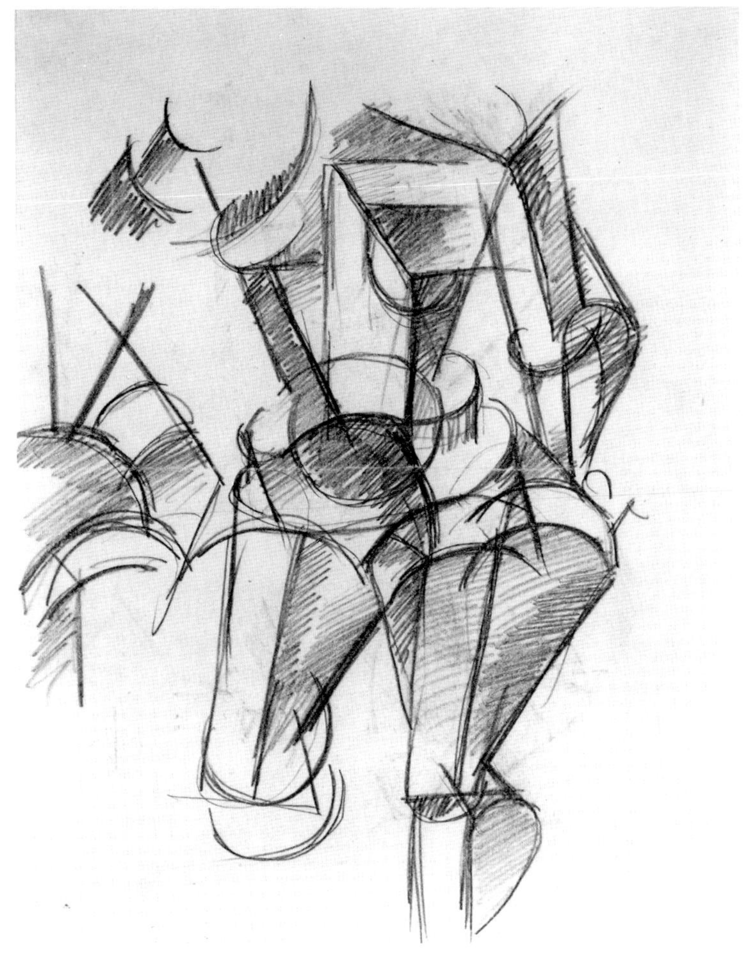

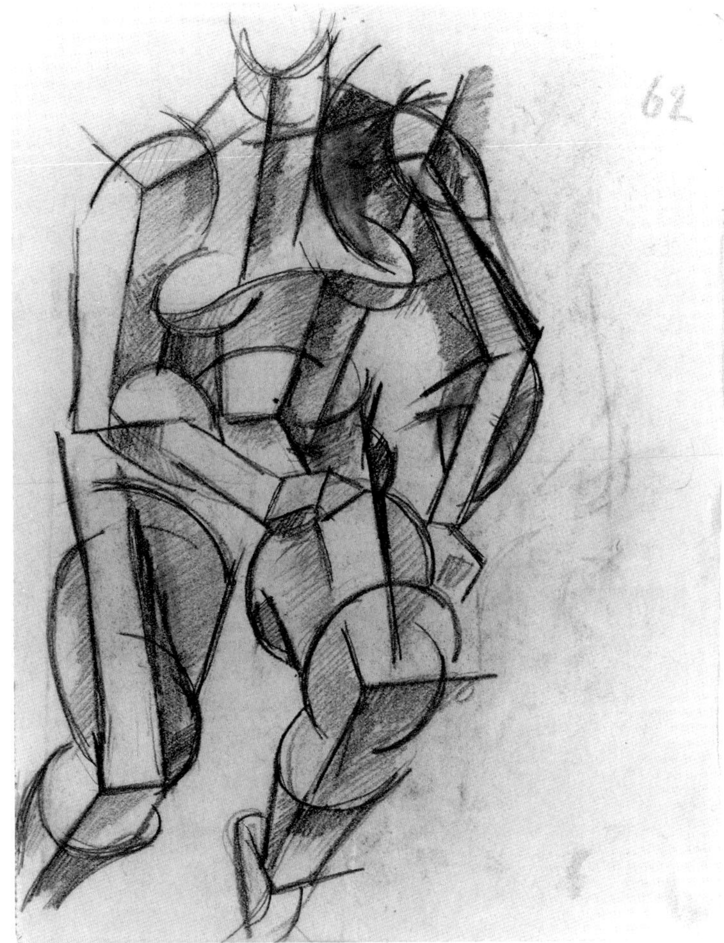

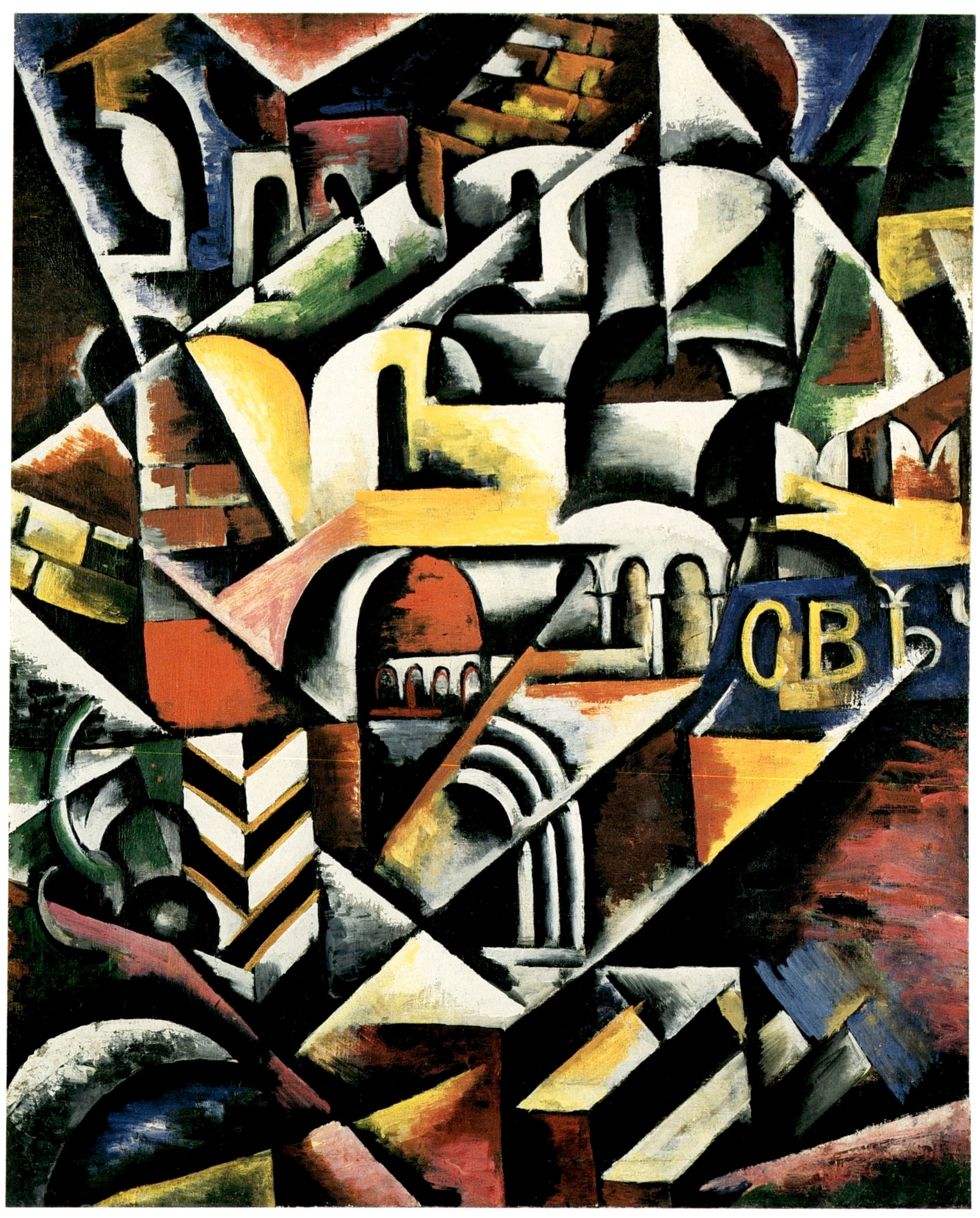

Cubist Cityscape
1914
Oil on canvas
41 × 34″

Objects from the Dyer's Shop (Early Morning)
1914
Oil on canvas
28 × 35″

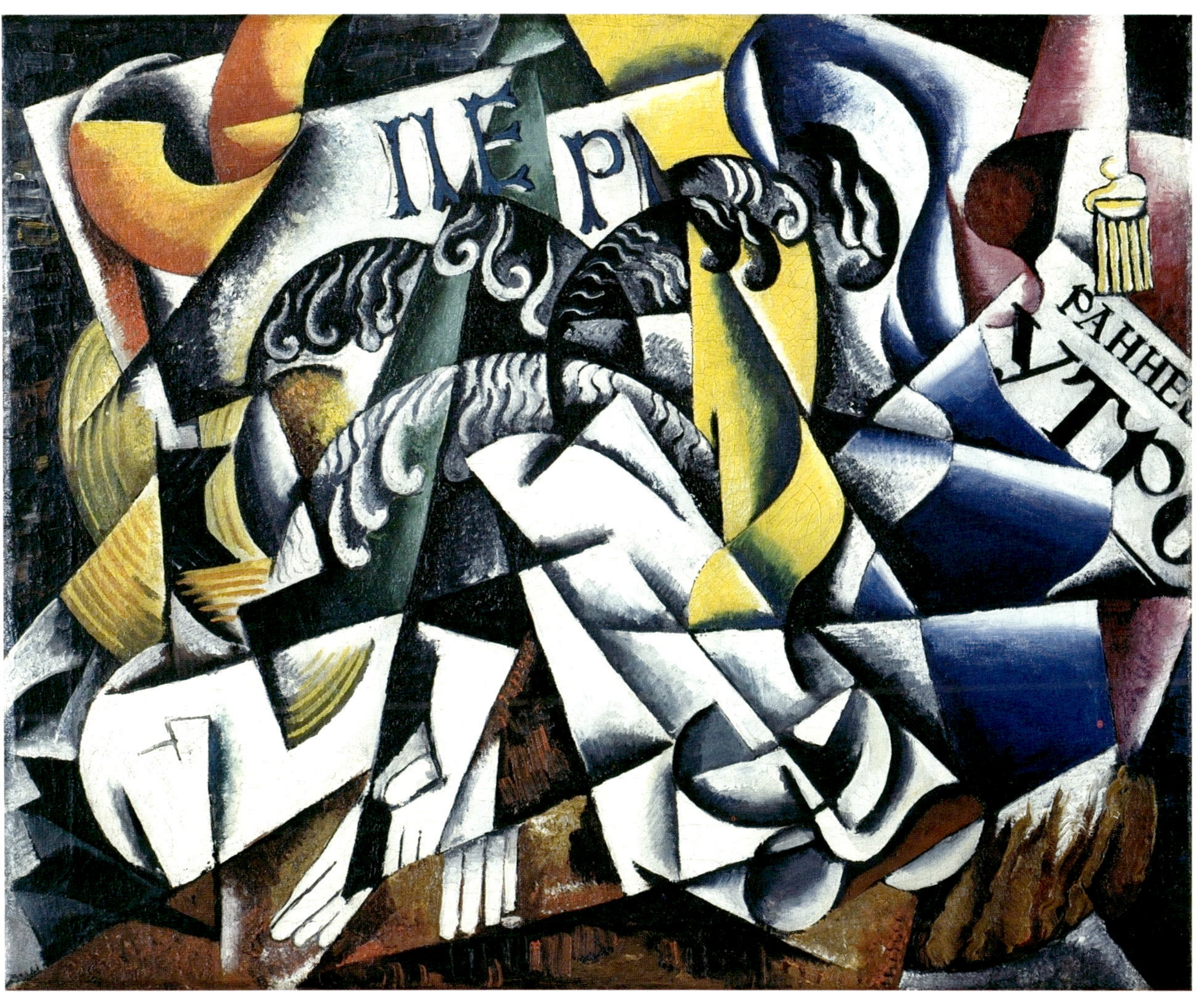

Italian Still Life
1914
Oil, plaster, and paper collage
on canvas
$24\frac{1}{4} \times 19''$

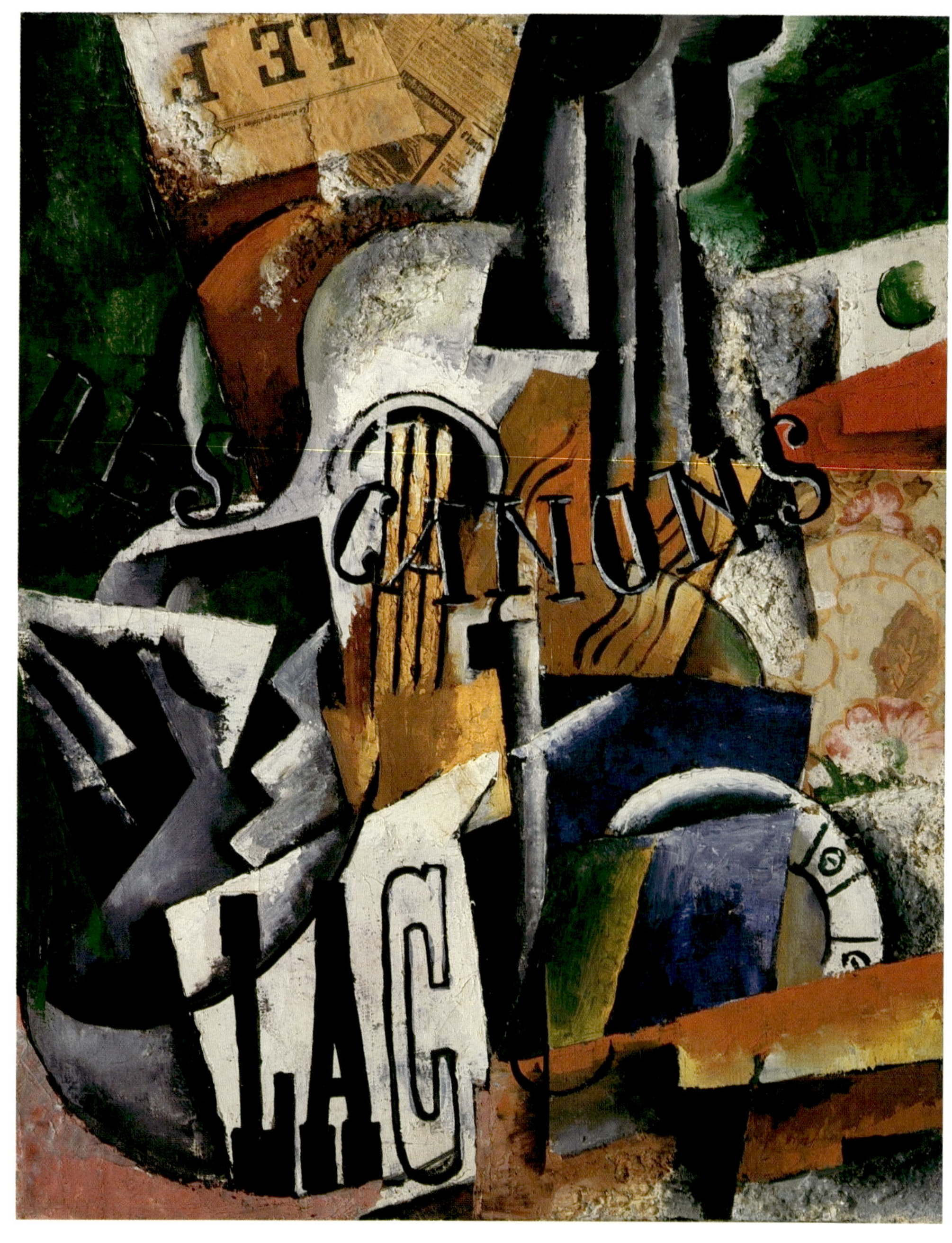

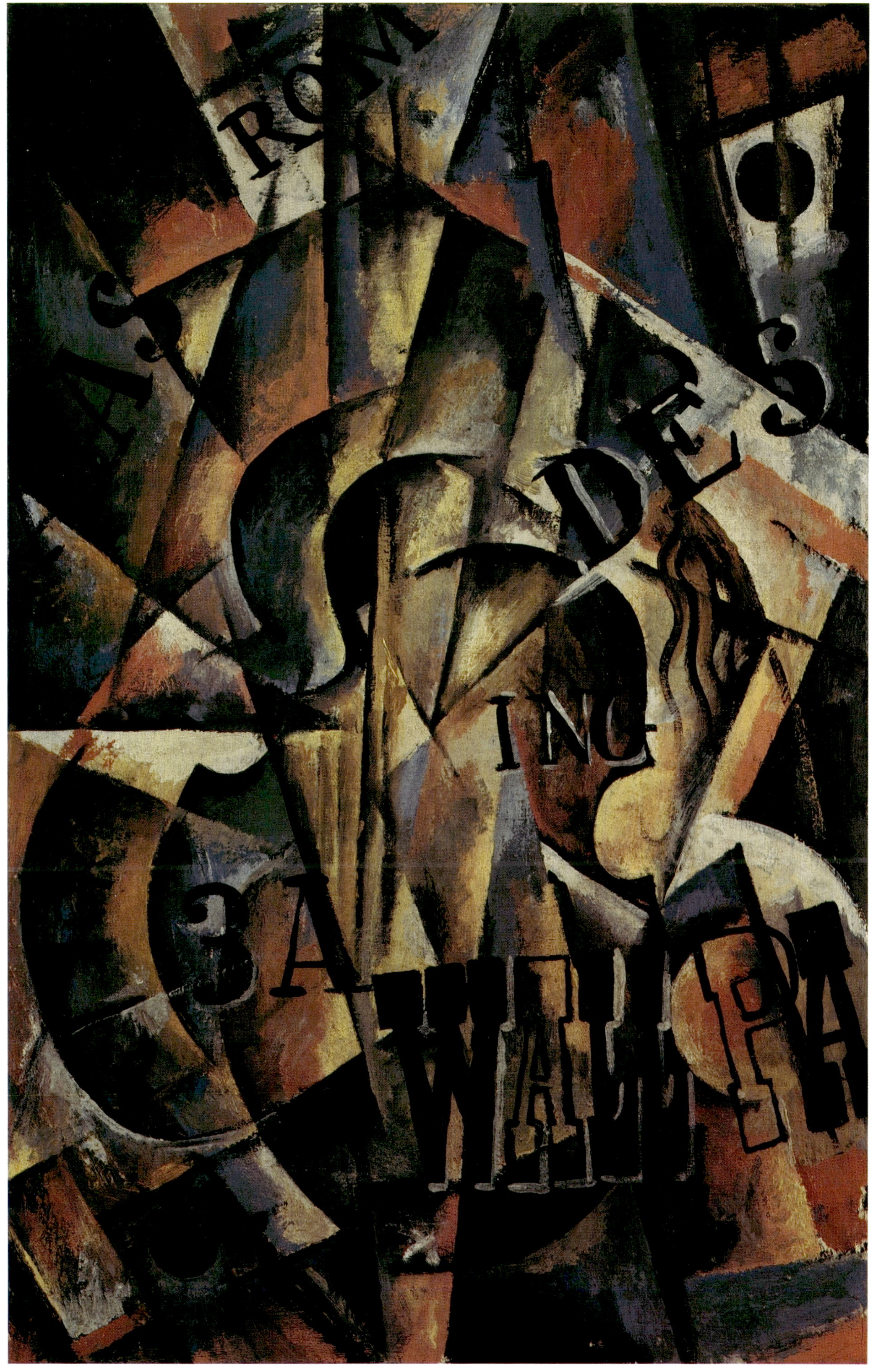

Still Life
1914
Oil on canvas
34⅝ × 22⅝"

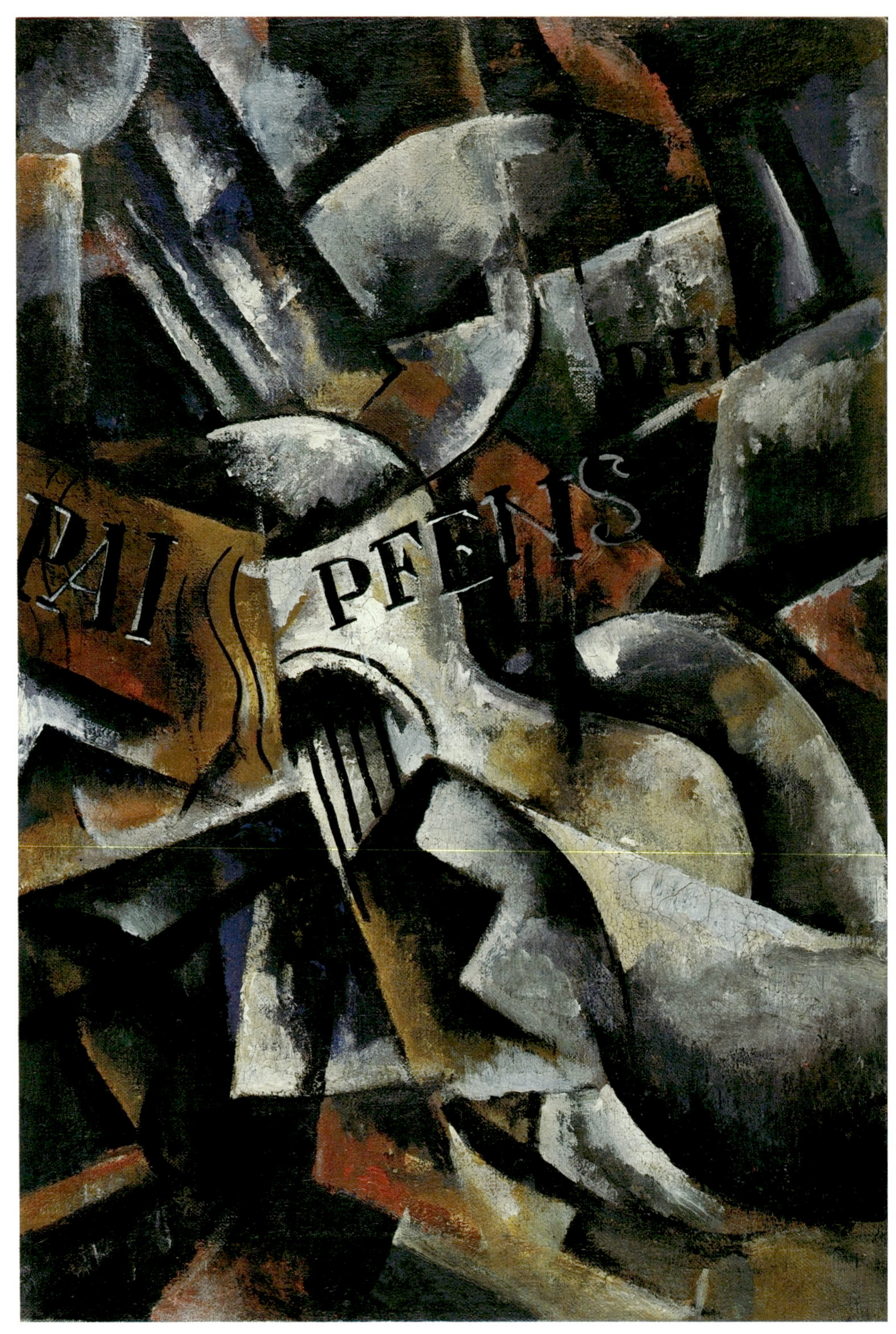

Still Life with Guitar
1914–15
Oil on canvas
26 × 18⅛″

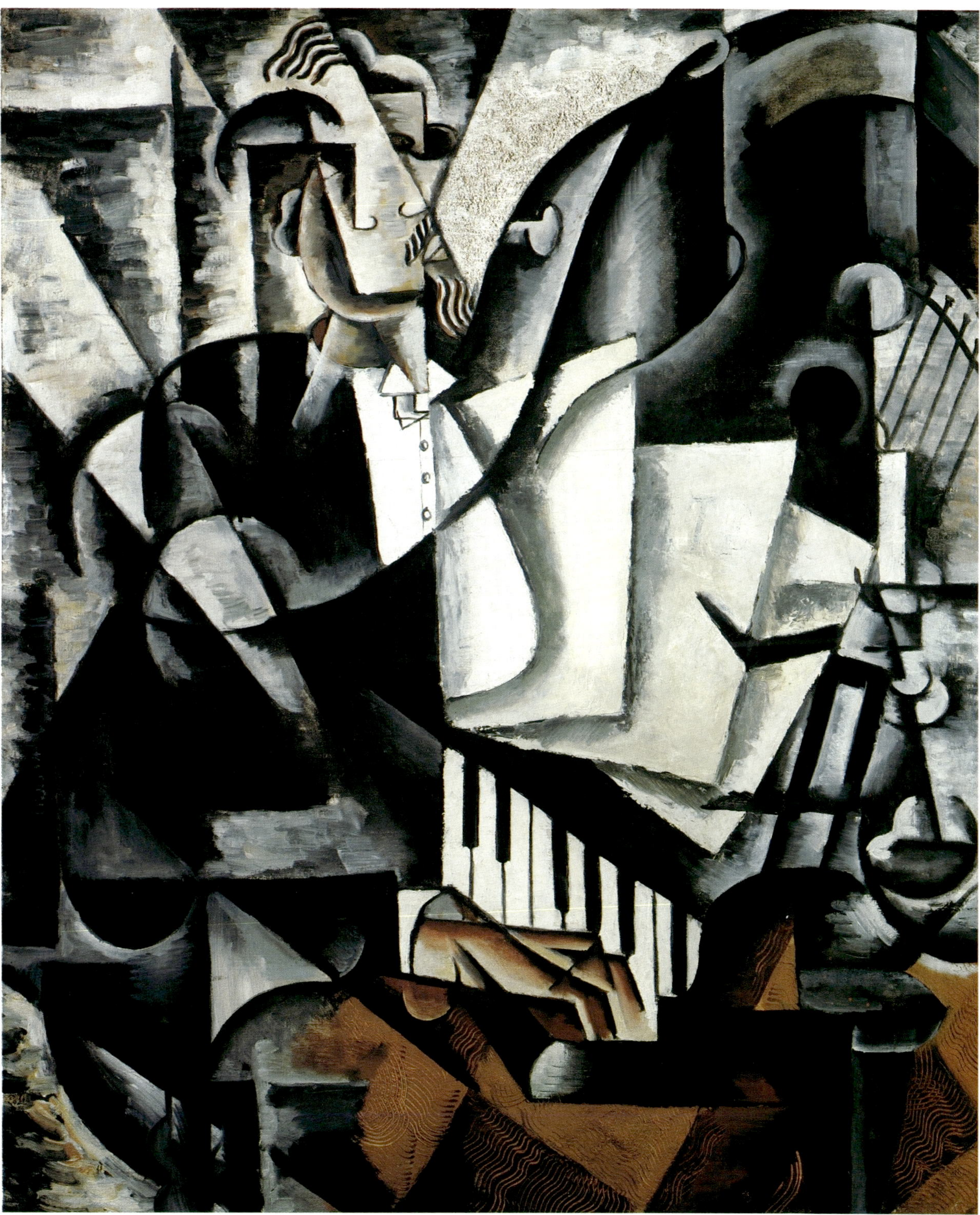

The Pianist
1915
Oil on canvas
$41\frac{7}{8} \times 34\frac{7}{8}$"

Lady with a Guitar
1915
Oil on canvas
42⅛ × 28⅛"

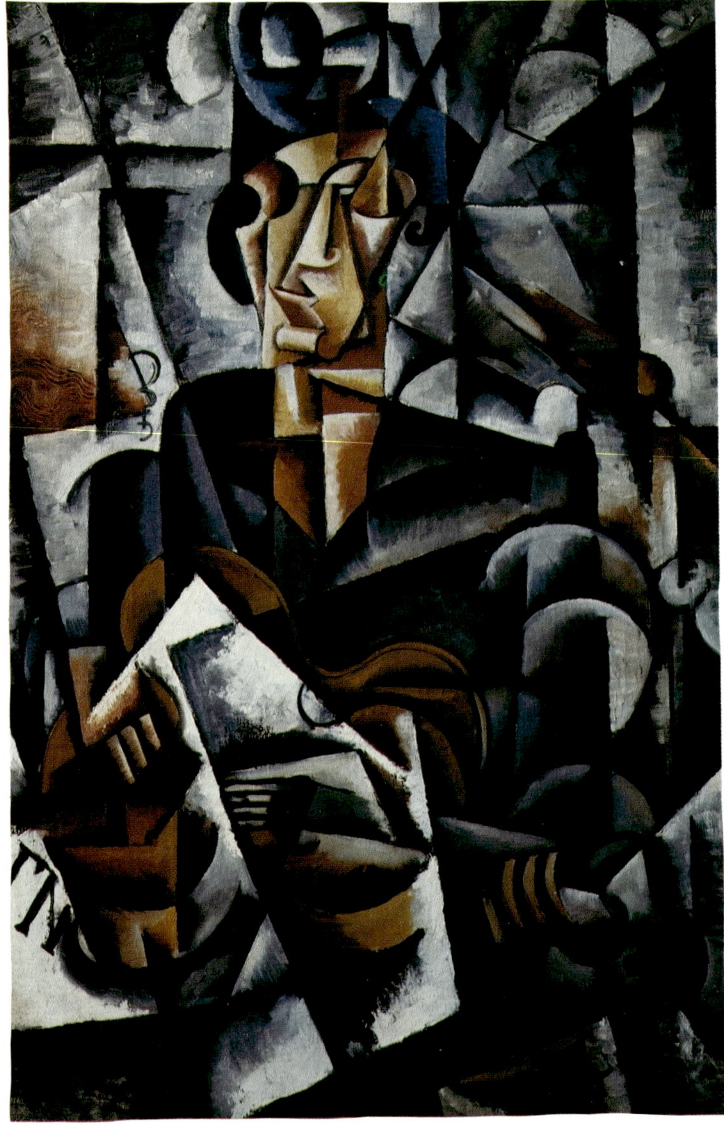

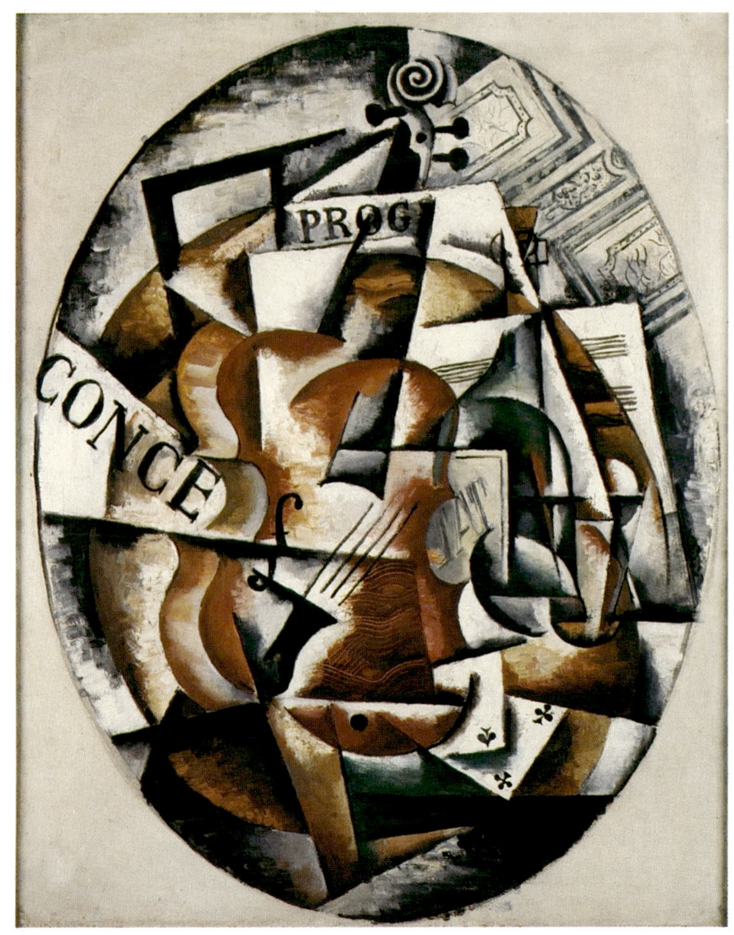

Violin
1915
Oil on canvas
34⅞ × 27¾"

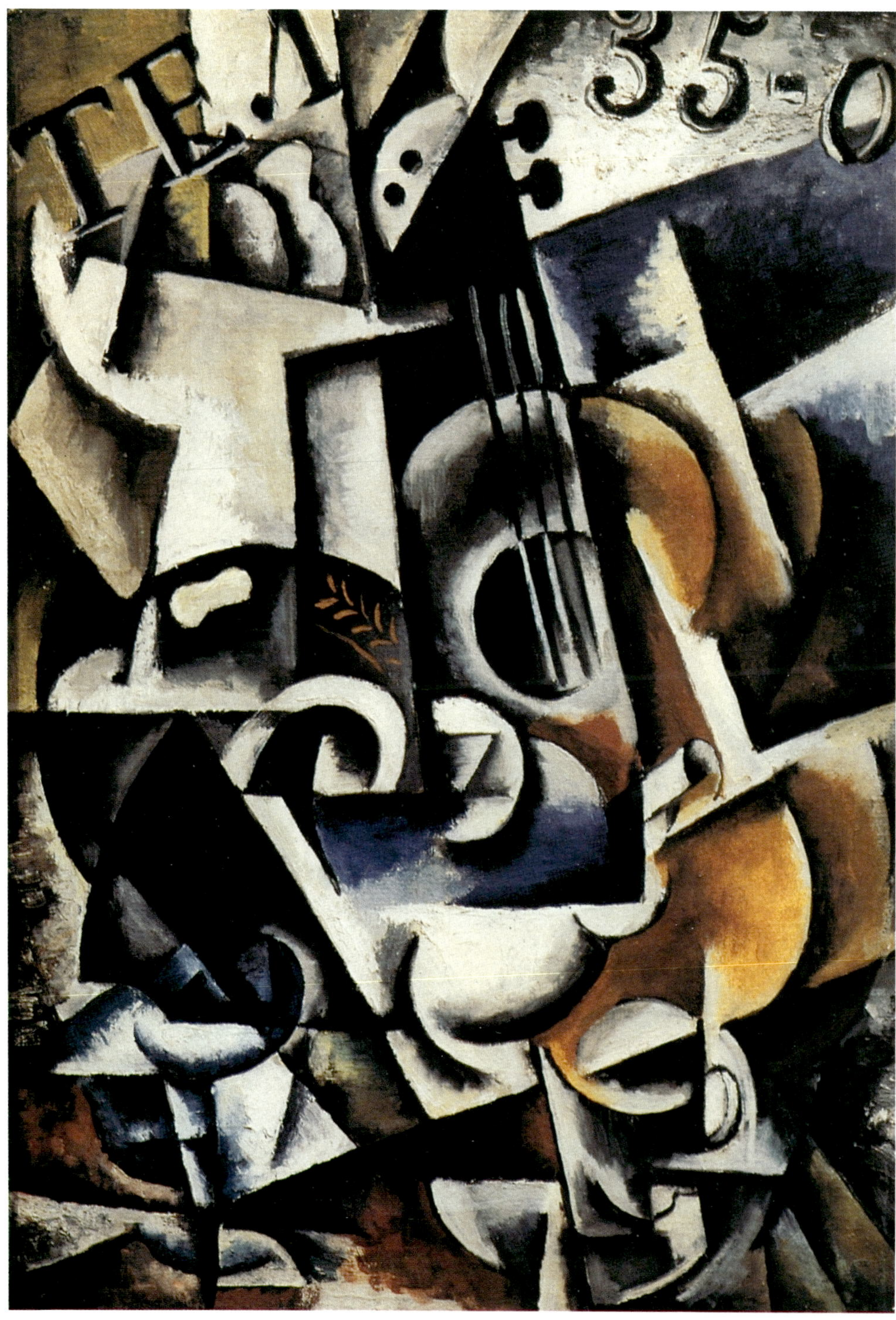

Objects
1915
Oil on canvas
24 × 17½″

Study for a Portrait
1915
Oil and marble dust
on canvas
27¾ × 18½"

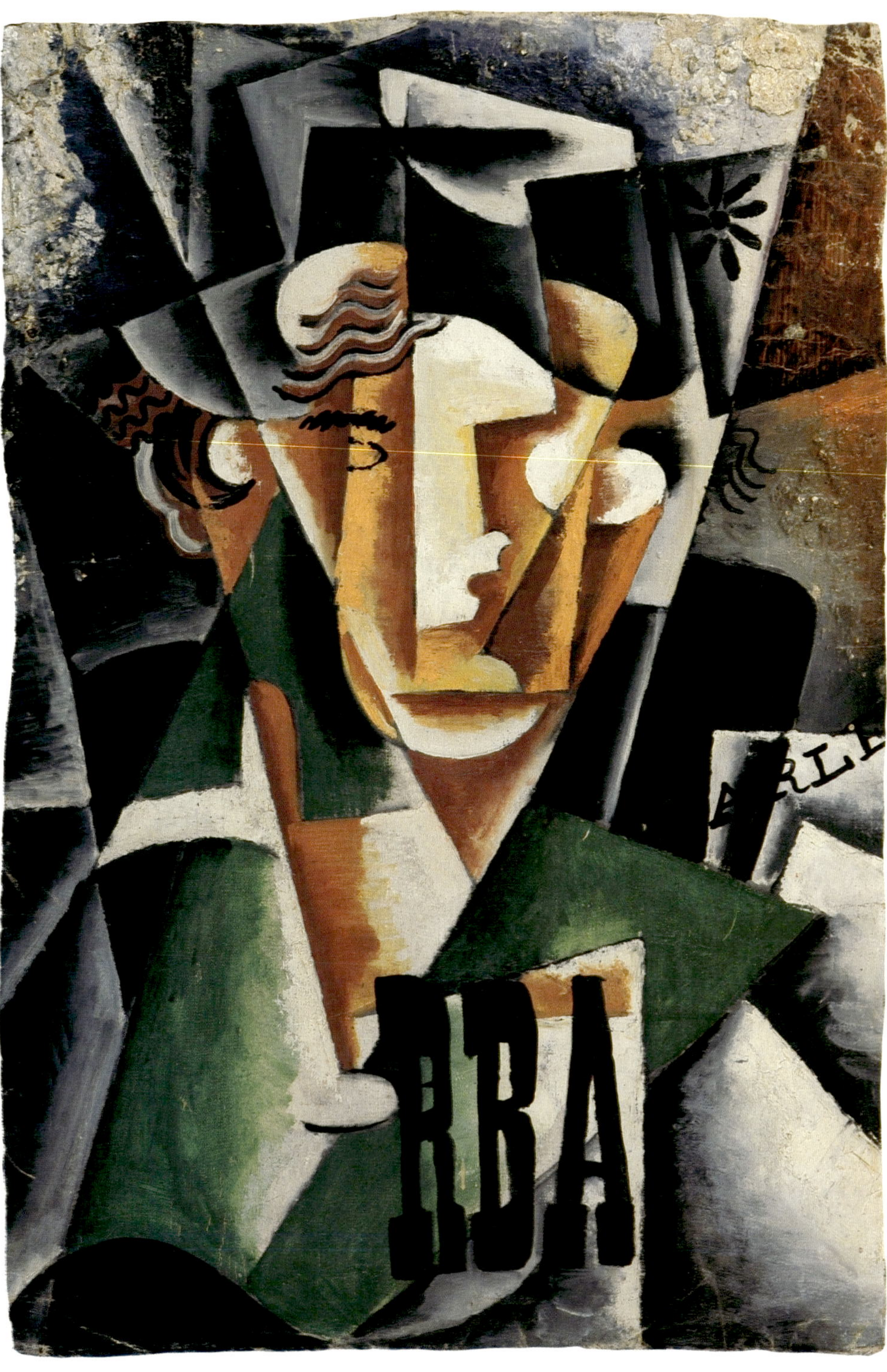

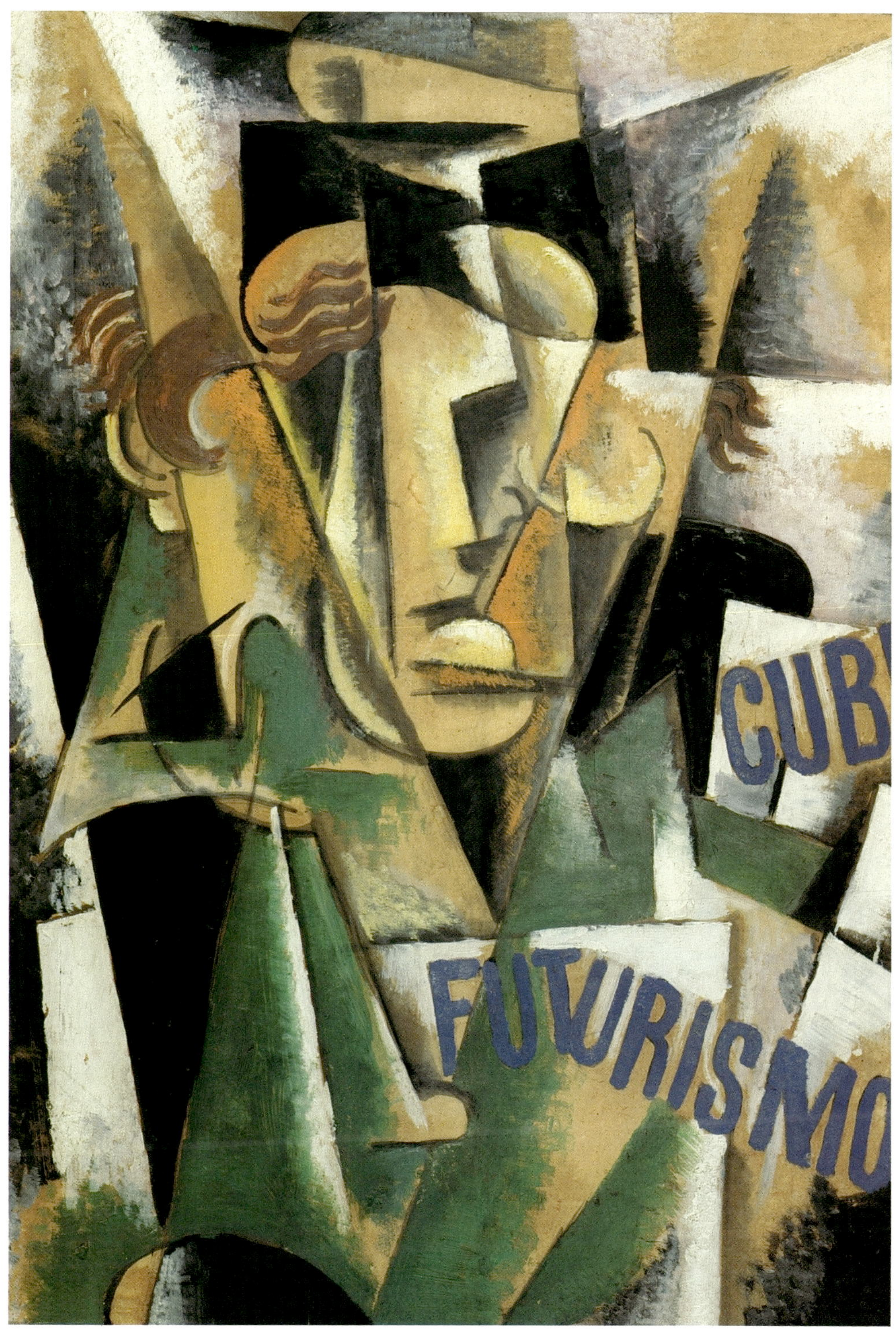

Portrait
1915
Oil on paperboard
23½ × 16⅜″

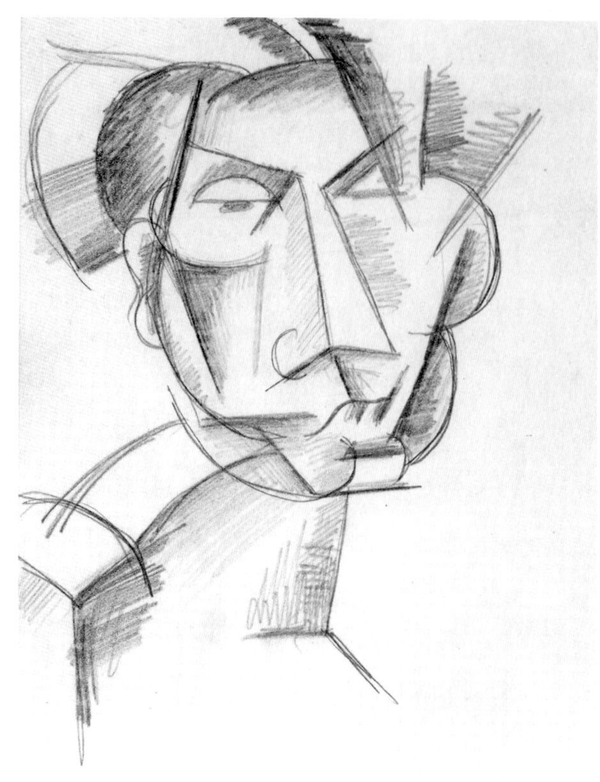

Study
1915
Pencil on paper
10½ × 8⅛″

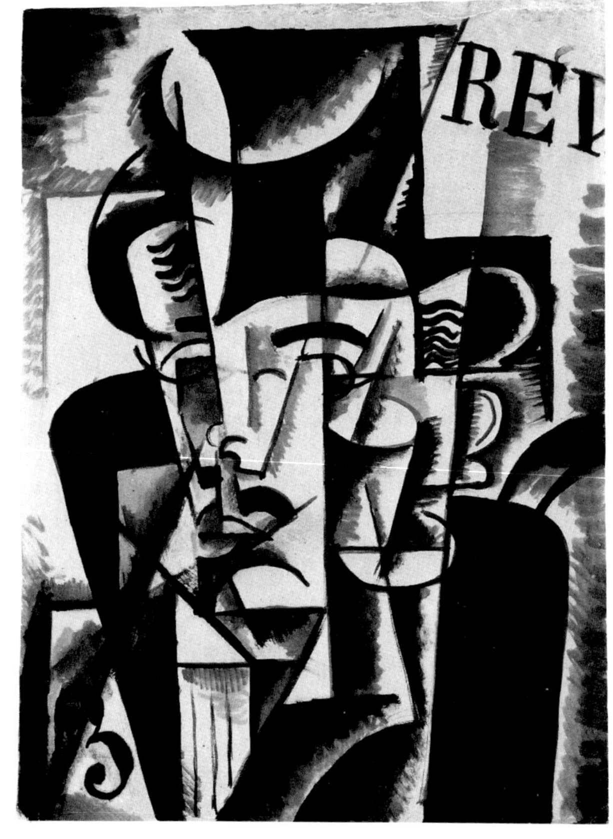

Study for
Portrait of a Philosopher
1915
Black gouache on pasteboard
20½ × 14⅞″

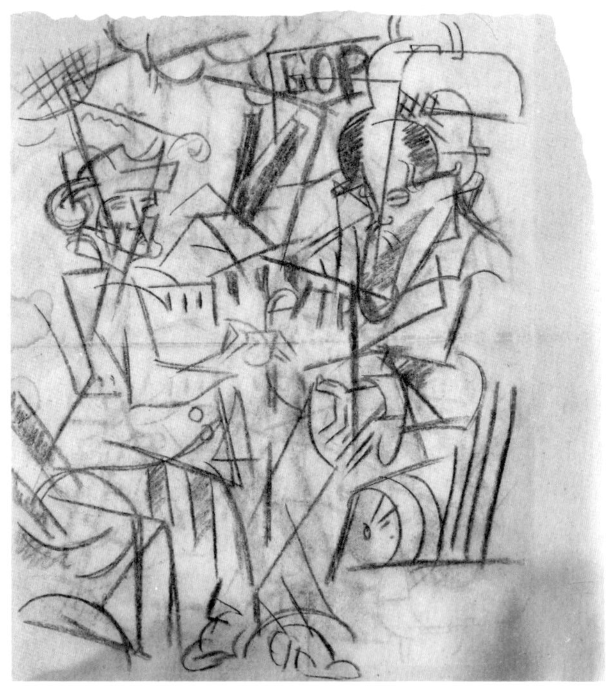

Study for a
Two-Figure Composition
1915
Charcoal on paper
17½ × 13⅞″

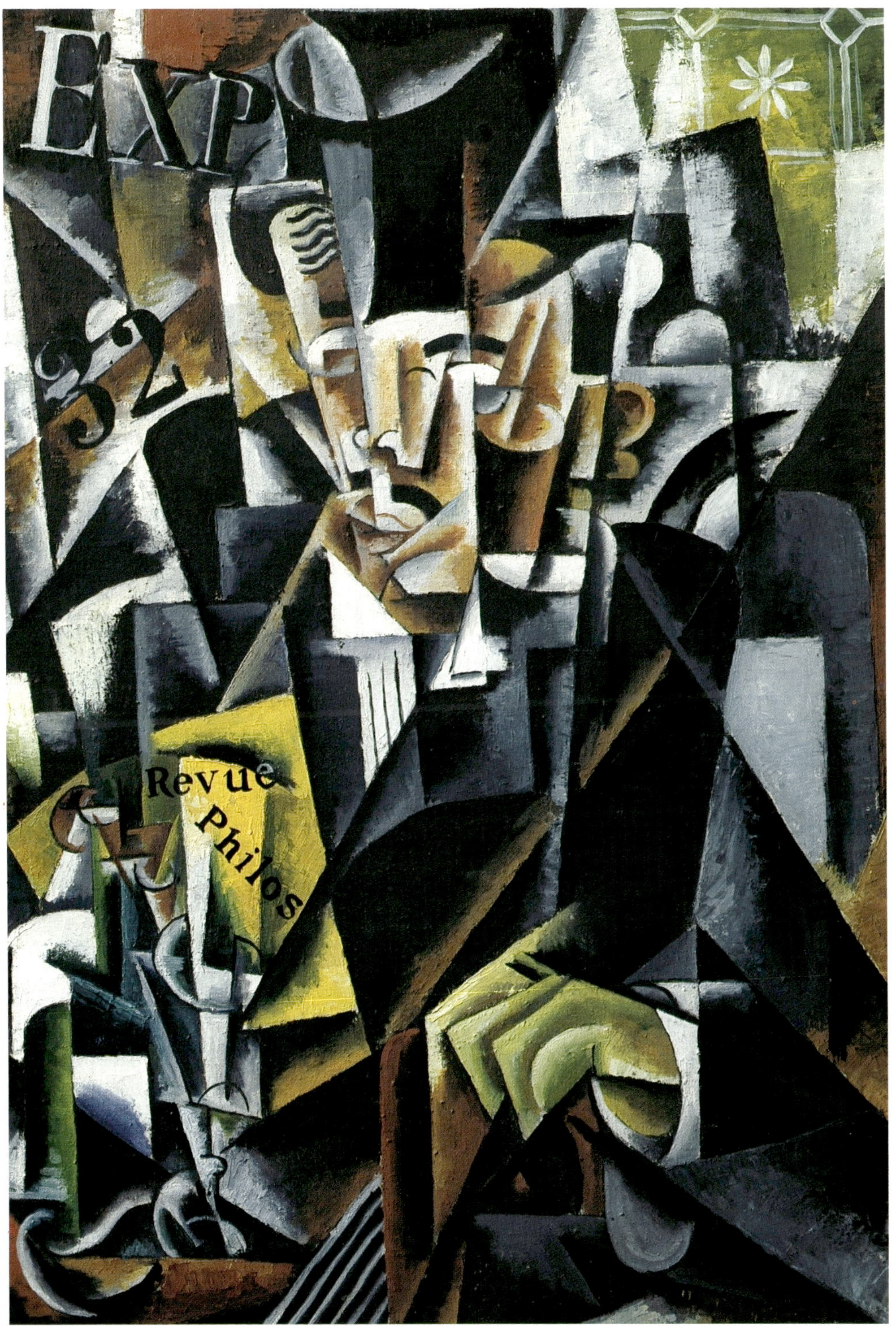

Portrait of a Philosopher
1915
Oil on canvas
35 × 24¾″

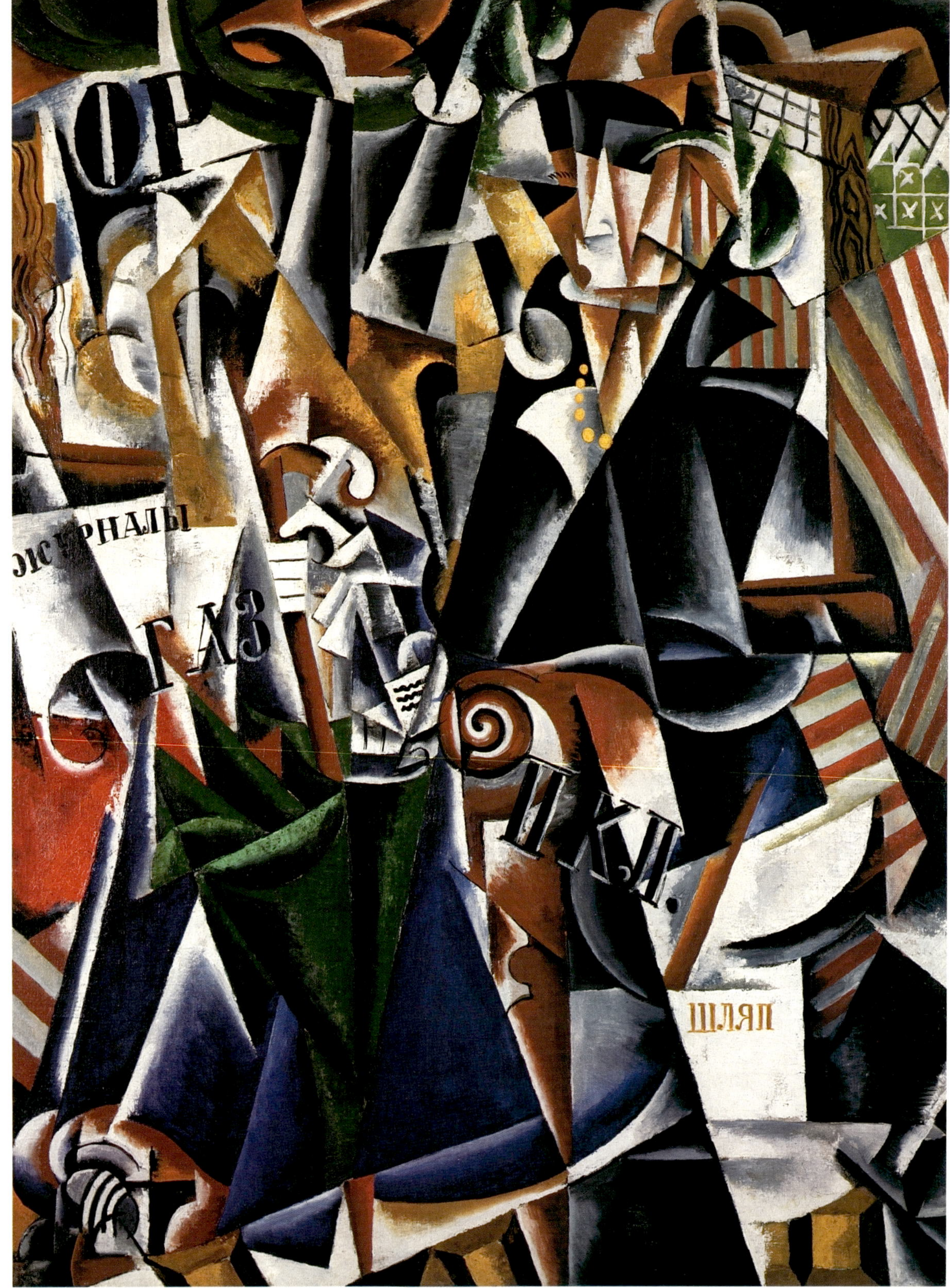

Traveling Woman
1915
Oil on canvas
$56 \times 41\frac{1}{2}''$

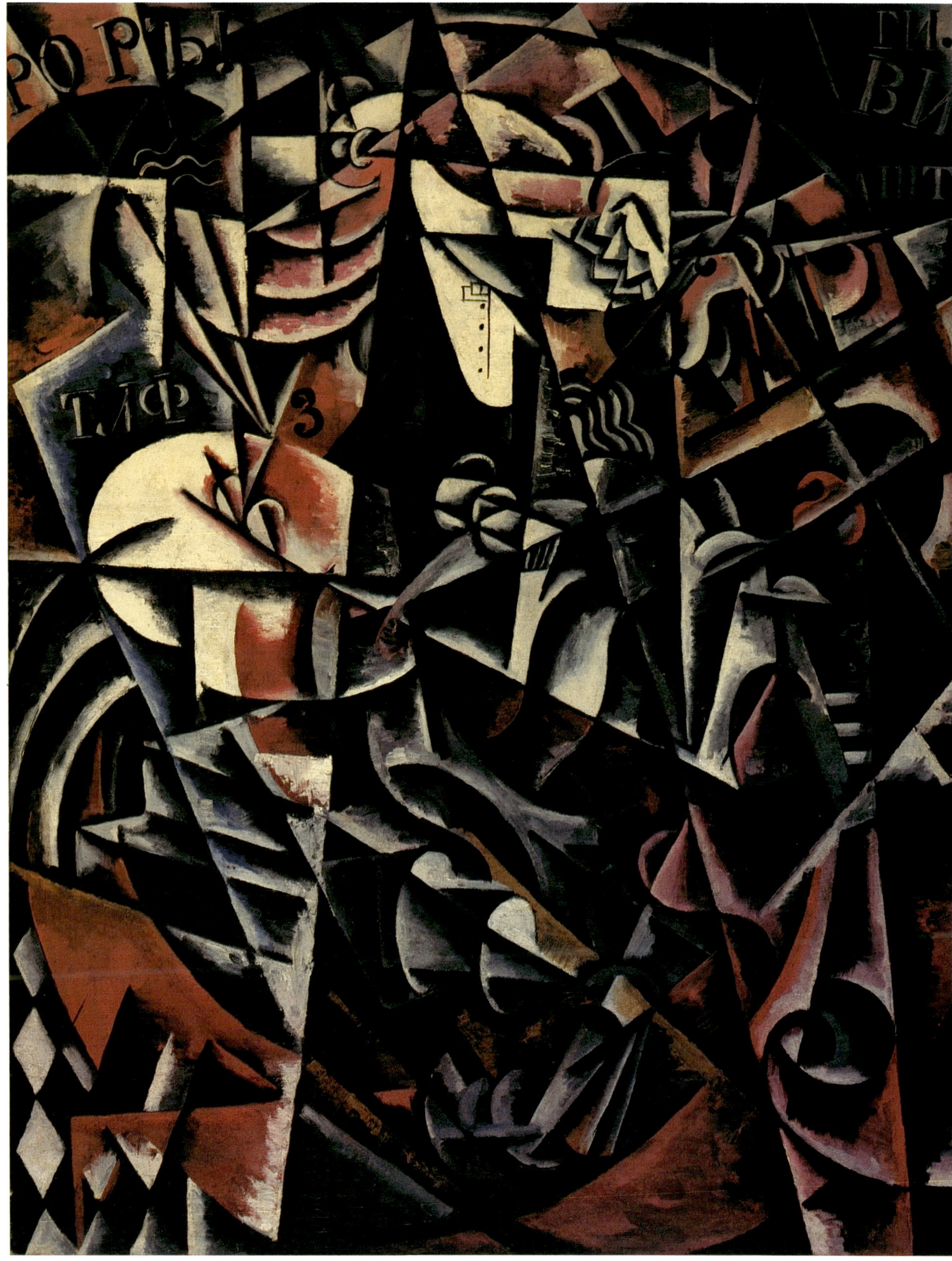

Traveling Woman
1915
Oil on canvas
62⅜ × 48½″

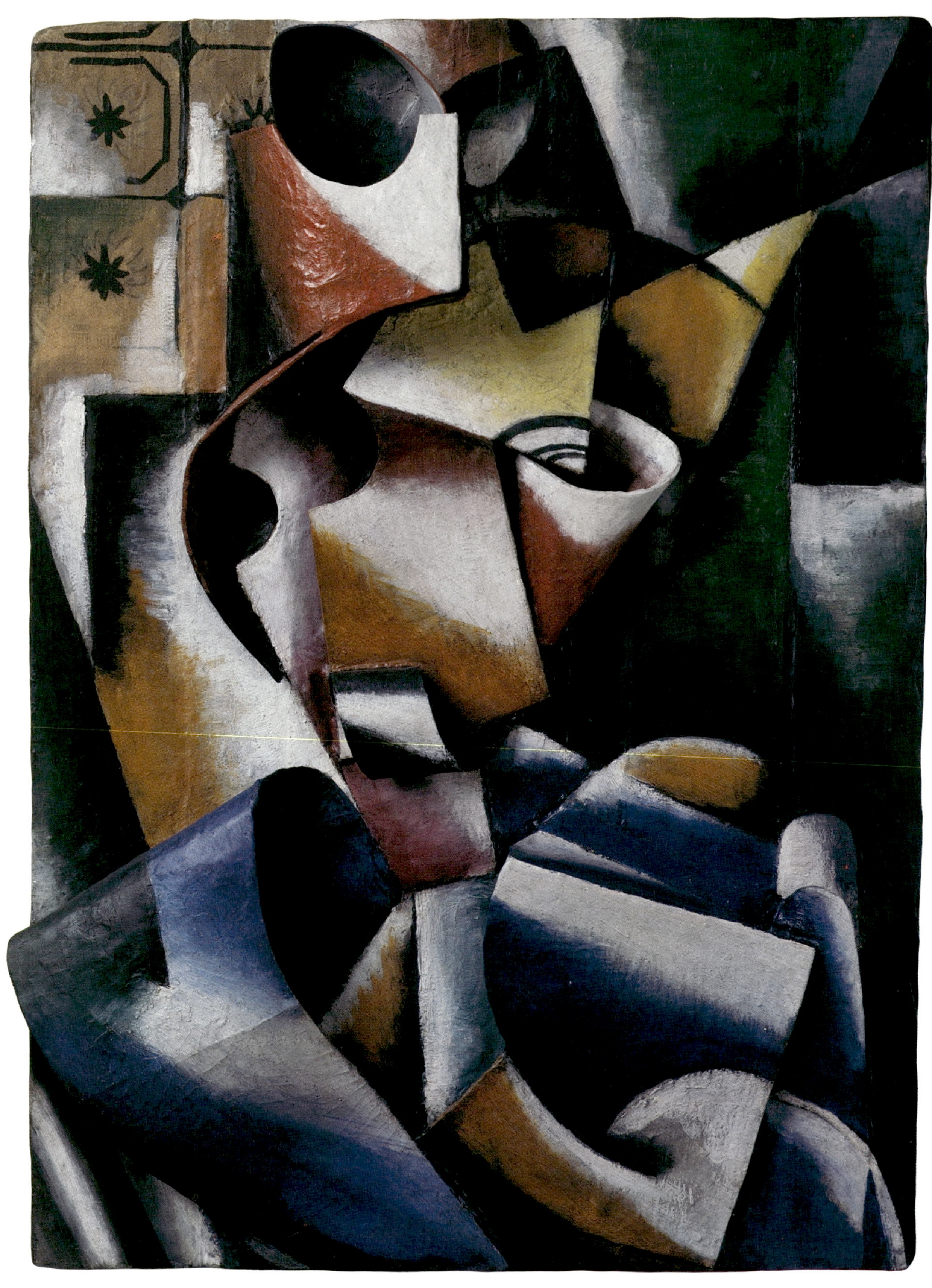

Portrait of a Lady (Plastic Drawing)
1915
Oil on paper and cardboard on wood
26⅛ × 19⅛″

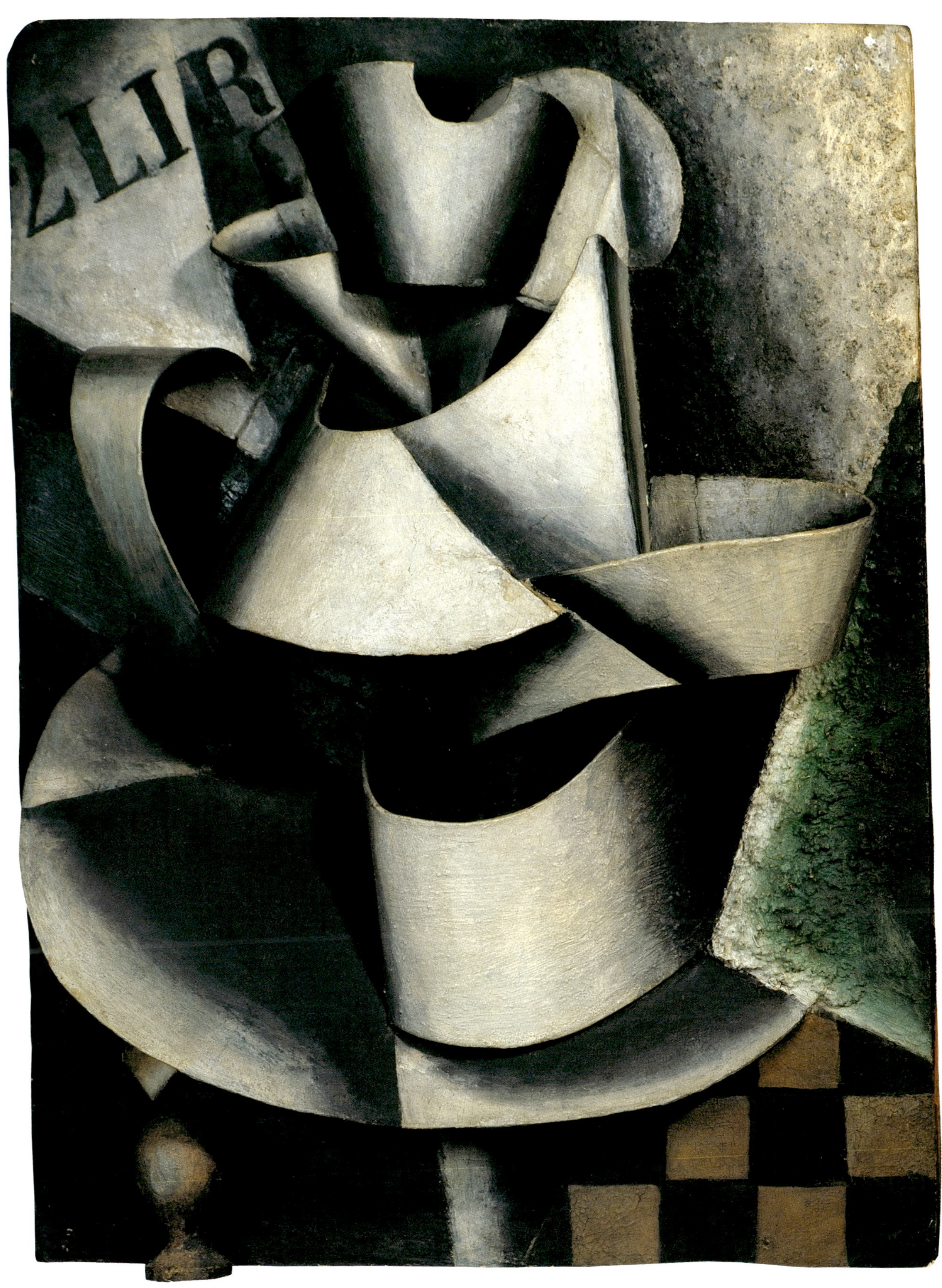

The Jug on the Table (Plastic Painting)
1915
Oil on cardboard
mounted on wood
$23\frac{1}{4} \times 17\frac{7}{8}$"

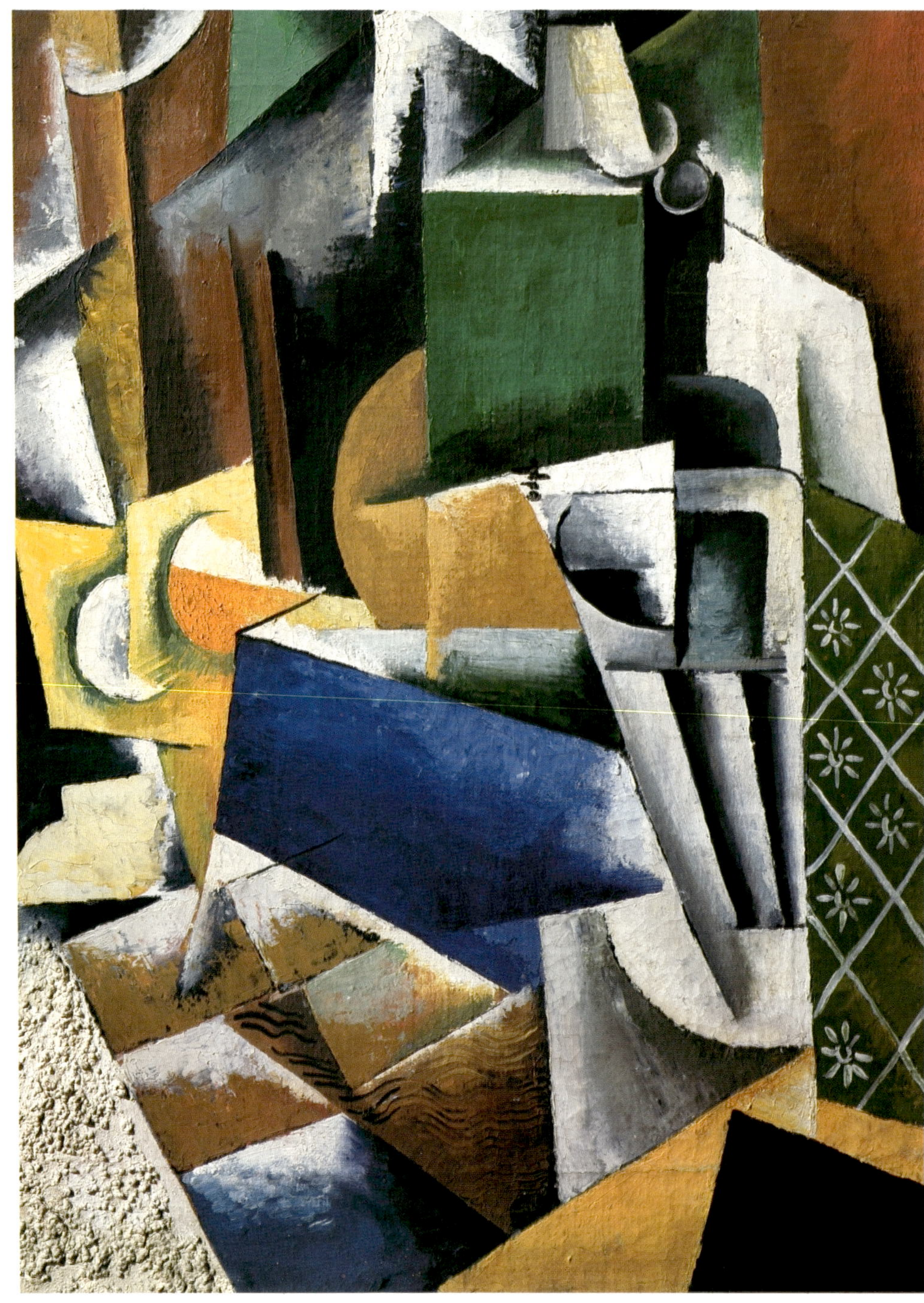

The Grocery Store
1916
Oil on canvas
21¼ × 16⅞″

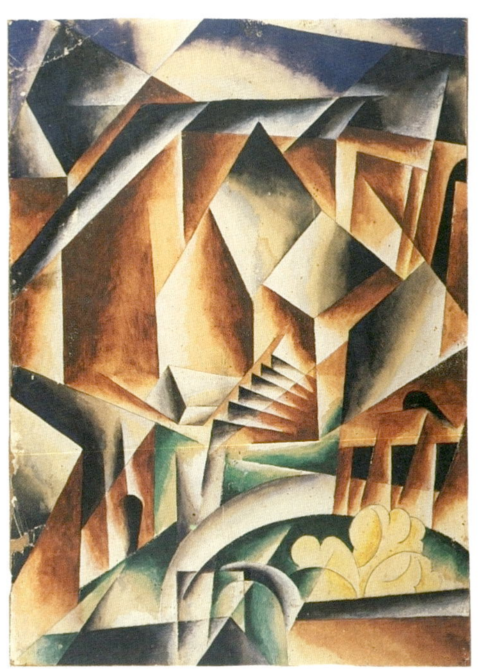

Box Factory
1916
Gouache on paper
mounted on board
16½ × 12¼″

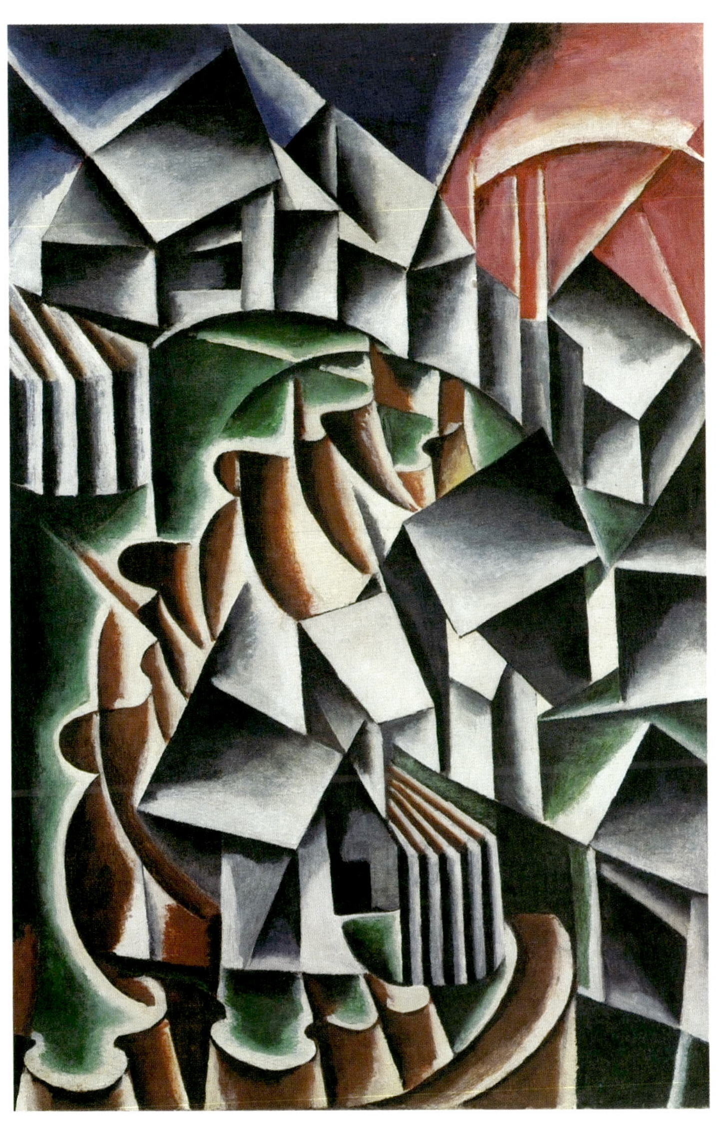

Birsk
1916
Oil on canvas
41¾ × 27⅜″

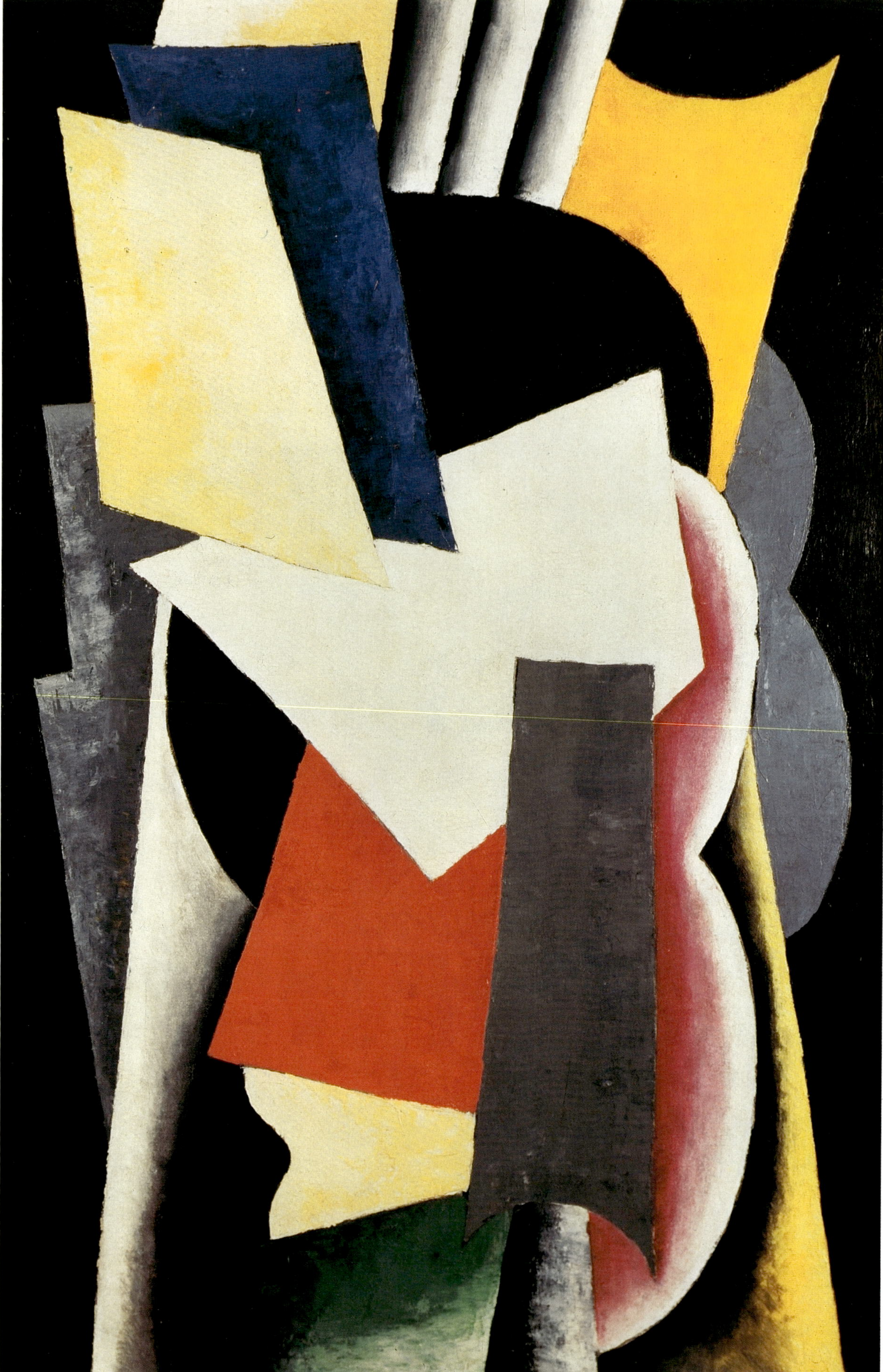

Painterly Architectonic (Still Life: Instruments)
1916
Oil on canvas
41½ × 27¼"

Painterly Architectonic
1918
Oil on canvas
$17\frac{3}{4} \times 20\frac{7}{8}$"

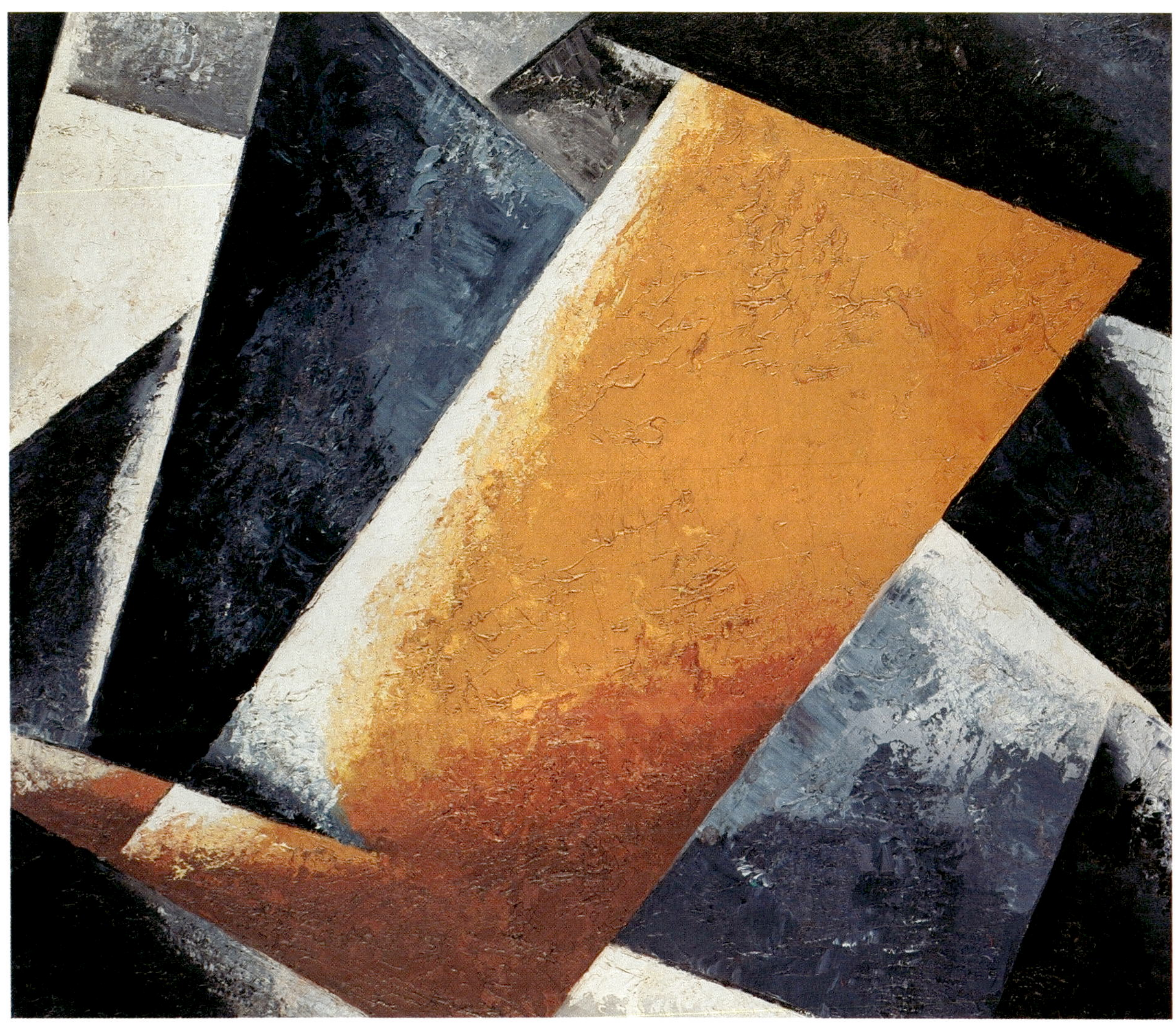

Painterly Architectonic with Three Stripes
1916
Oil on canvas
42⅛ × 35″

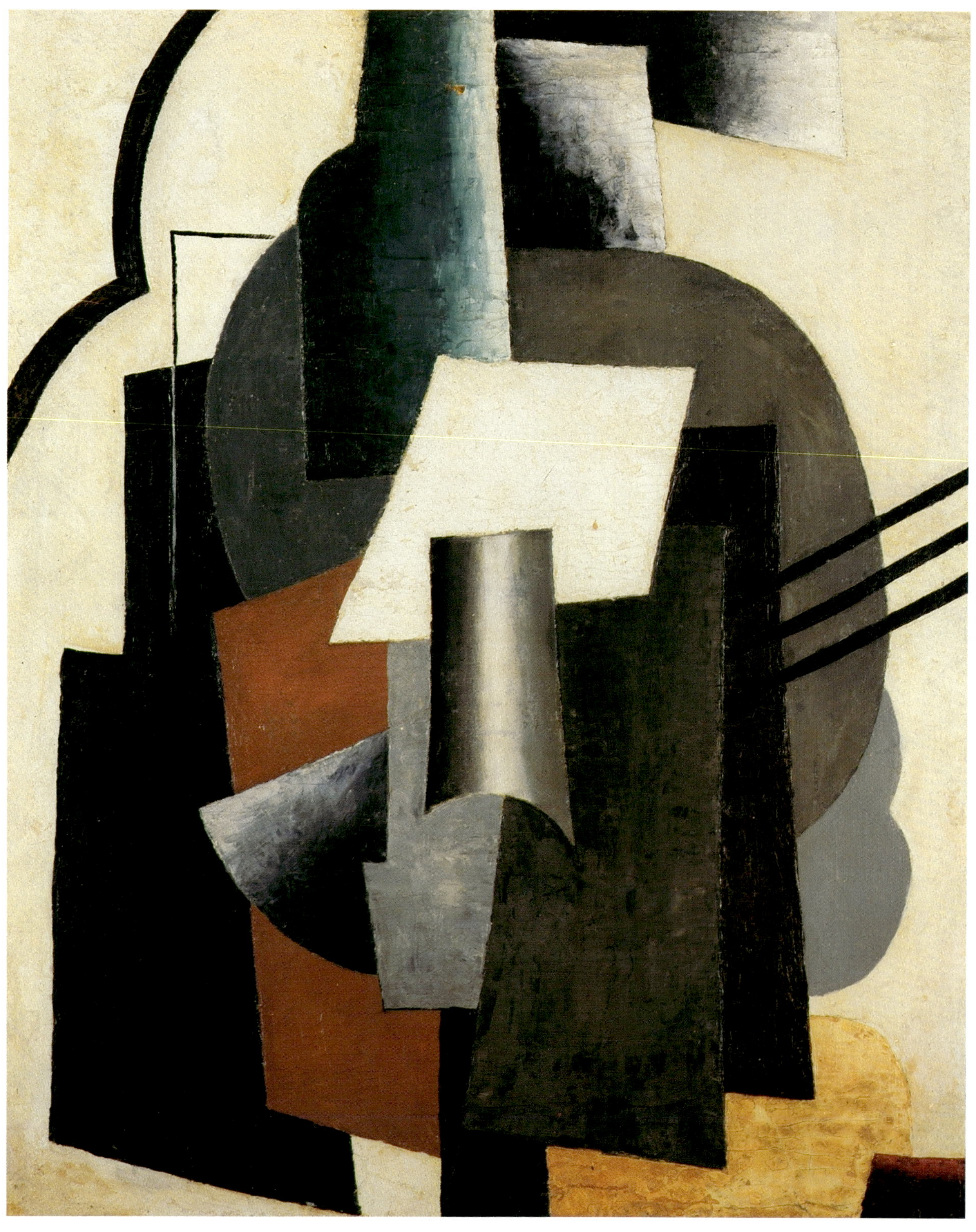

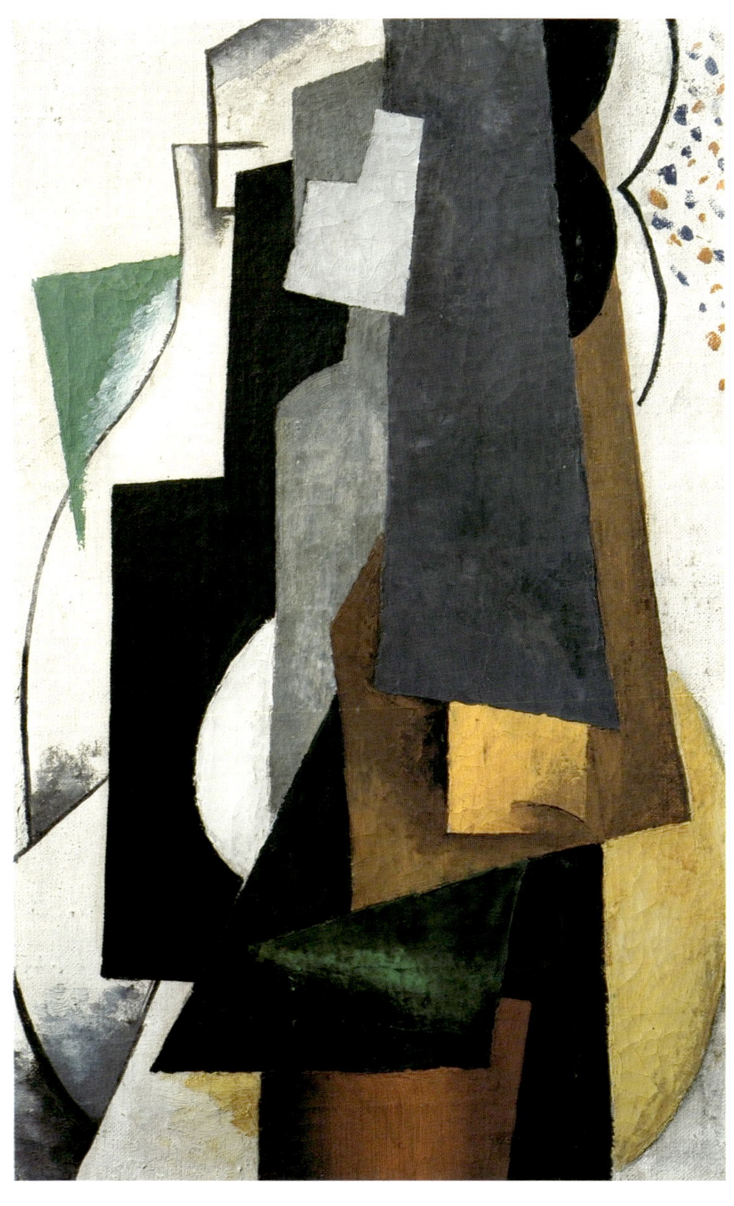

Painterly Architectonic
1916
Oil on canvas
20⅛ × 13″

Painterly Architectonic with Yellow Board
1916
Oil on canvas
34½ × 30⅝″

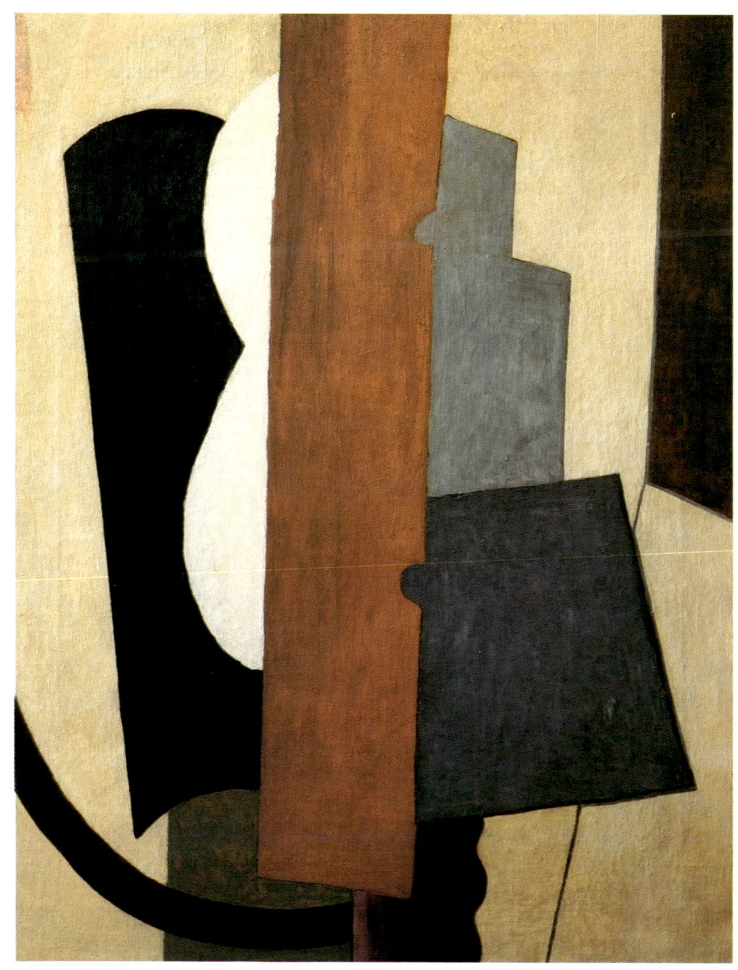

Painterly Architectonic:
Black, Red, Gray
1916
Oil on canvas
35⅛ × 27⅞"

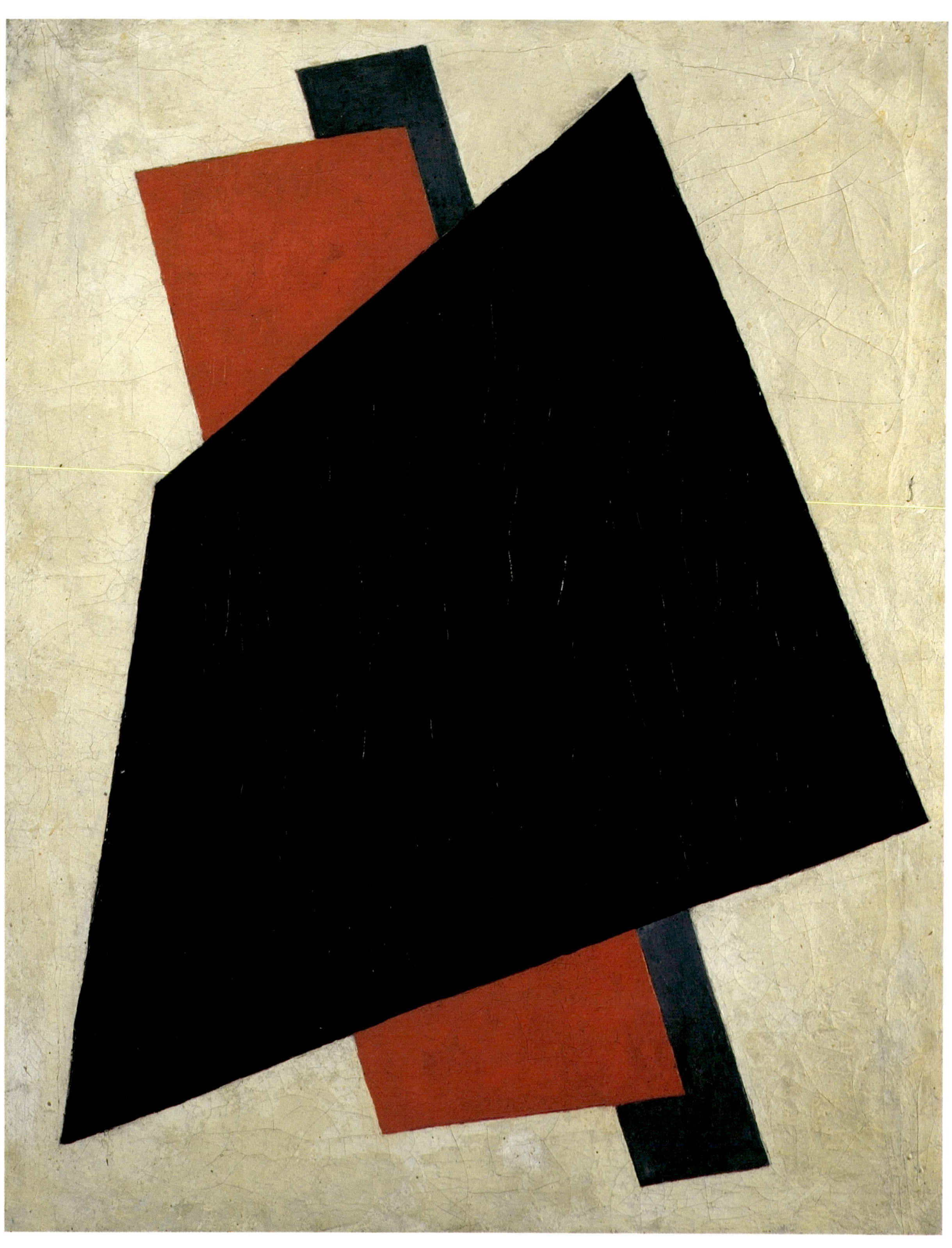

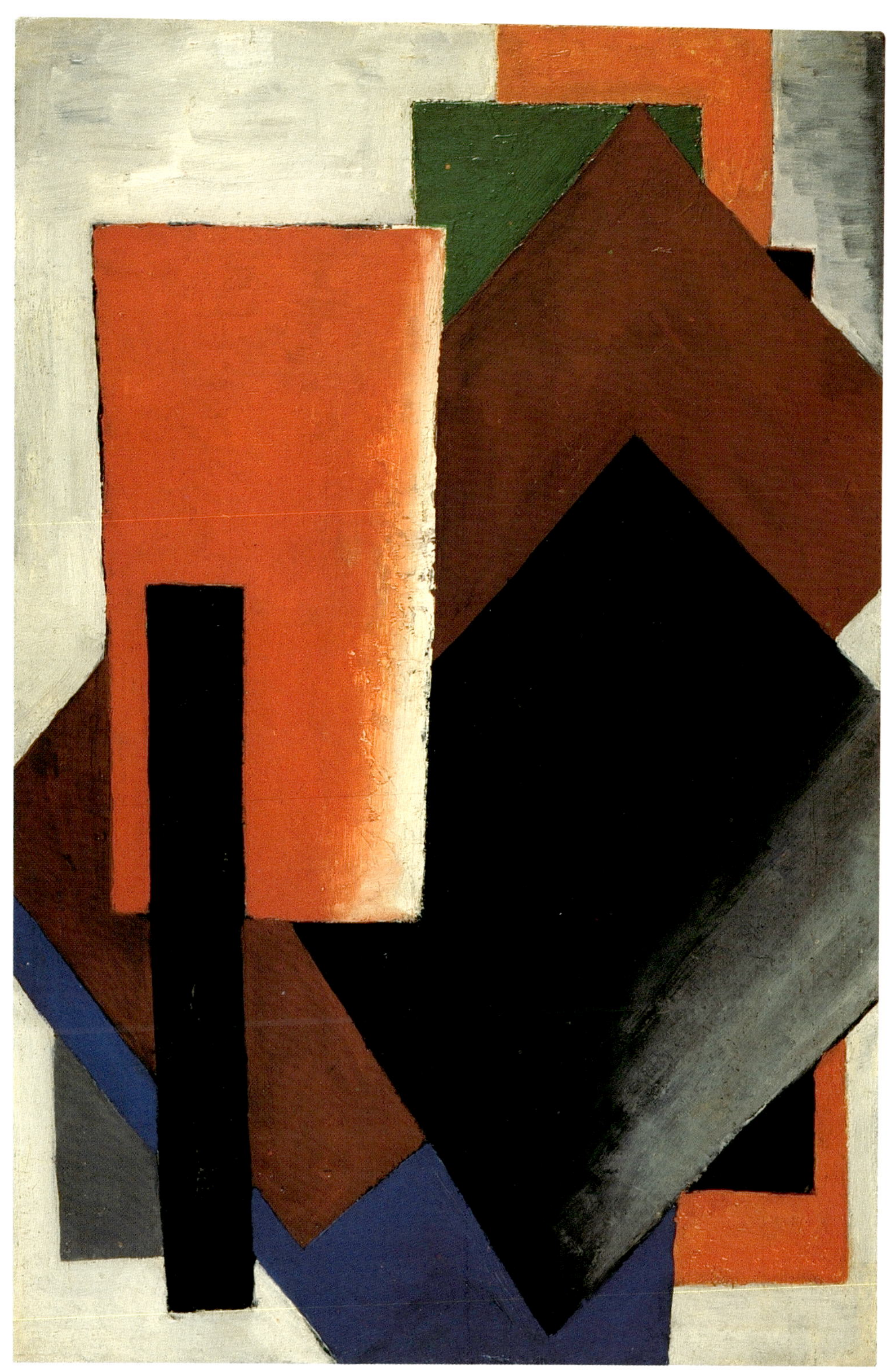

Painterly Architectonic
1916
Oil on board
$23\frac{1}{2} \times 15\frac{1}{2}$"

(recto)
Painterly Architectonic
1916–17
Oil on canvas
62½ × 49⅛″

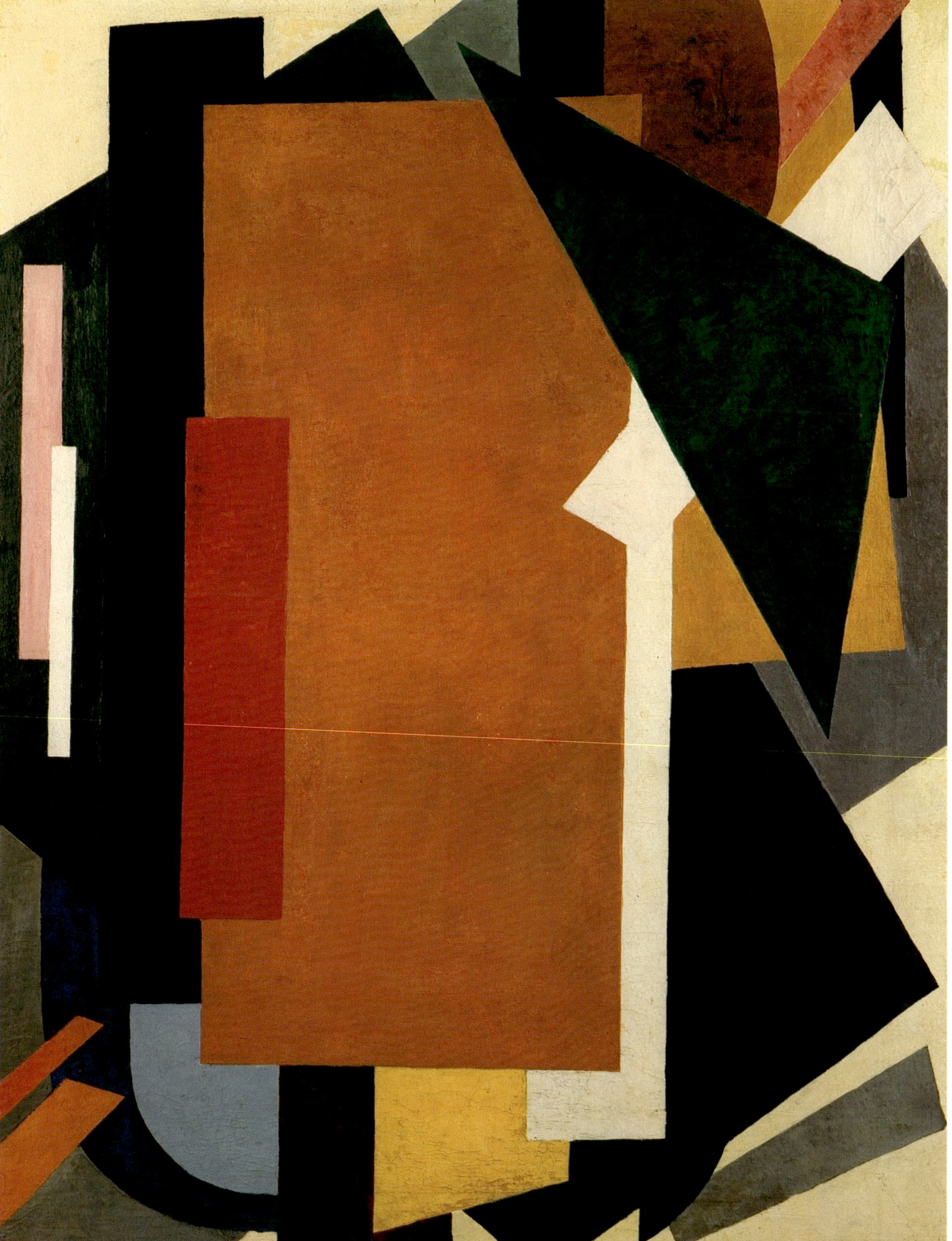

(verso)
Painterly Construction
1920
Oil on canvas
62½ × 49⅛"

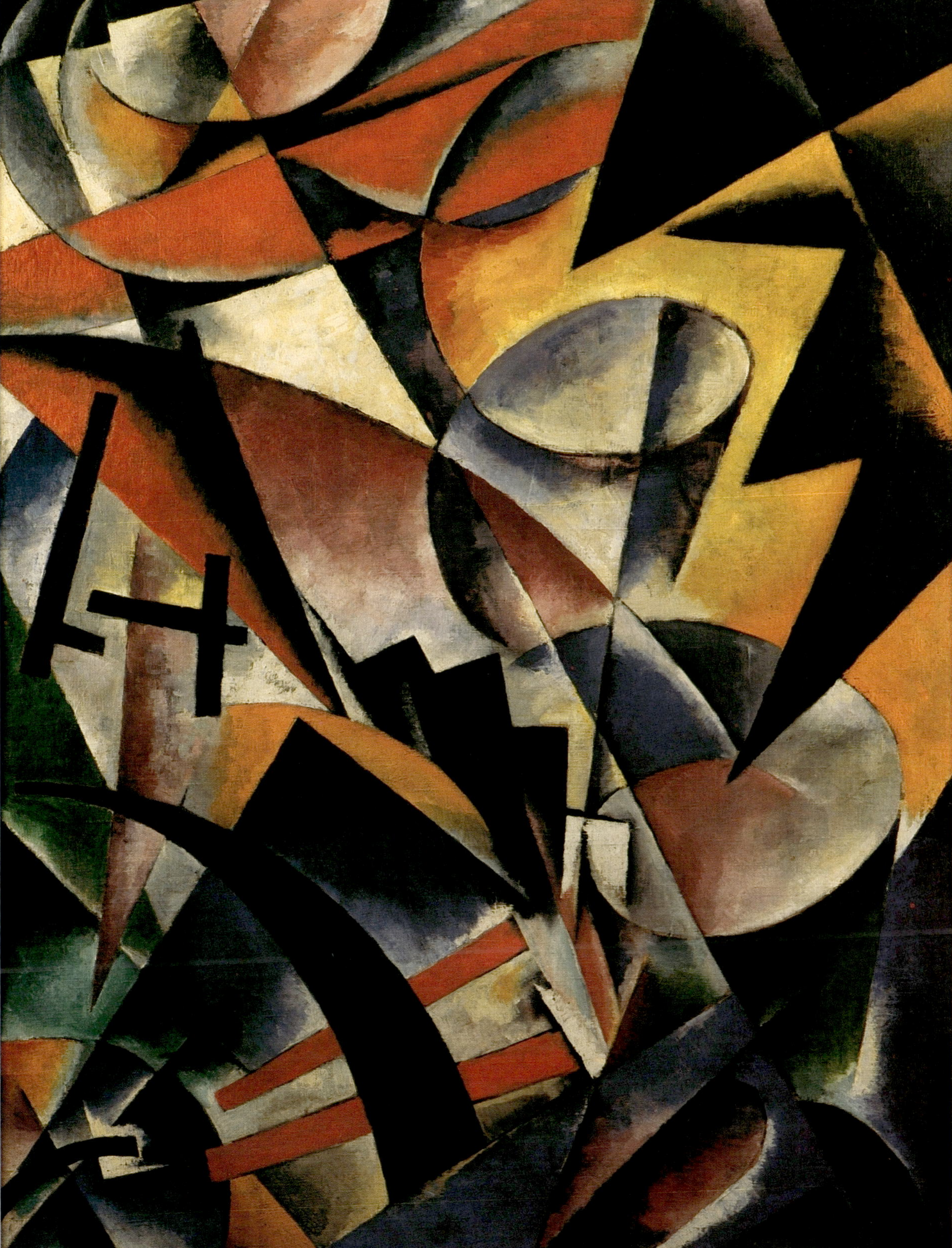

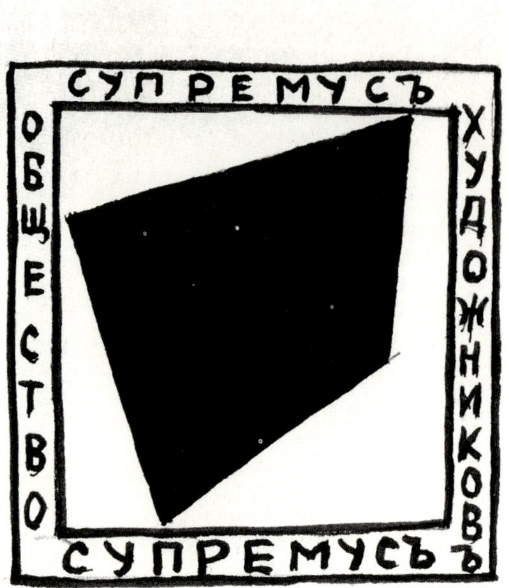

Cover Design for the Society of Painters Supremus
1916–17
Ink on paper
3½ × 3⅛"

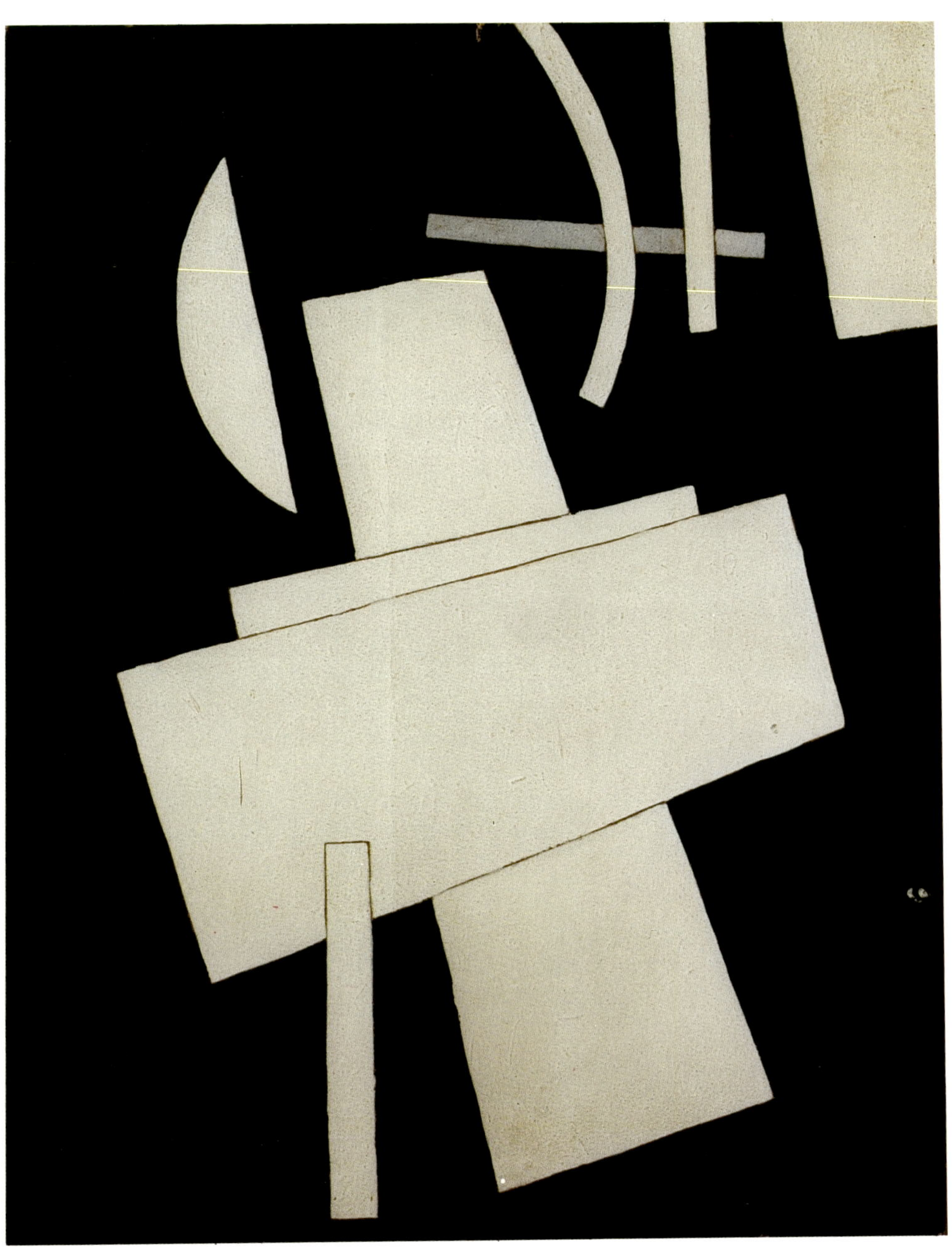

Untitled
c. 1916–17
Gouache on cardboard
19½ × 15½"

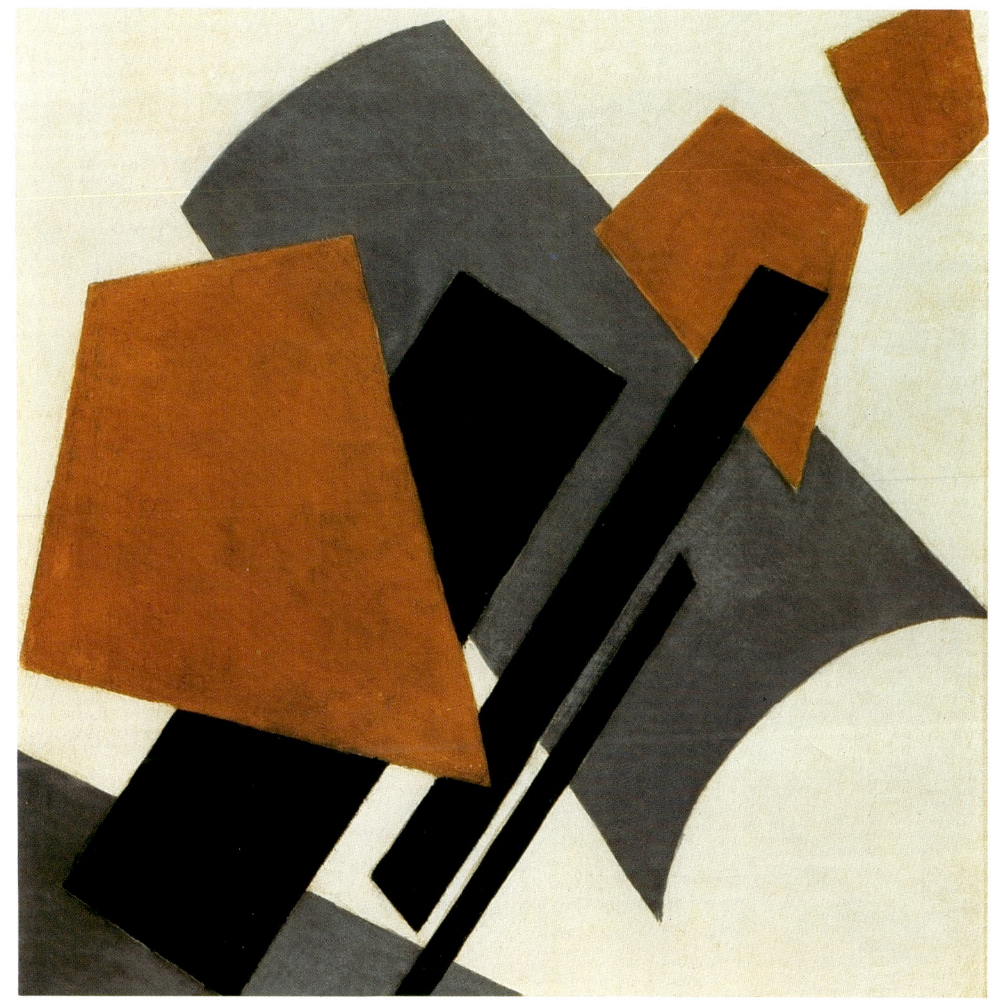

Painterly Architectonic
1916–17
Oil on canvas
17⅛ × 17¼″

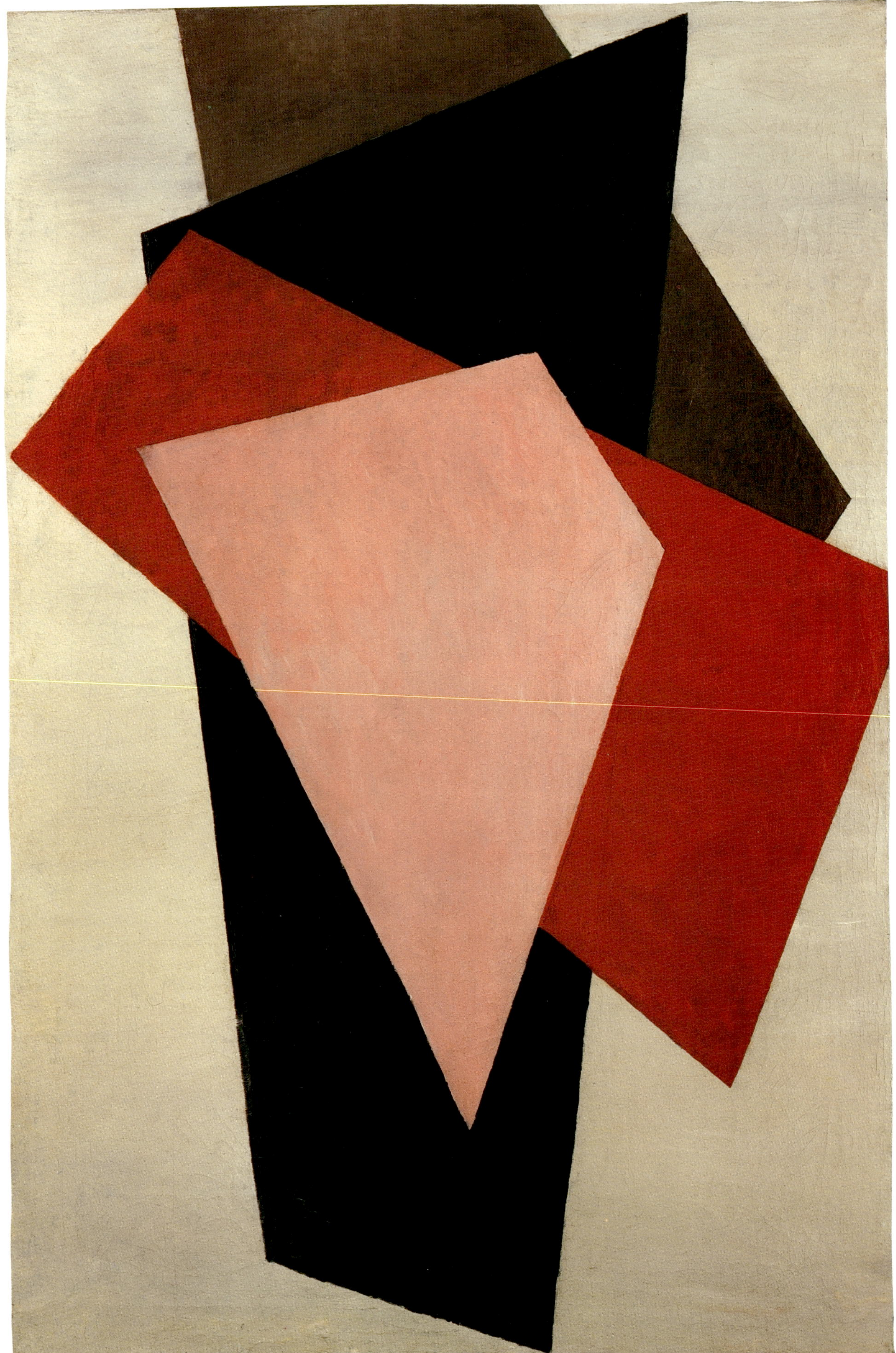

Pictorial Architectonic
1916–17
Oil on canvas
41½ × 27¾″

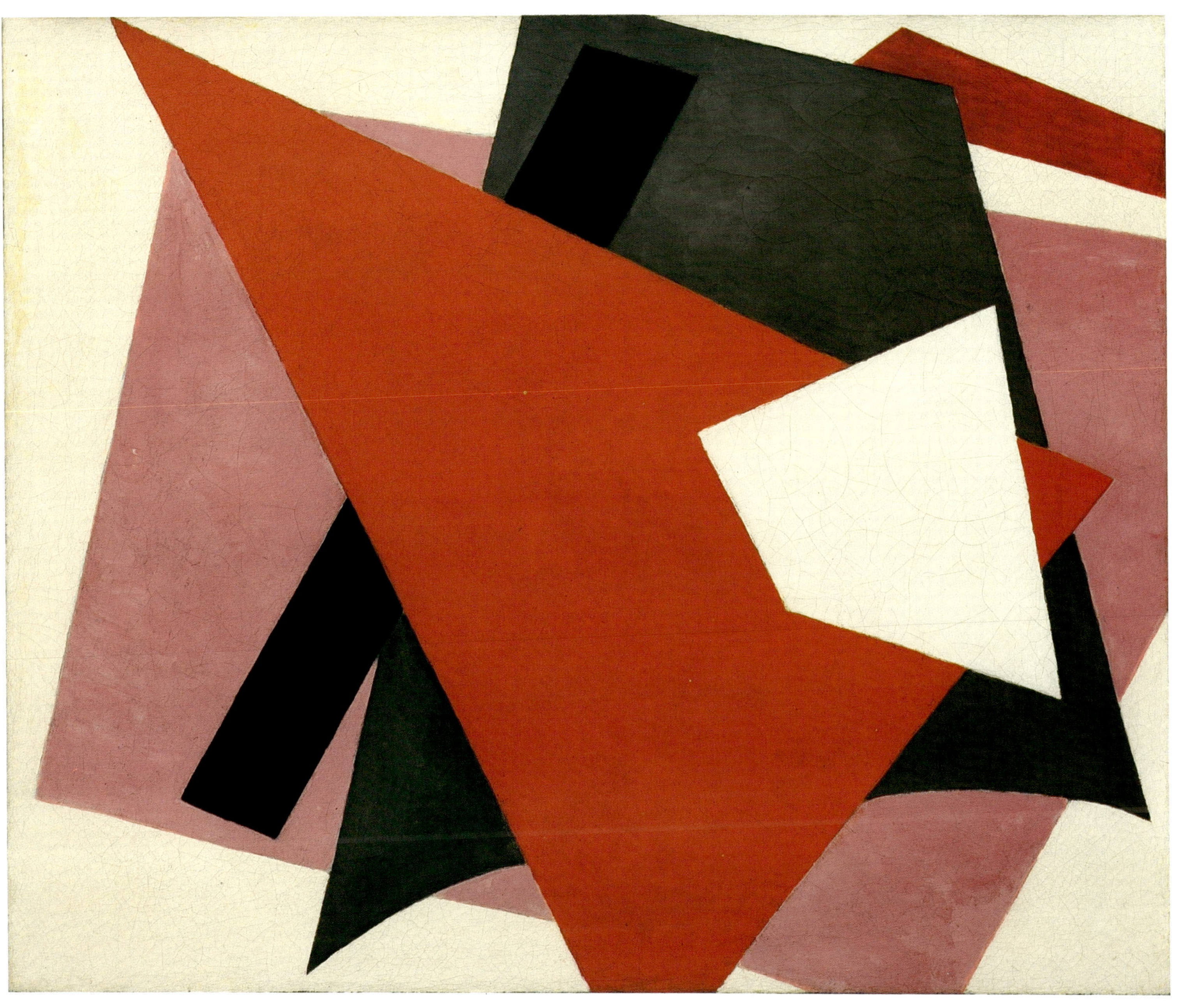

Painterly Architectonic
1917
Oil on canvas
31½ × 38⅝"

Untitled
1917
Cut-and-pasted paper
mounted on paper
$9\frac{3}{8} \times 6\frac{1}{8}$″

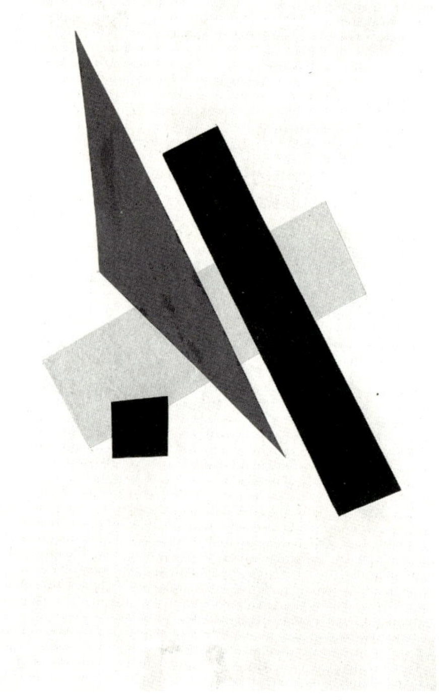

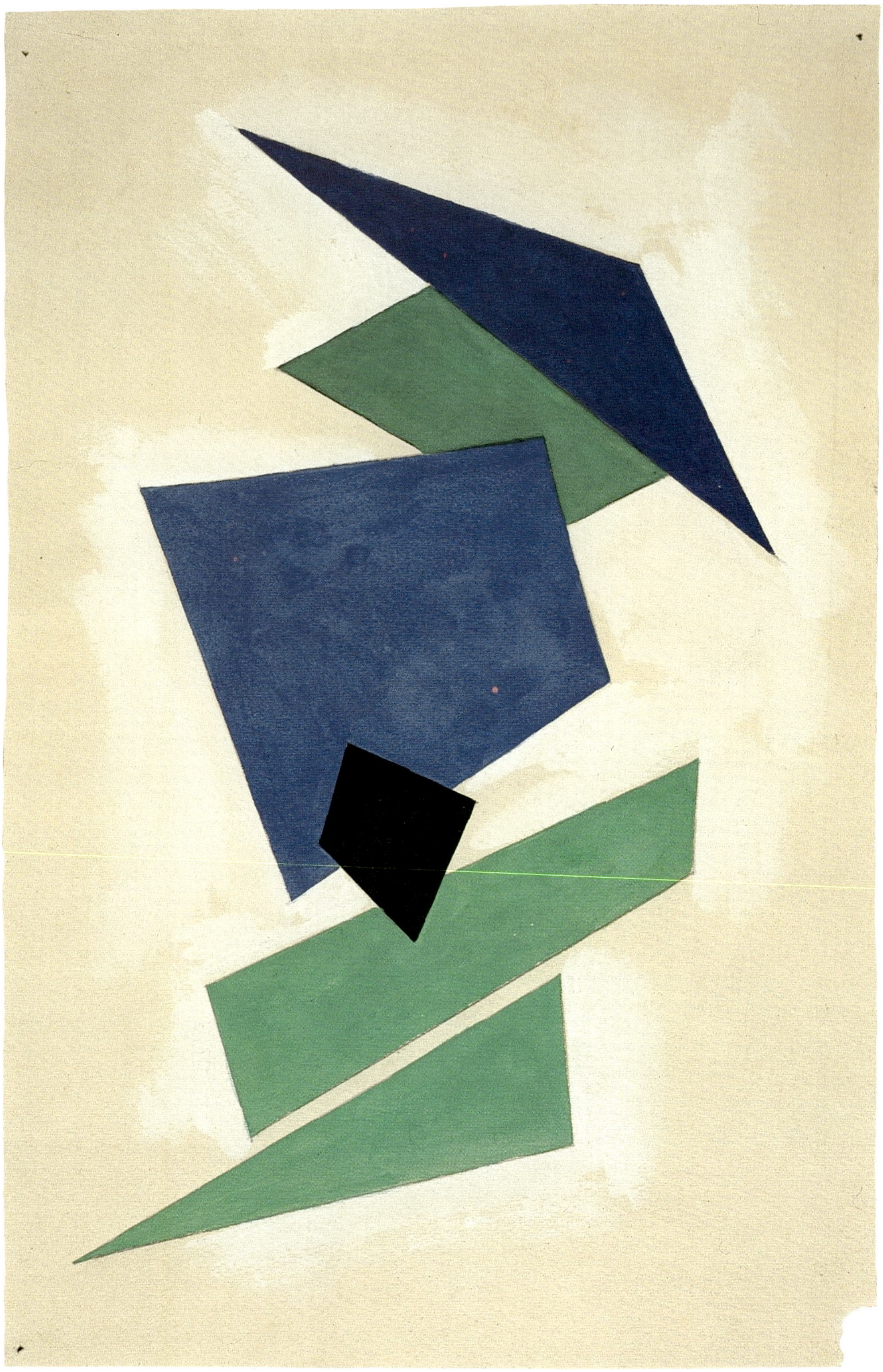

Composition
1917
Gouache on paper
$13\frac{1}{8} \times 9\frac{5}{8}$″

Composition
1917
Gouache on paper
13⅝ × 10¾″

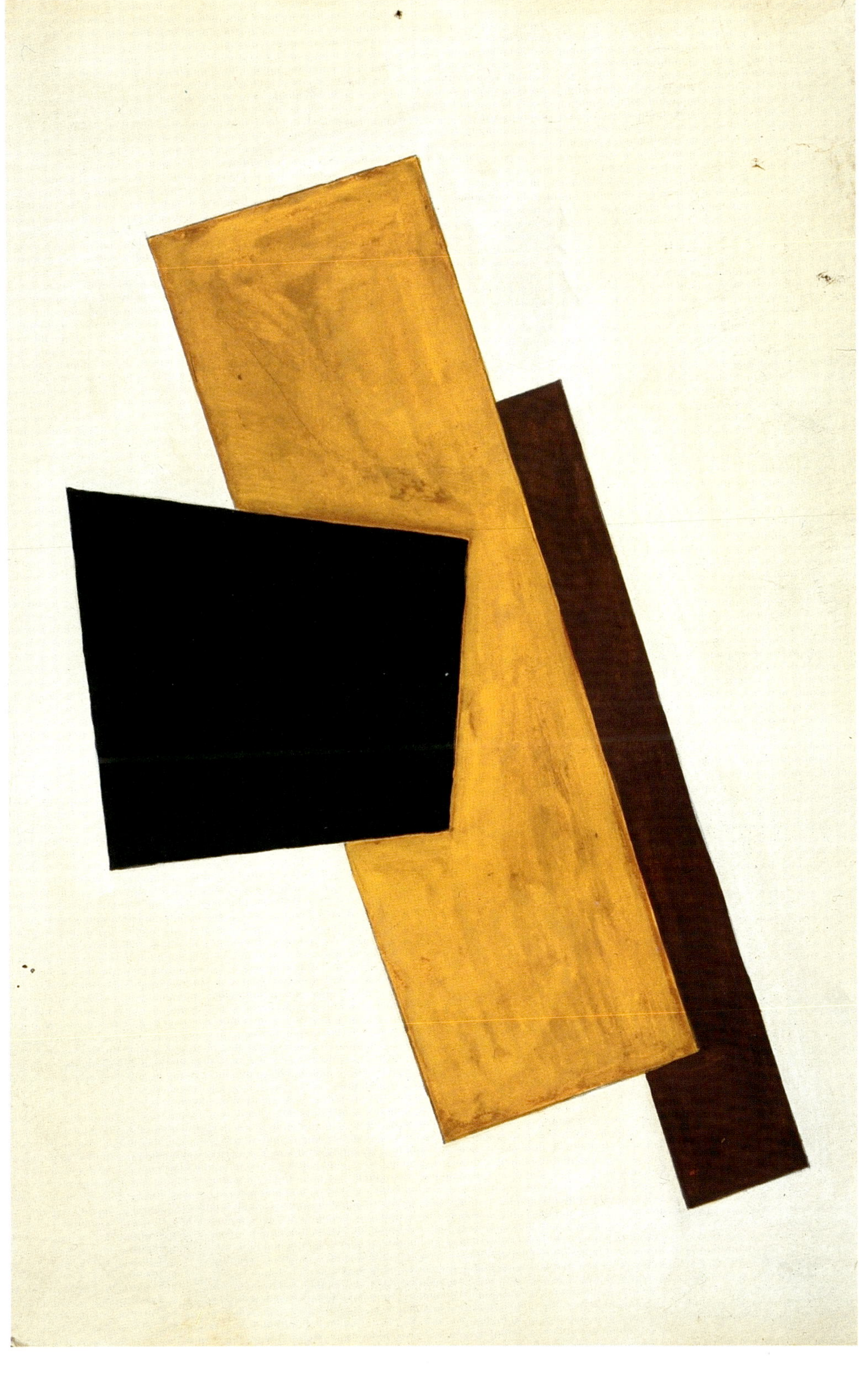

Untitled
1917
Pencil and colored pencil
on paper
13⅛ × 9⅝″

Untitled
c. 1917–19
Gouache, watercolor,
and pencil on paper
12⅞ × 9⅝″

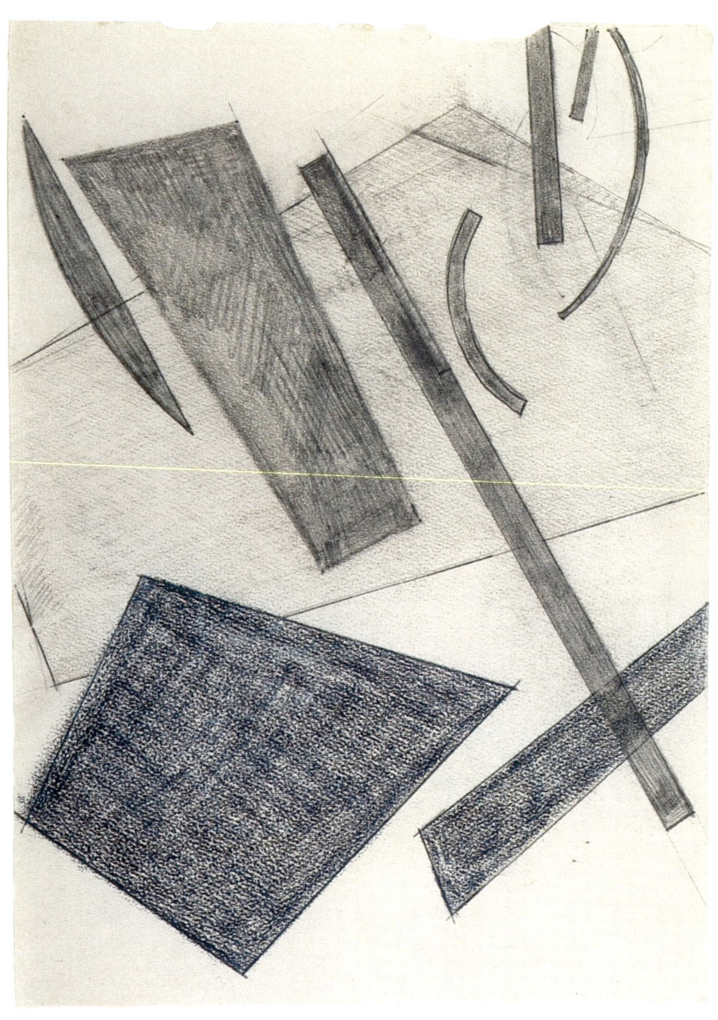

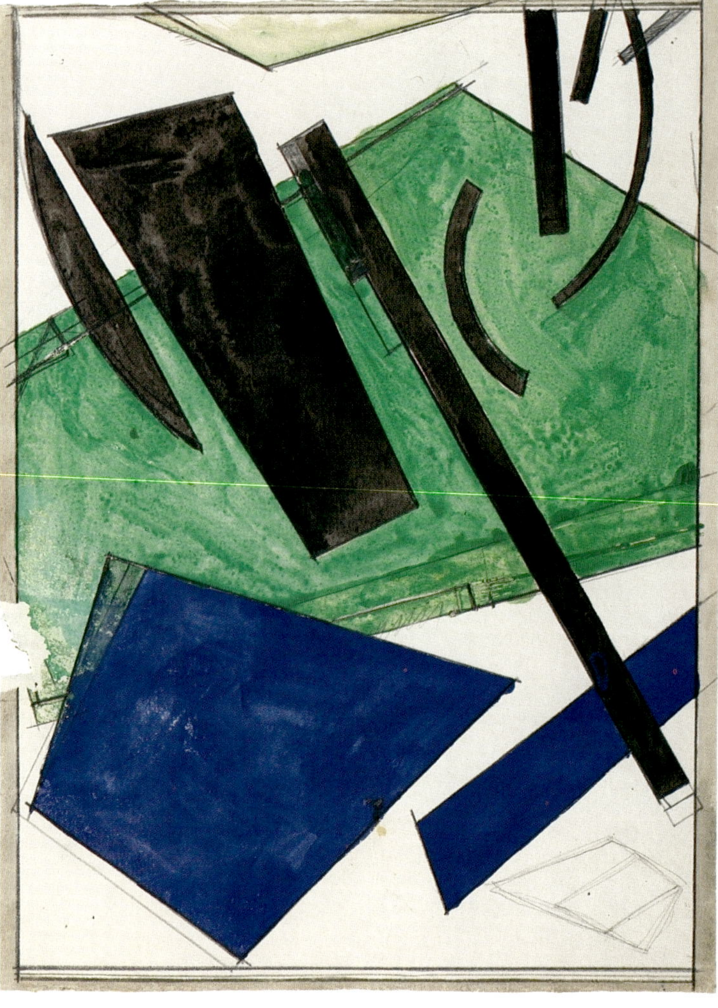

Portfolio:
Six Prints
c. 1917–19
Seven linoleum cuts, printed in color

a. (cover) $16\frac{3}{8} \times 11\frac{3}{4}$″

b. $13\frac{3}{4} \times 10\frac{1}{8}$″

c. $13\frac{1}{2} \times 10\frac{1}{4}$″

d. $13\frac{1}{2} \times 10\frac{1}{4}$″

following page:
e. $12\frac{7}{8} \times 9\frac{1}{2}$″

f. $13\frac{1}{2} \times 10\frac{1}{4}$″

g. $13\frac{3}{8} \times 10\frac{1}{4}$″

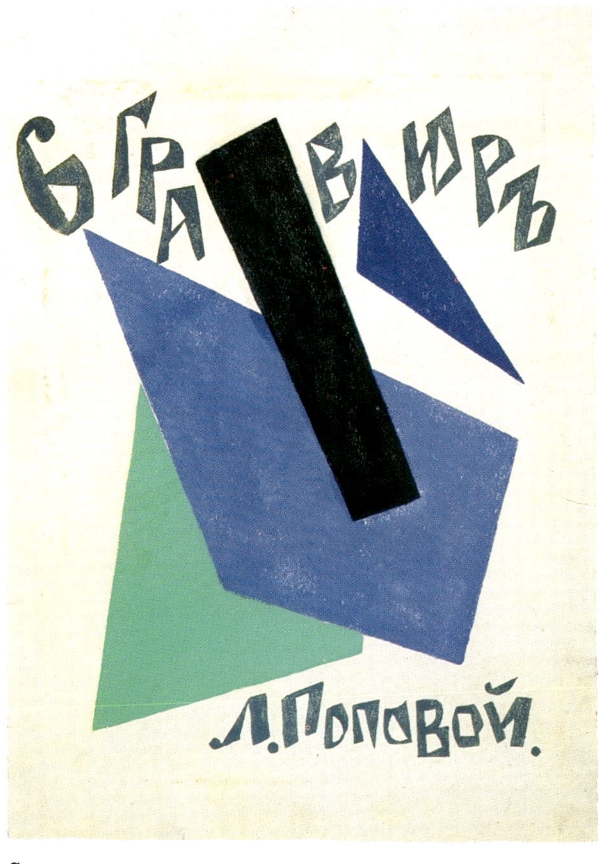

a.

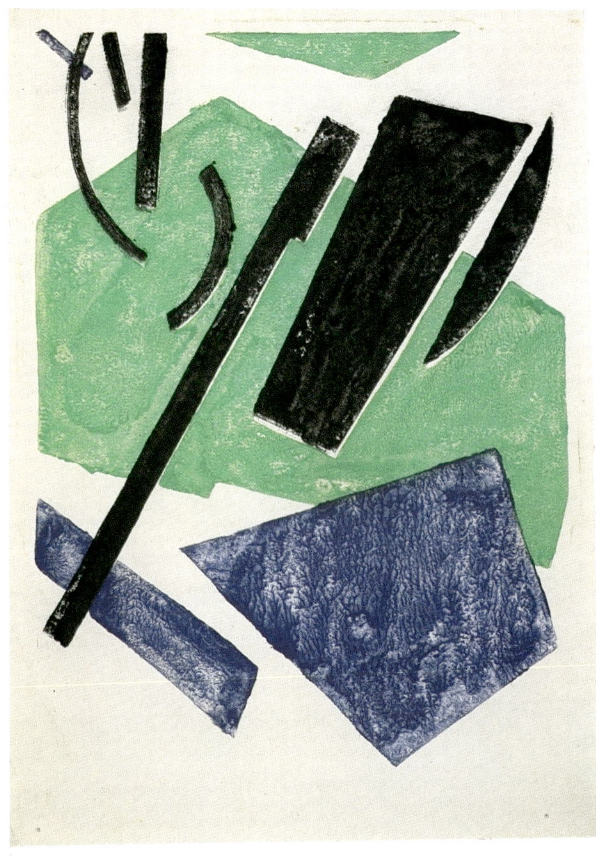
b.

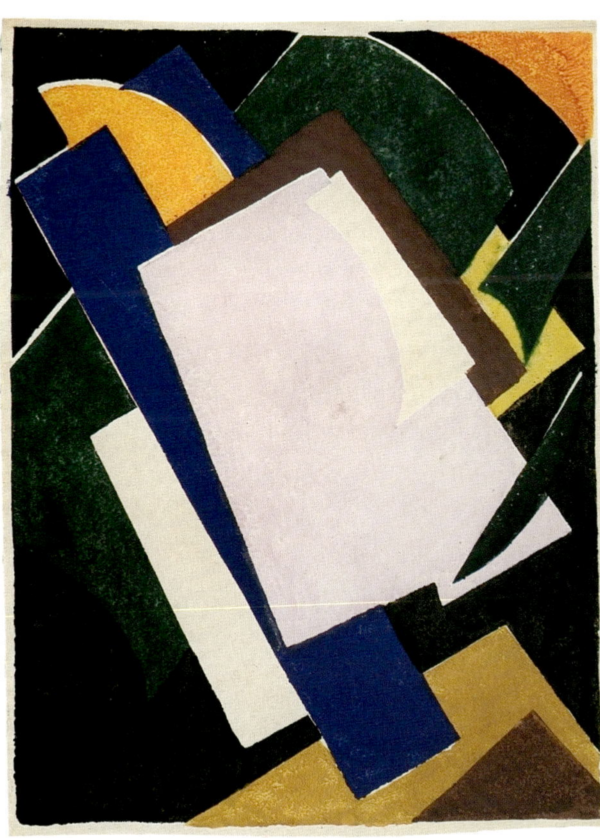
c.

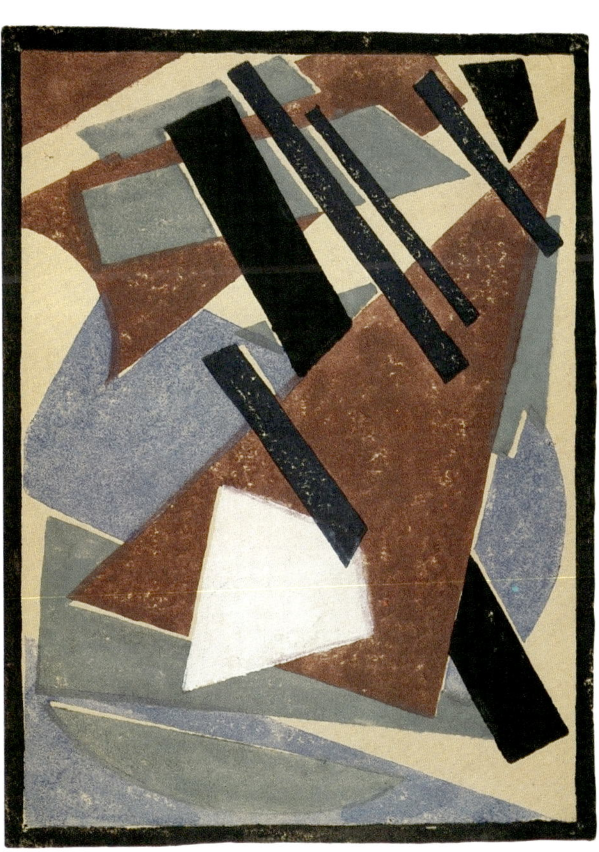
d.

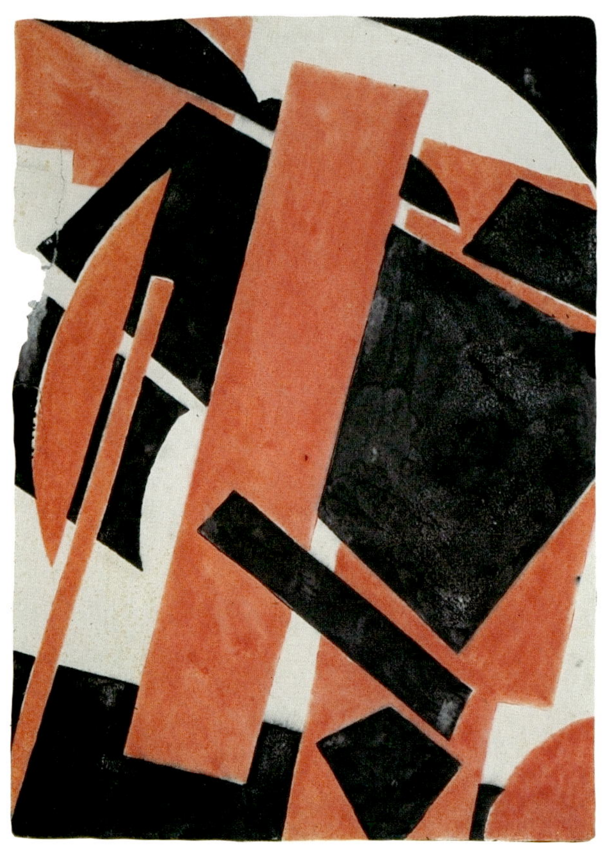
e.

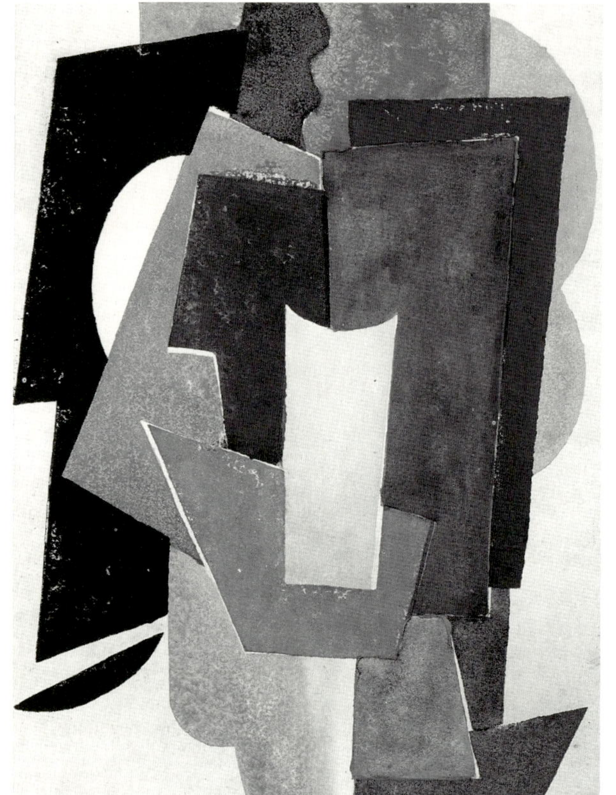
f.

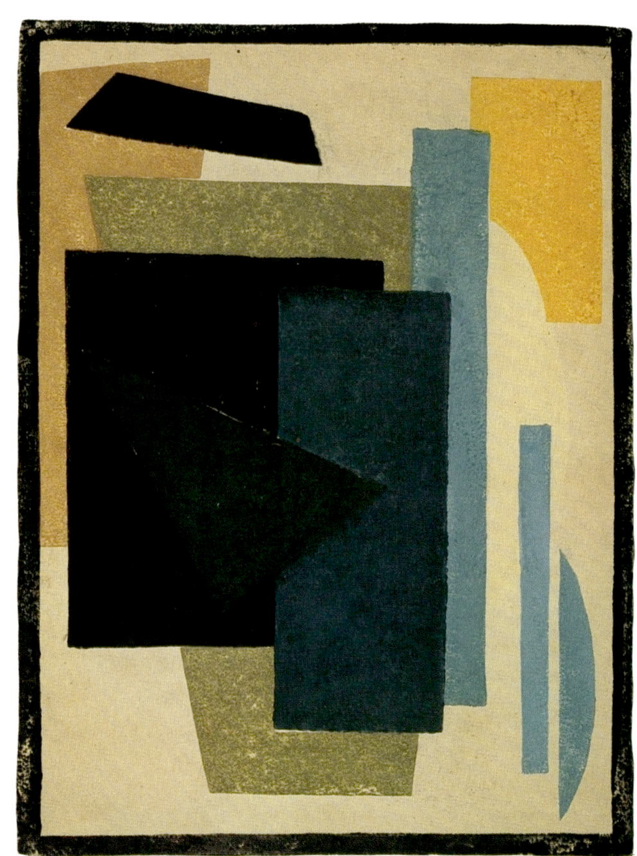
g.

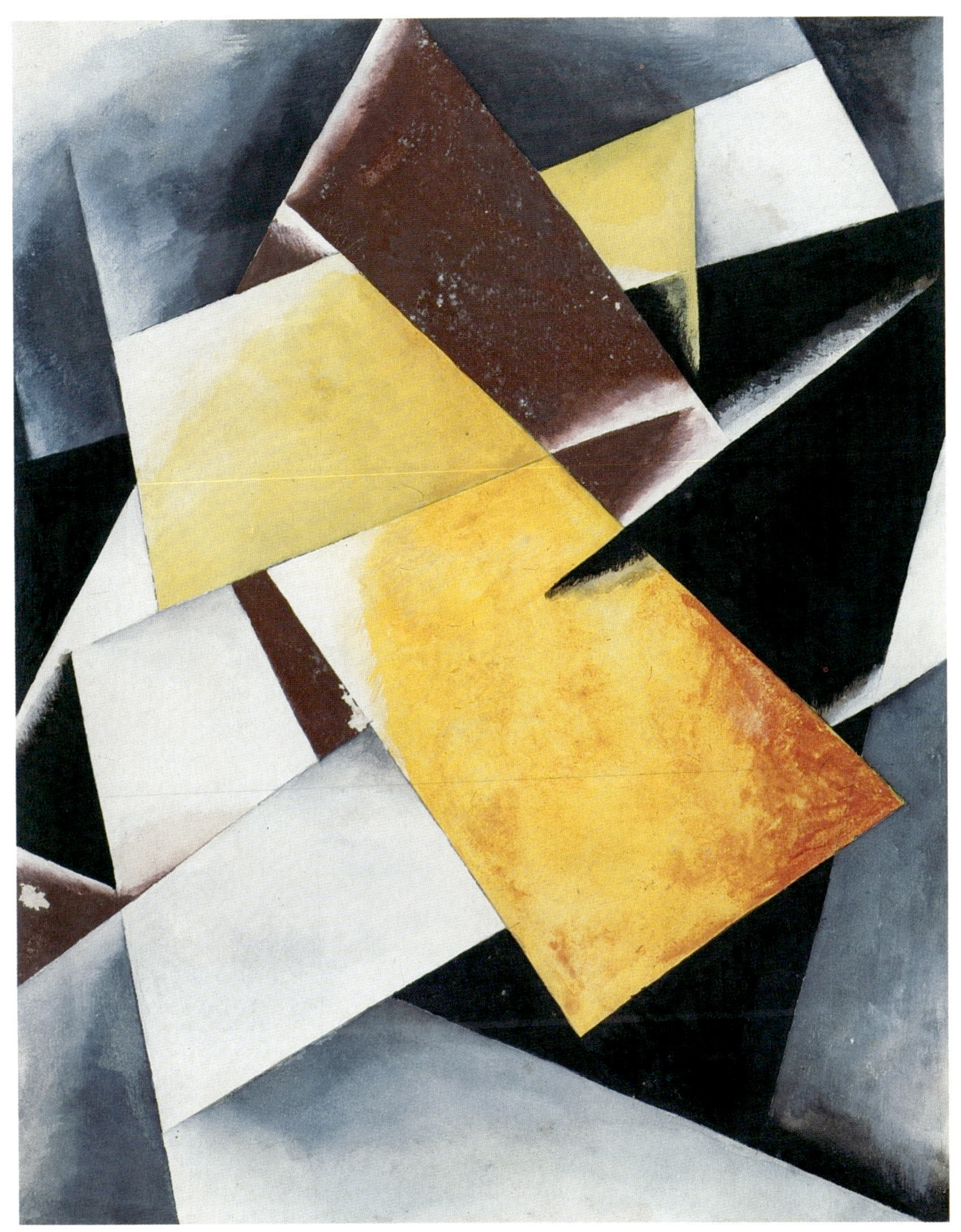

Painterly Architectonic
1918
Gouache and watercolor
with touches of varnish
on paper
11½ × 9¼″

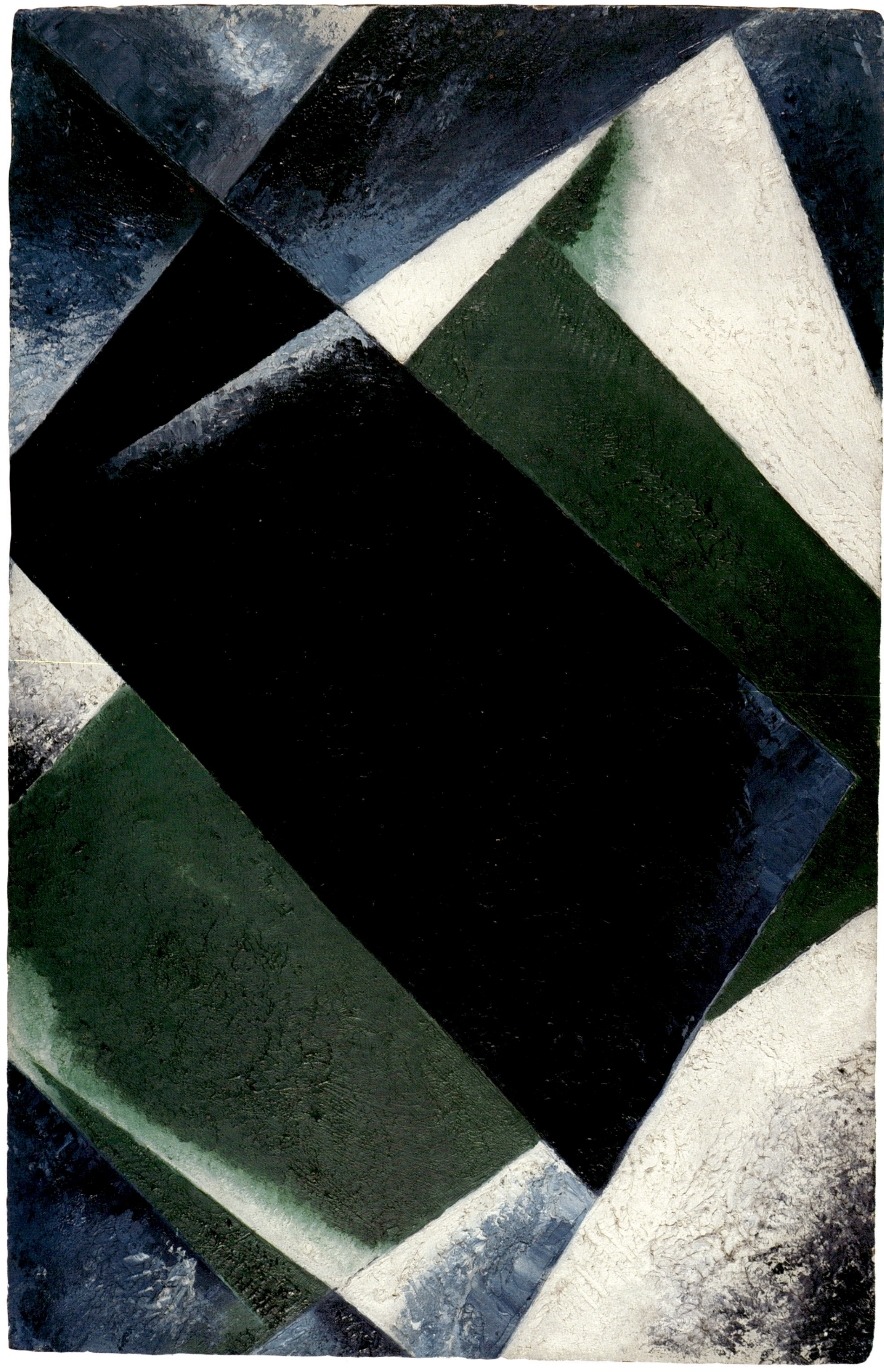

Painterly Architectonic
1918
Oil on board
23⅜ × 15½″

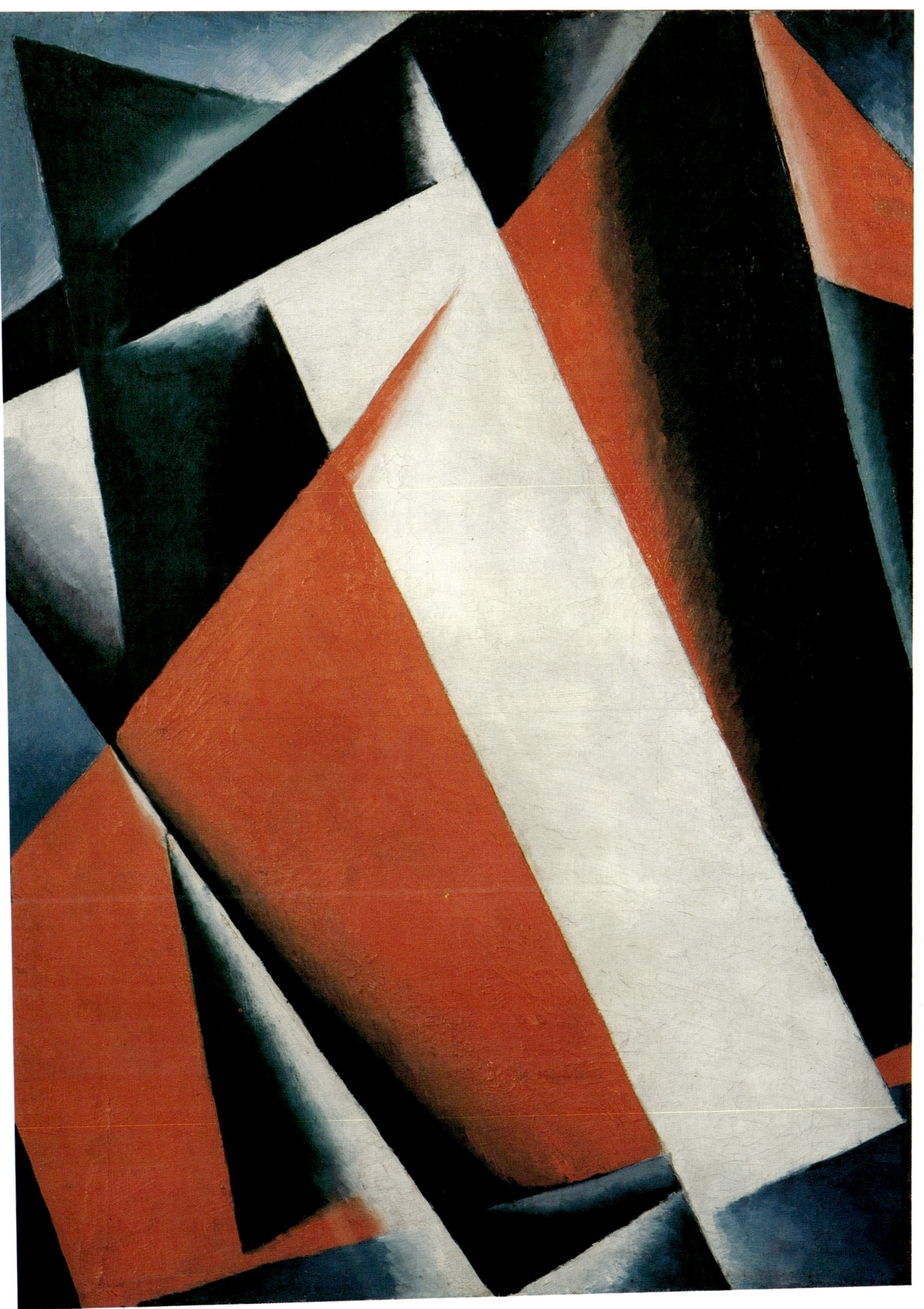

Painterly Architectonic
1918
Oil on canvas
24½ × 17½″

Painterly Architectonic
1918
Oil on canvas
22⅞ × 20⅞"

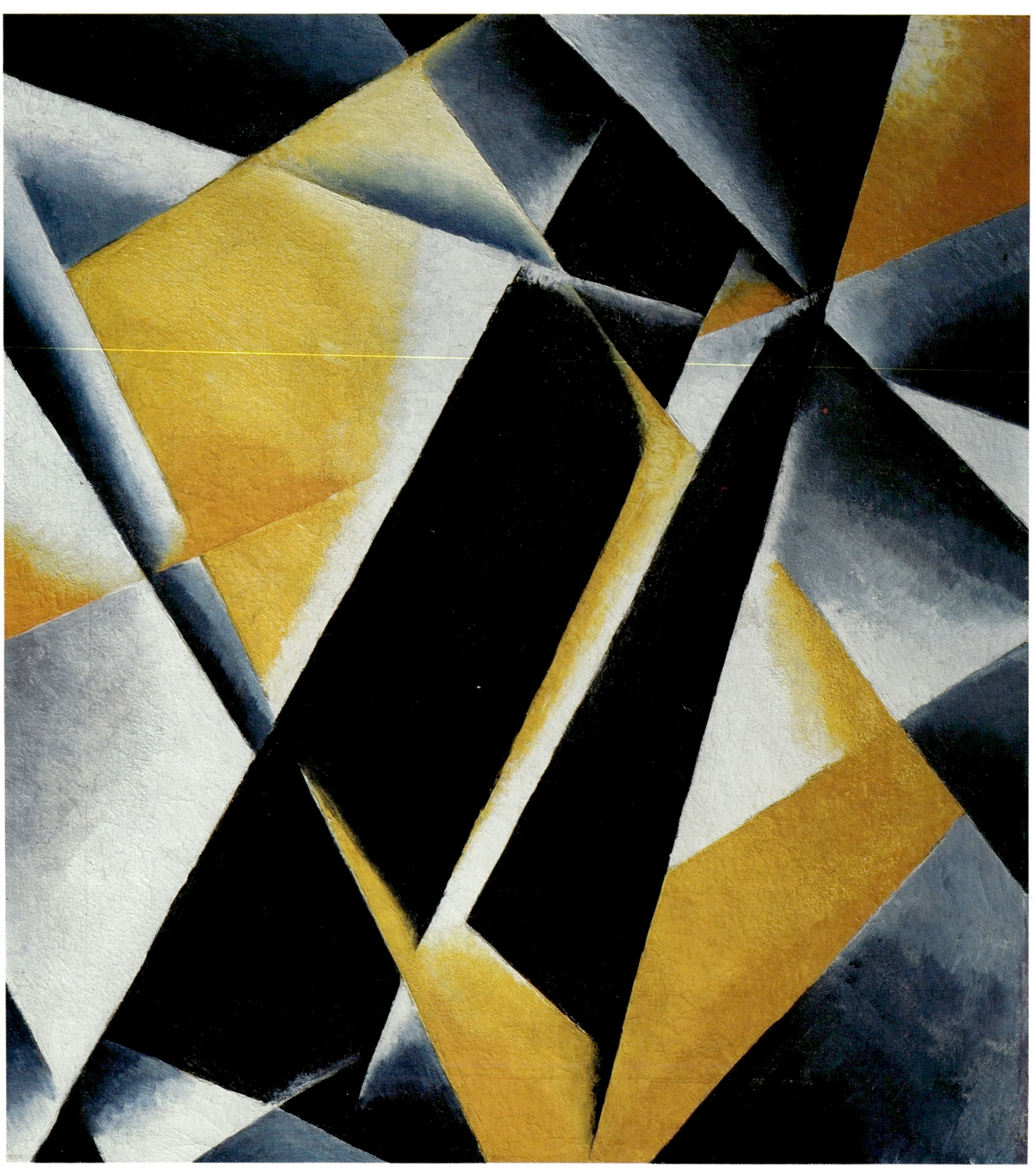

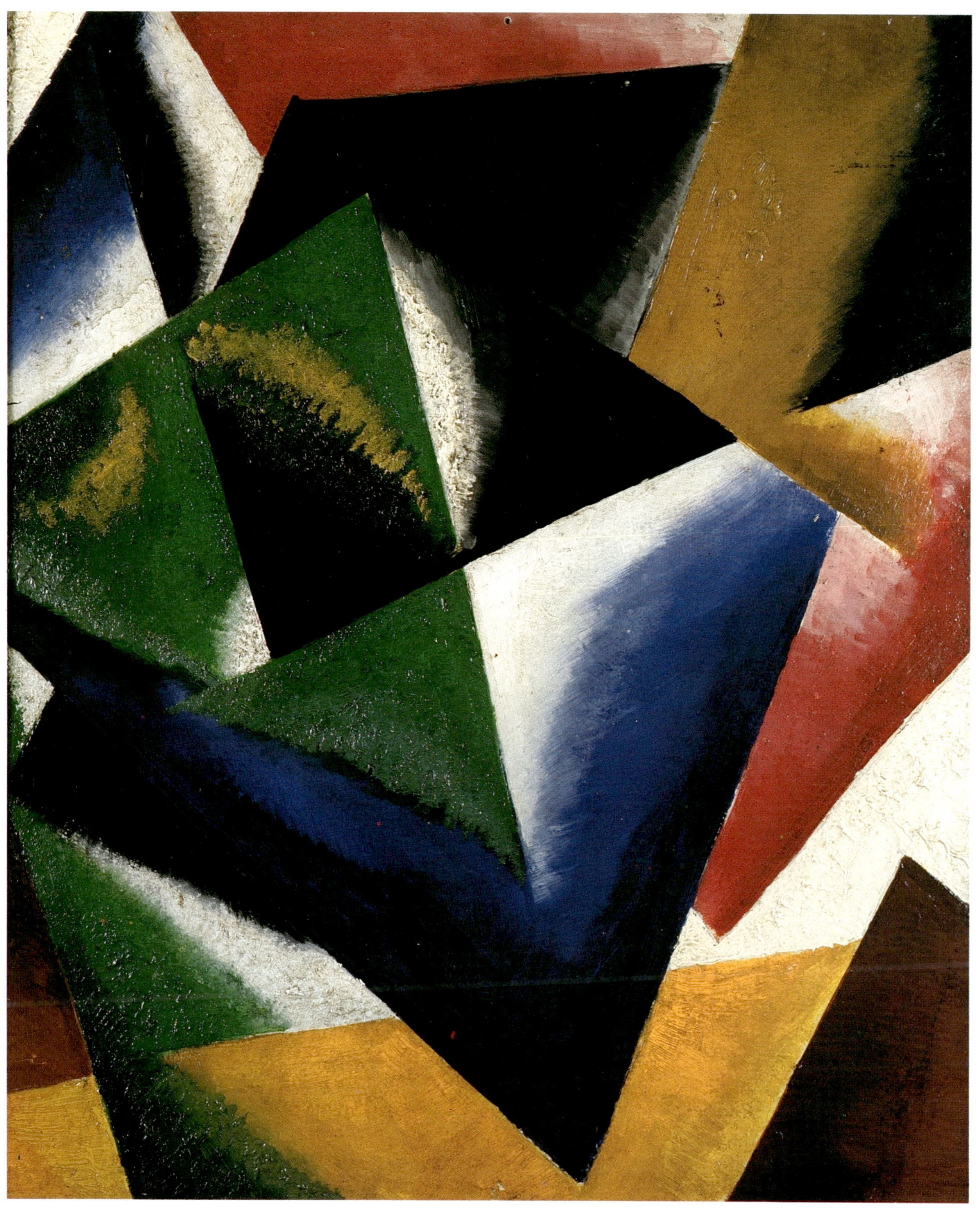

Painterly Architectonic
1918
Oil on board
20½ × 17½″

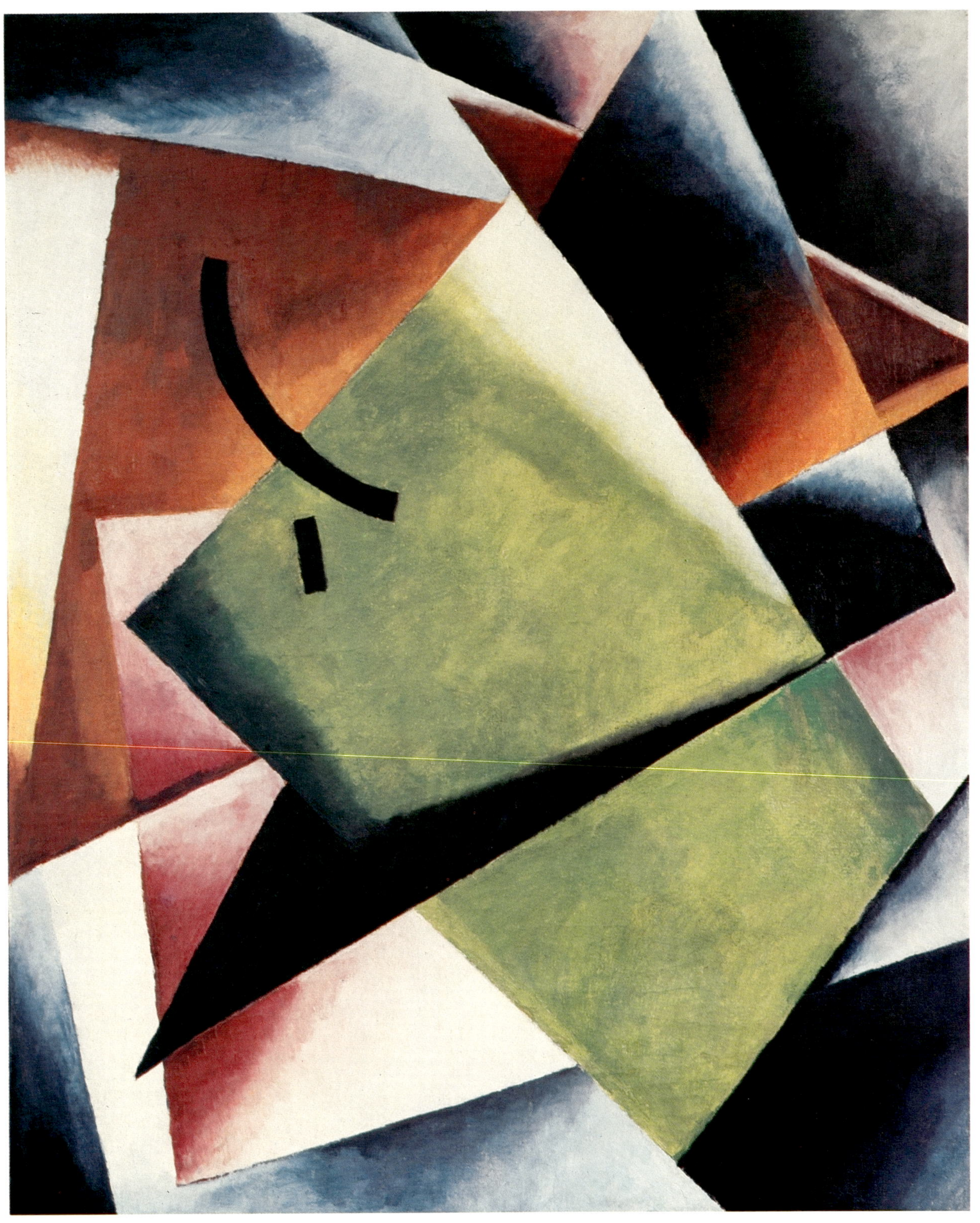

Painterly Architectonic
1918–19
Oil on canvas
$27\frac{7}{8} \times 22\frac{7}{8}''$

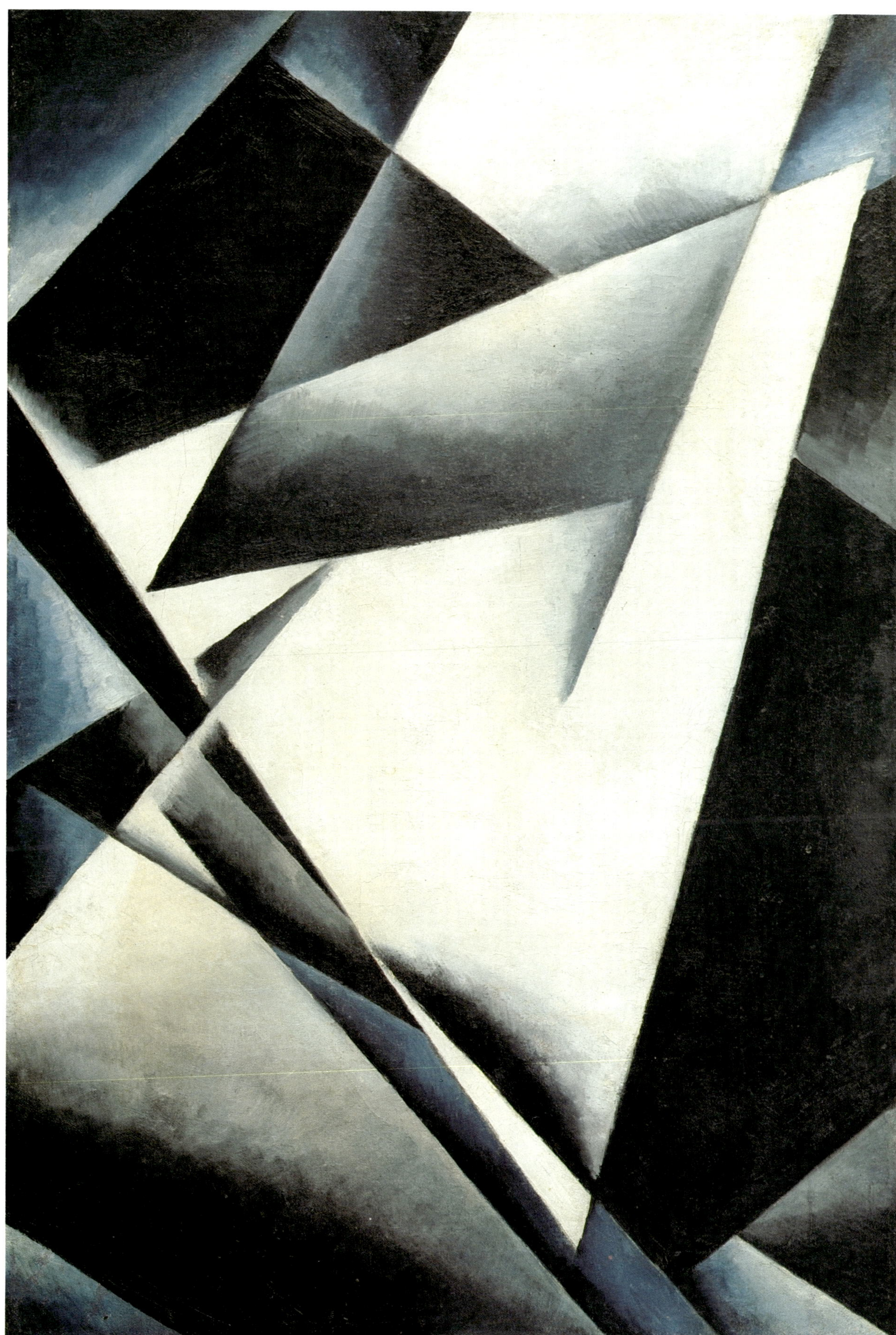

Painterly Architectonic
1918–19
Oil on canvas
$28\frac{3}{4} \times 18\frac{7}{8}$″

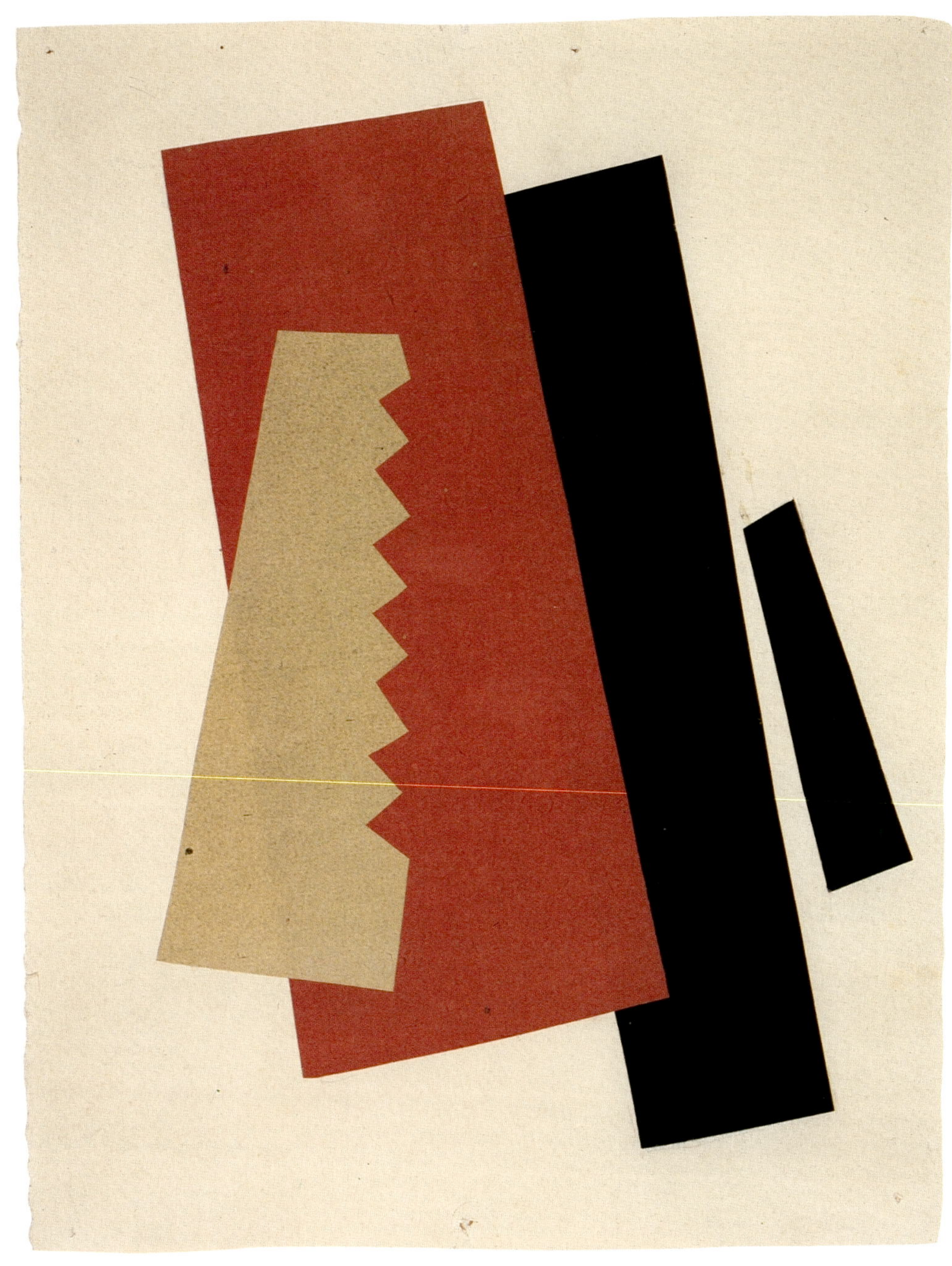

Composition
1920
Gouache and paper collage on paper
11¾ × 9⅛"

Composition
1920
Gouache and paper collage on paper
17½ × 11¾"

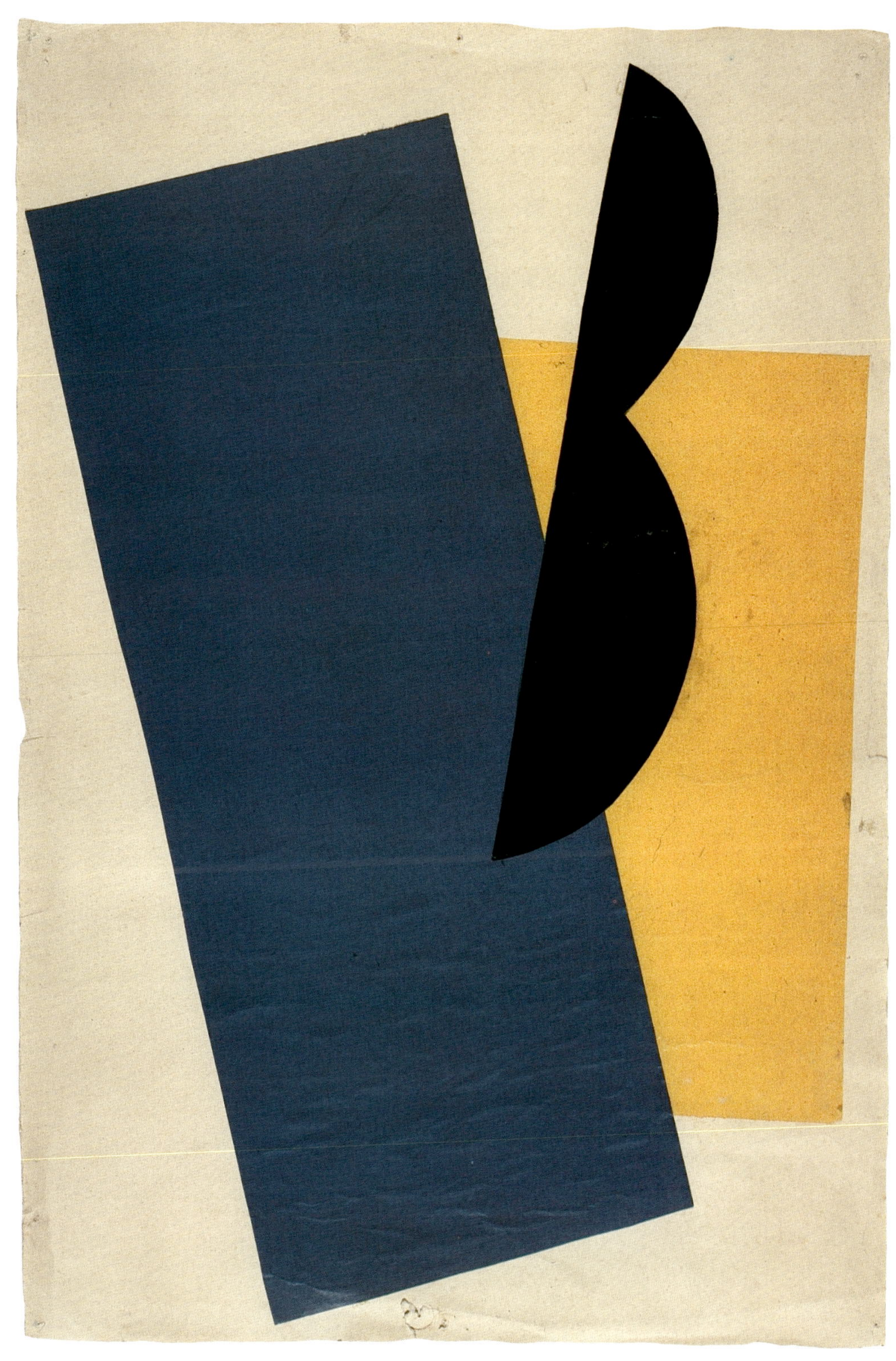

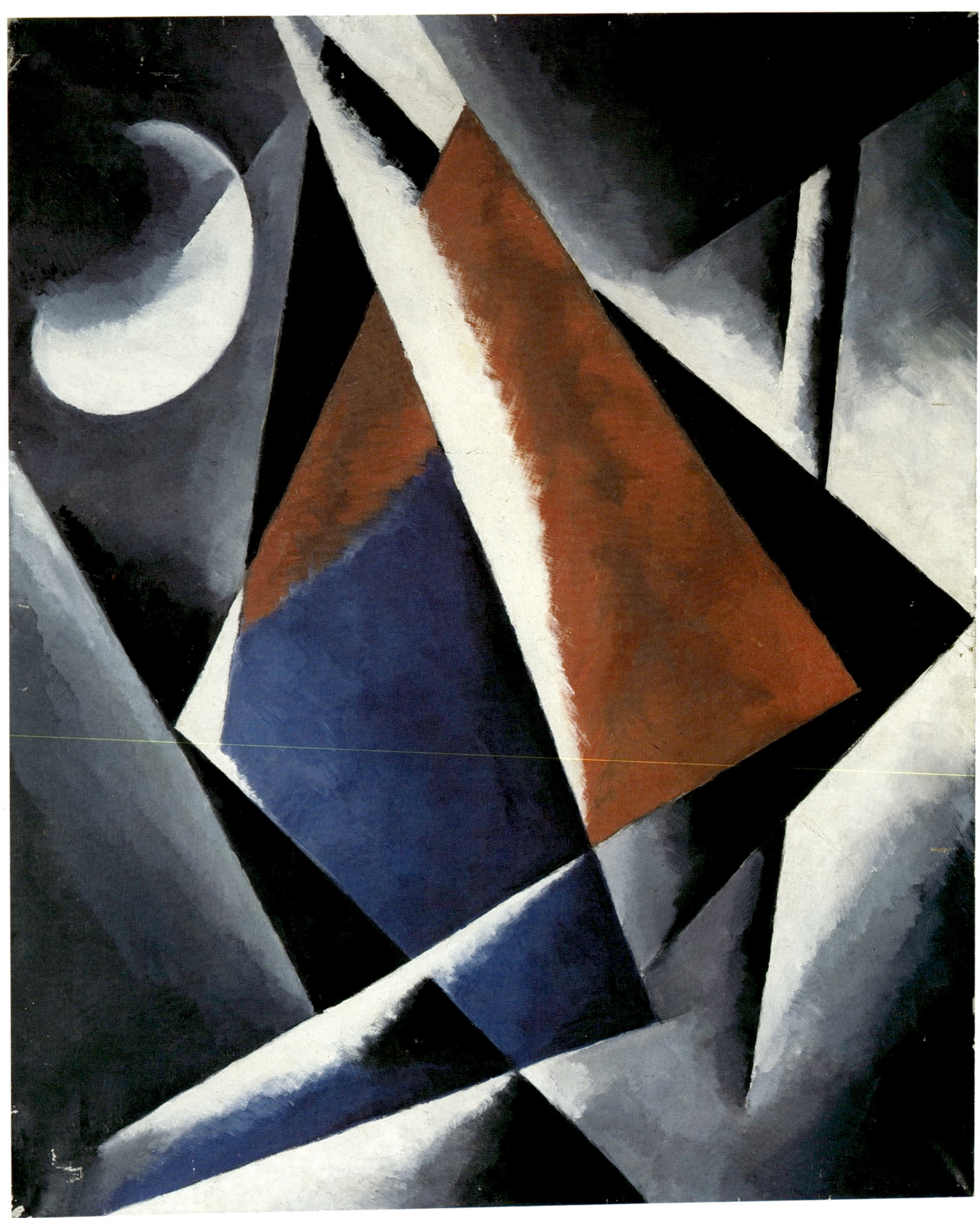

Construction
1920
Oil on canvas
42 × 34⅞″

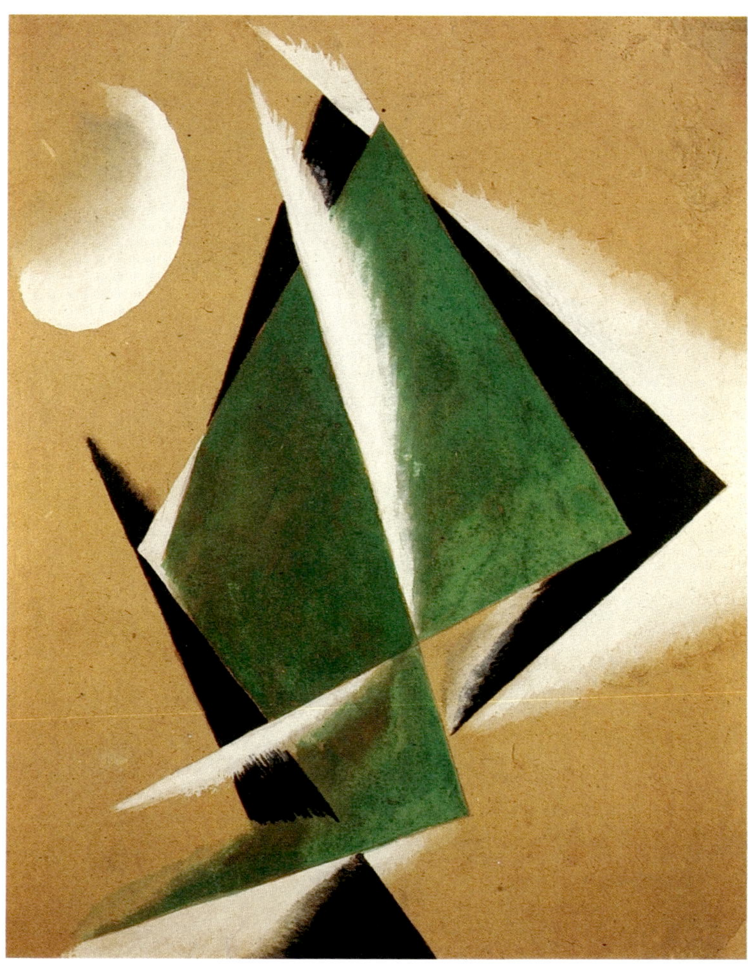

Construction with White Crescent
1920–21
Gouache on cardboard
13⅛ × 10⅝″

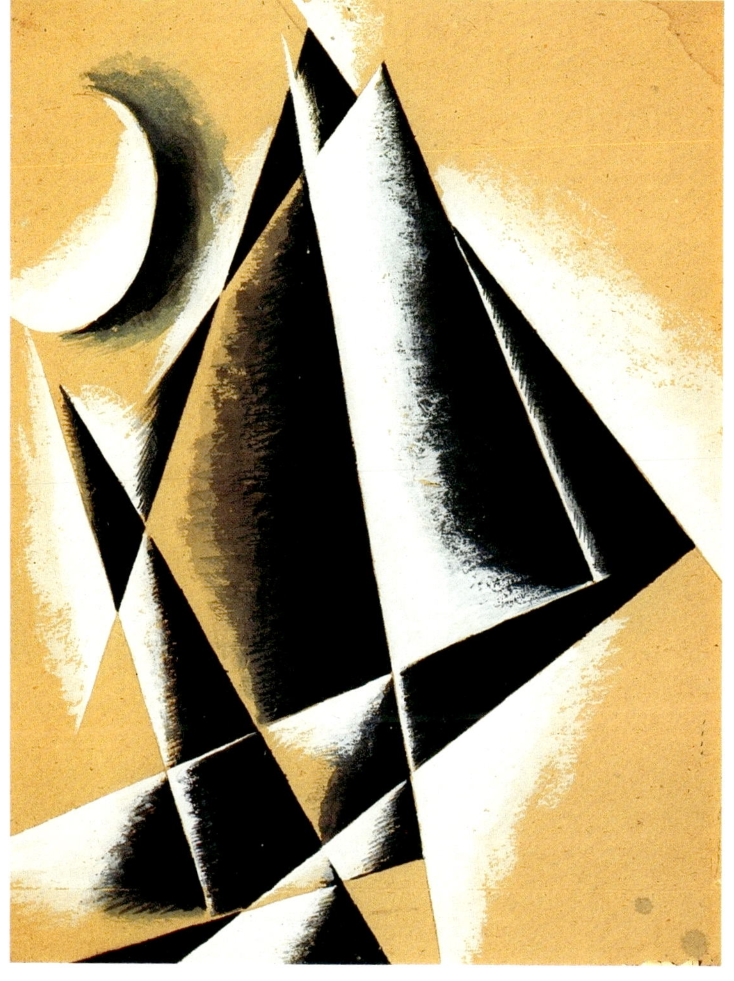

Construction with White Crescent
1921
Gouache on board
13¼ × 10¼″

Space-Force Construction
1921
Colored crayons on paper
10⅞ × 8⅛″

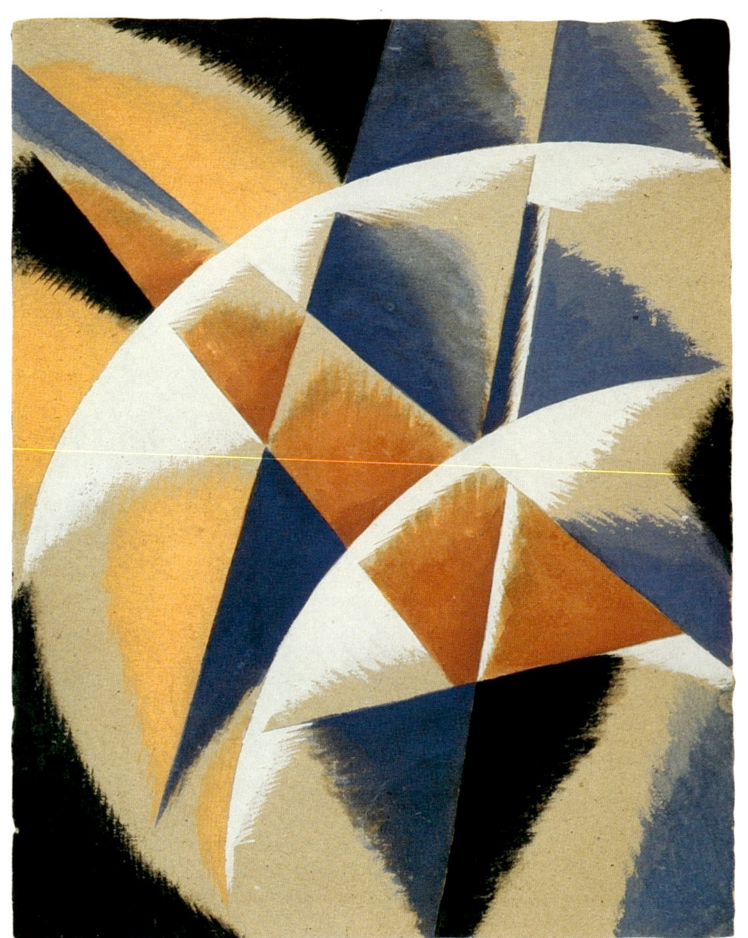

Composition
1921
Gouache on paper
13½ × 10⅞″

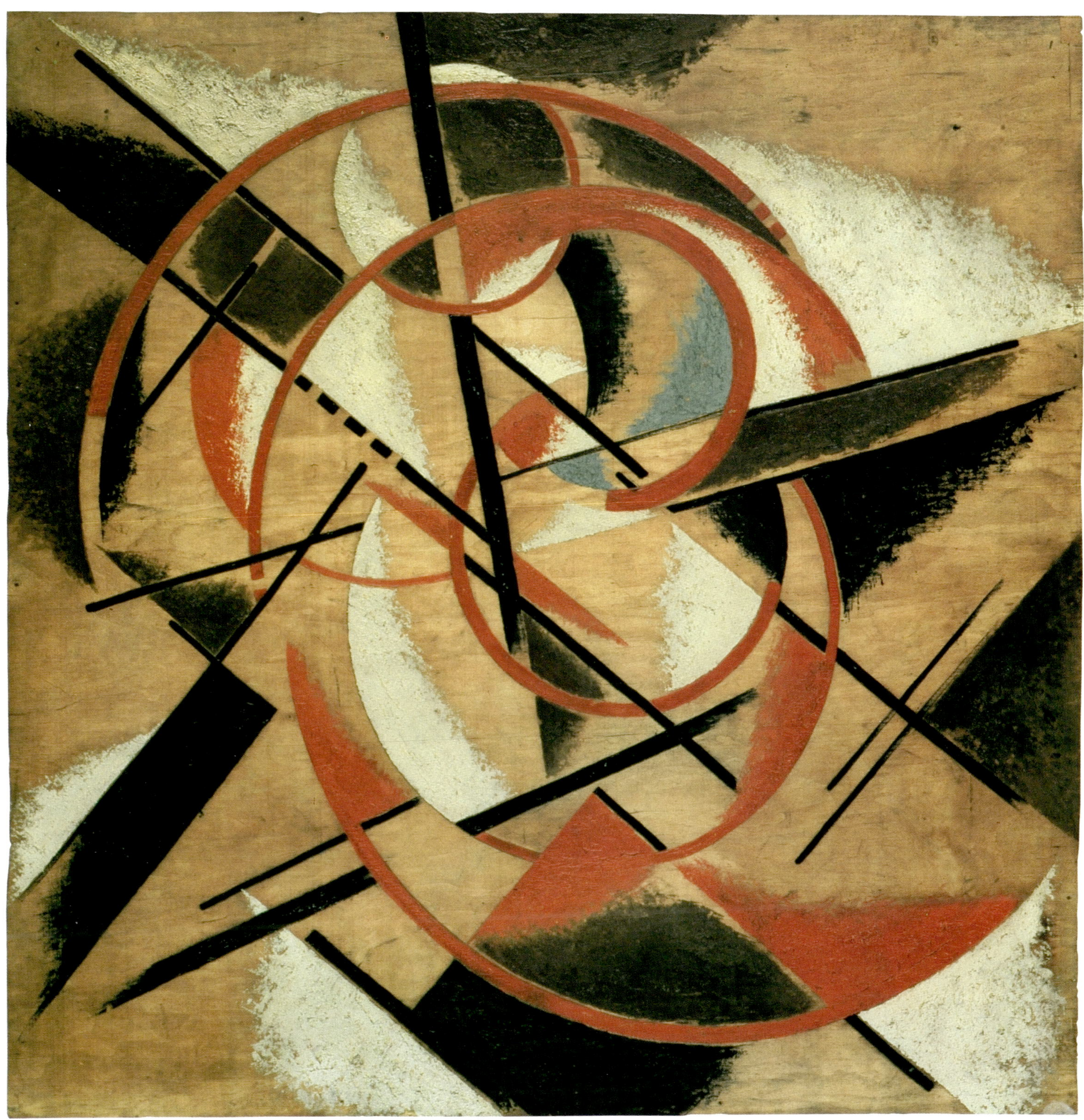

Space-Force Construction
1921
Oil with marble dust
on plywood
44⅜ × 44⅜″

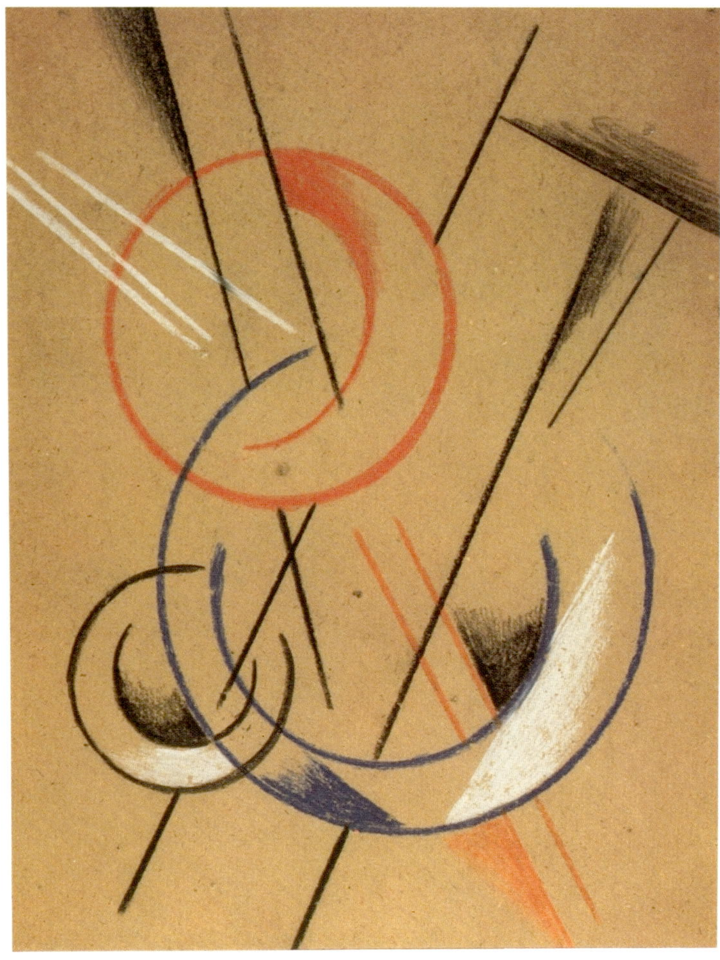

Space-Force Construction
1921
Colored pencil on paper
13⅞ × 8½"

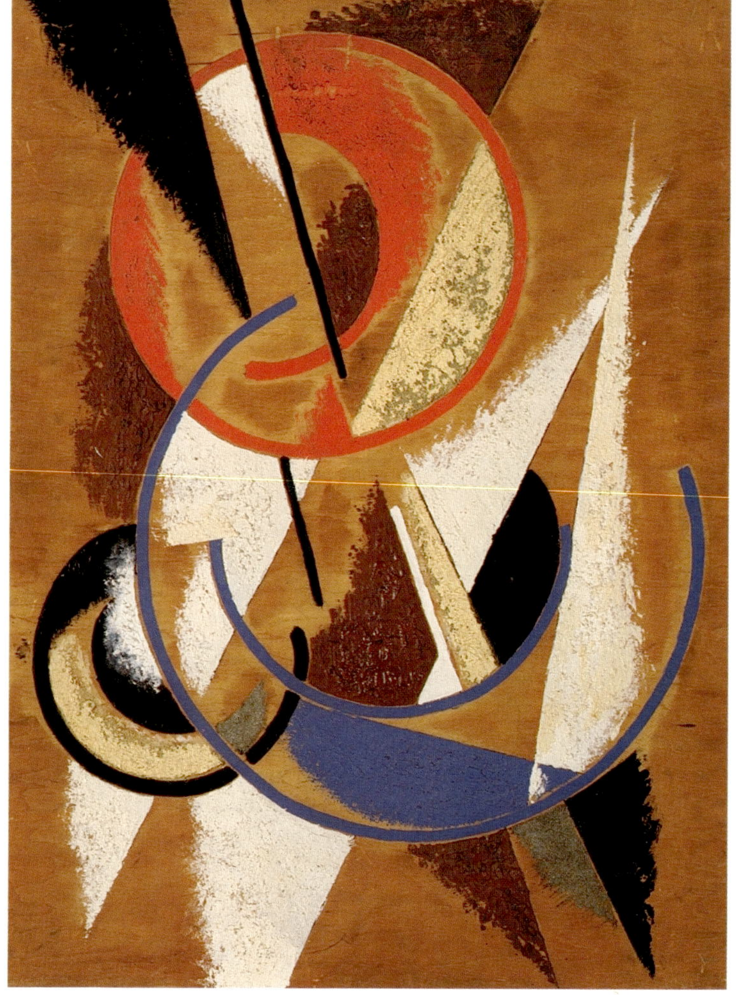

Space-Force Construction
1921
Oil with bronze powder and marble dust on plywood
27⅝ × 20⅜"

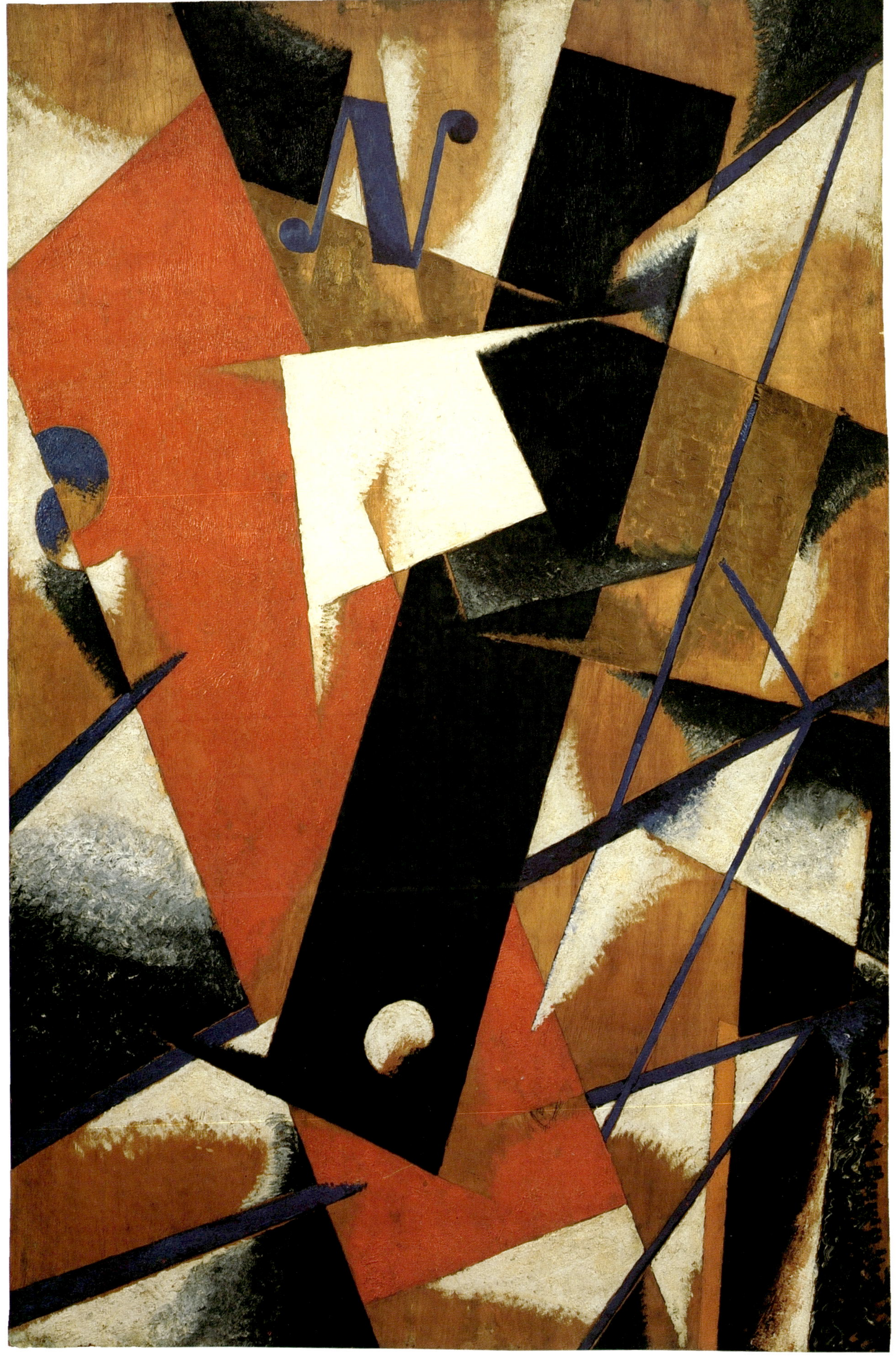

Space-Force Construction
1921
Oil over pencil on plywood
$48\frac{7}{8} \times 32\frac{1}{4}$"

Constructivist Composition
1921
Oil on board
$36\frac{5}{8} \times 24\frac{1}{4}''$

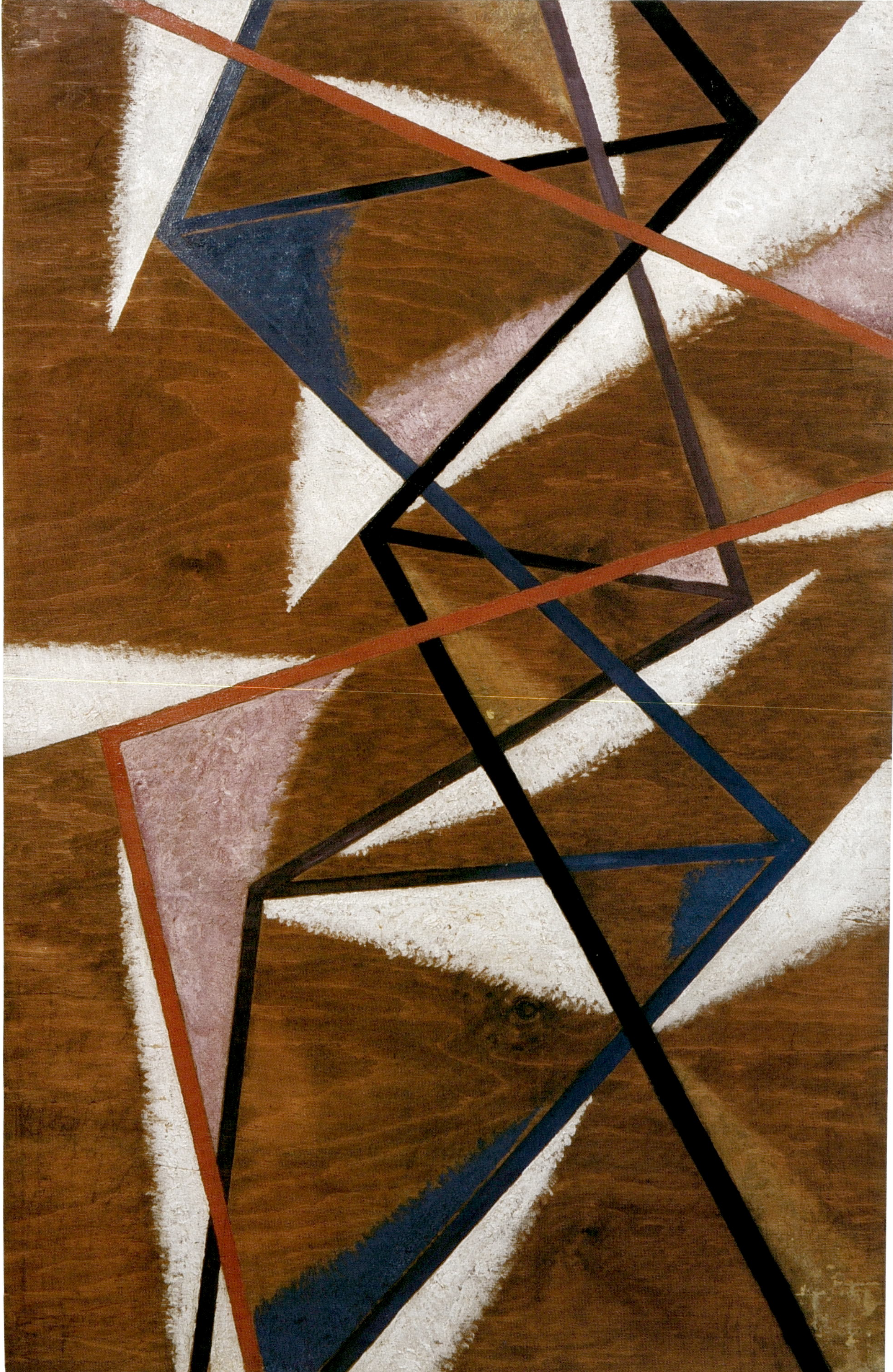

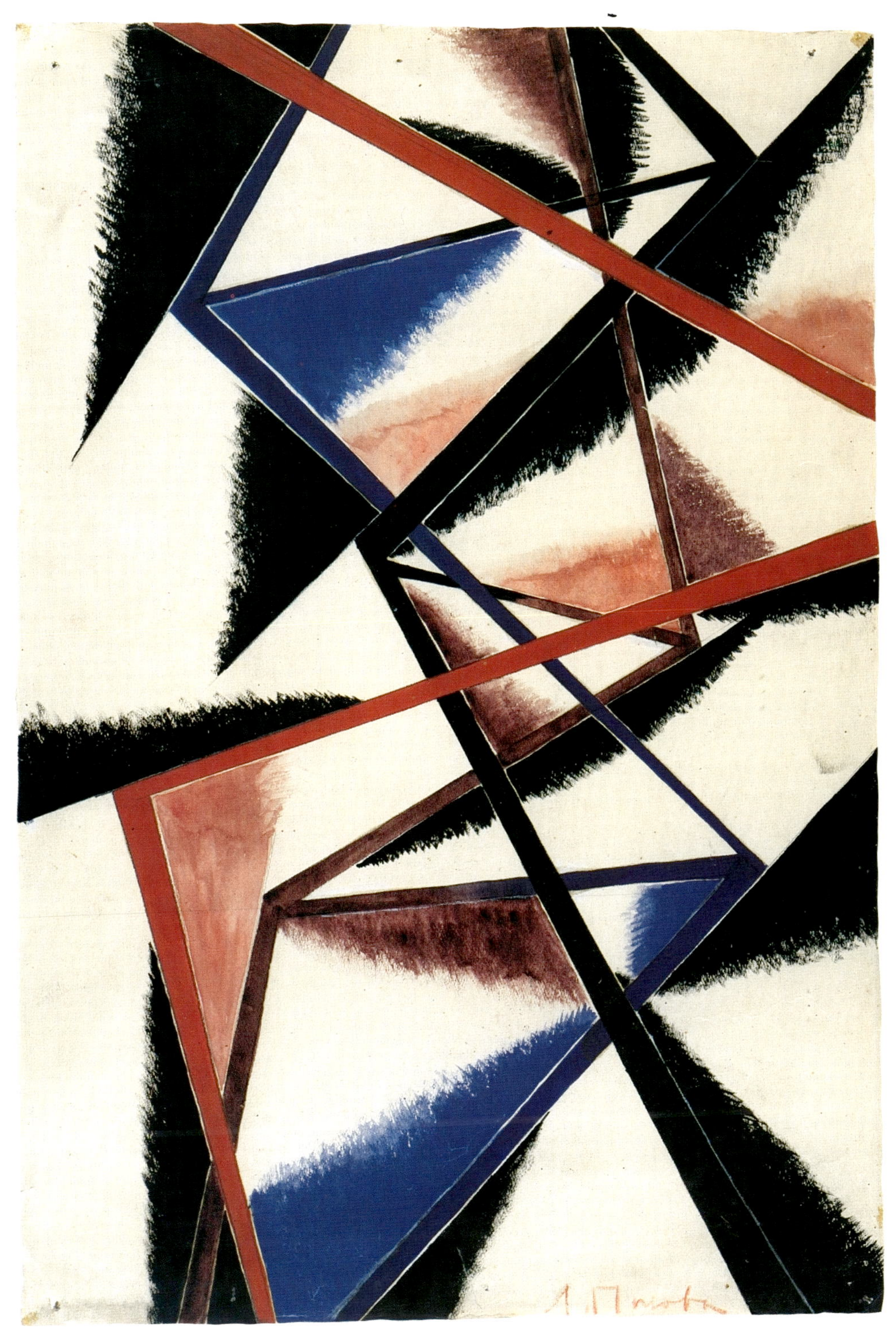

Composition No. 47
1921
Gouache, watercolor,
India ink, and
pencil on paper
20 × 13¾″

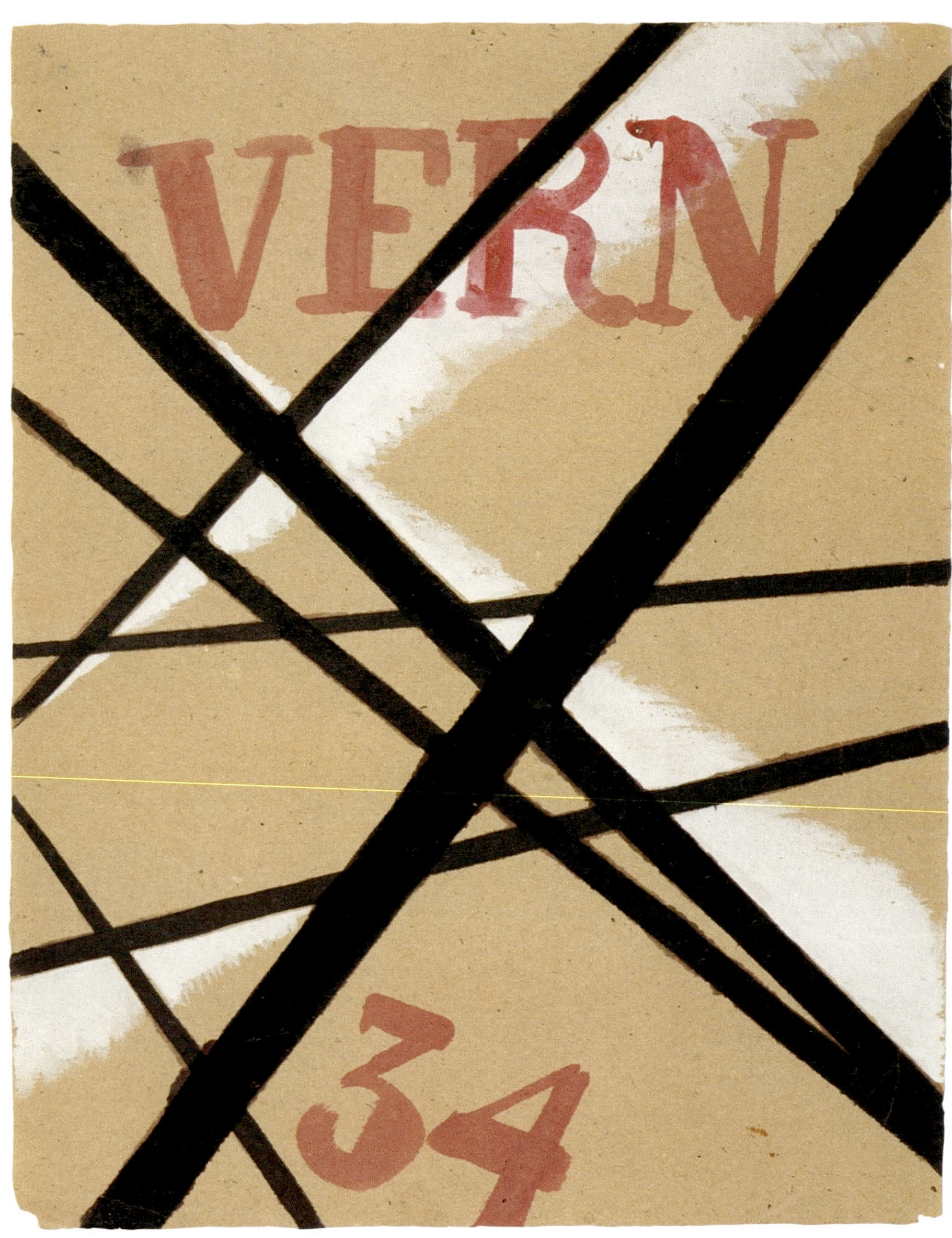

Vern 34
c. 1921
Watercolor and gouache
on paper
13¾ × 10¾″

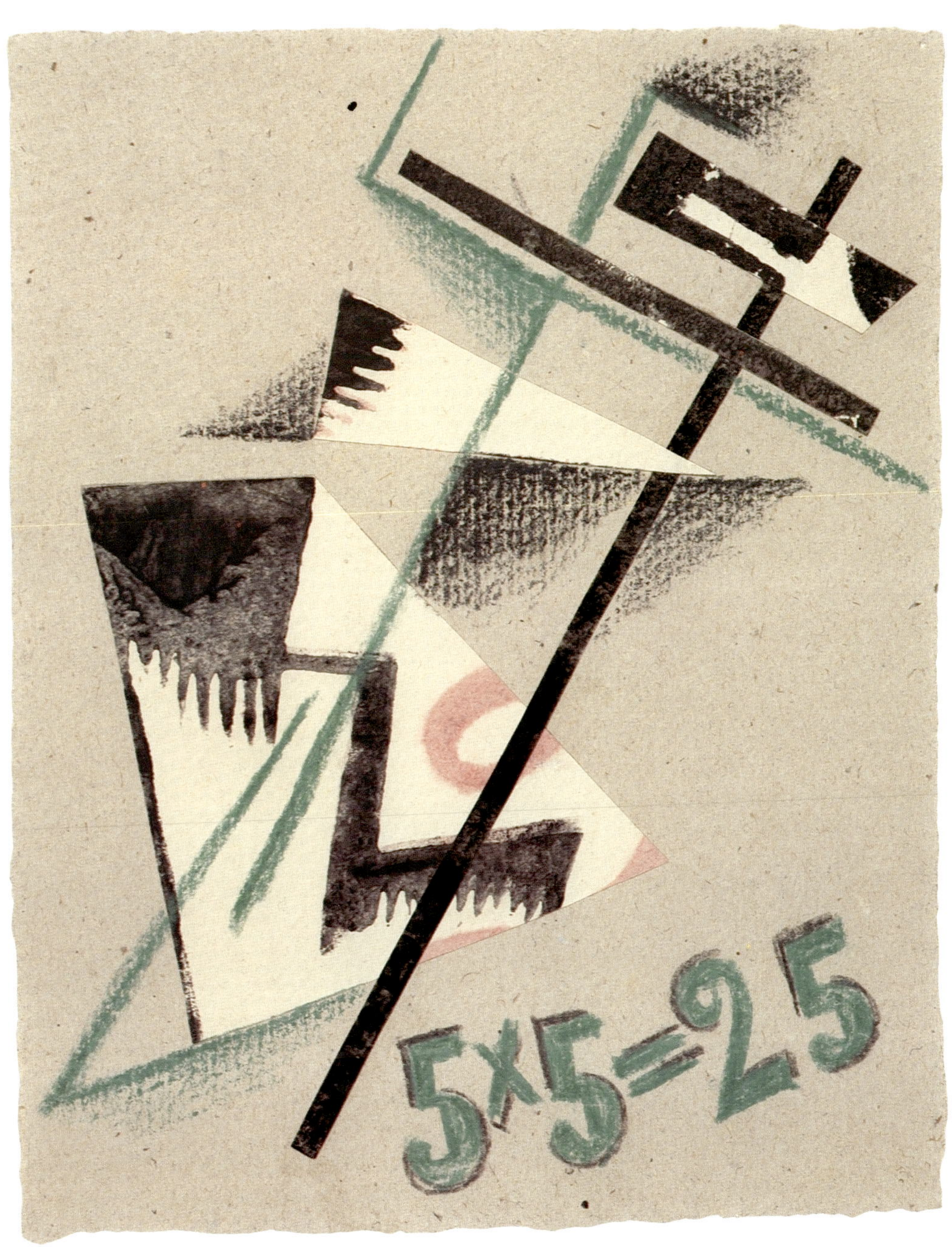

Design for Cover
of Exhibition Catalogue
5 × 5 = 25
1921
Collage, India ink, and
colored crayons on gray paper
8½ × 6¾″

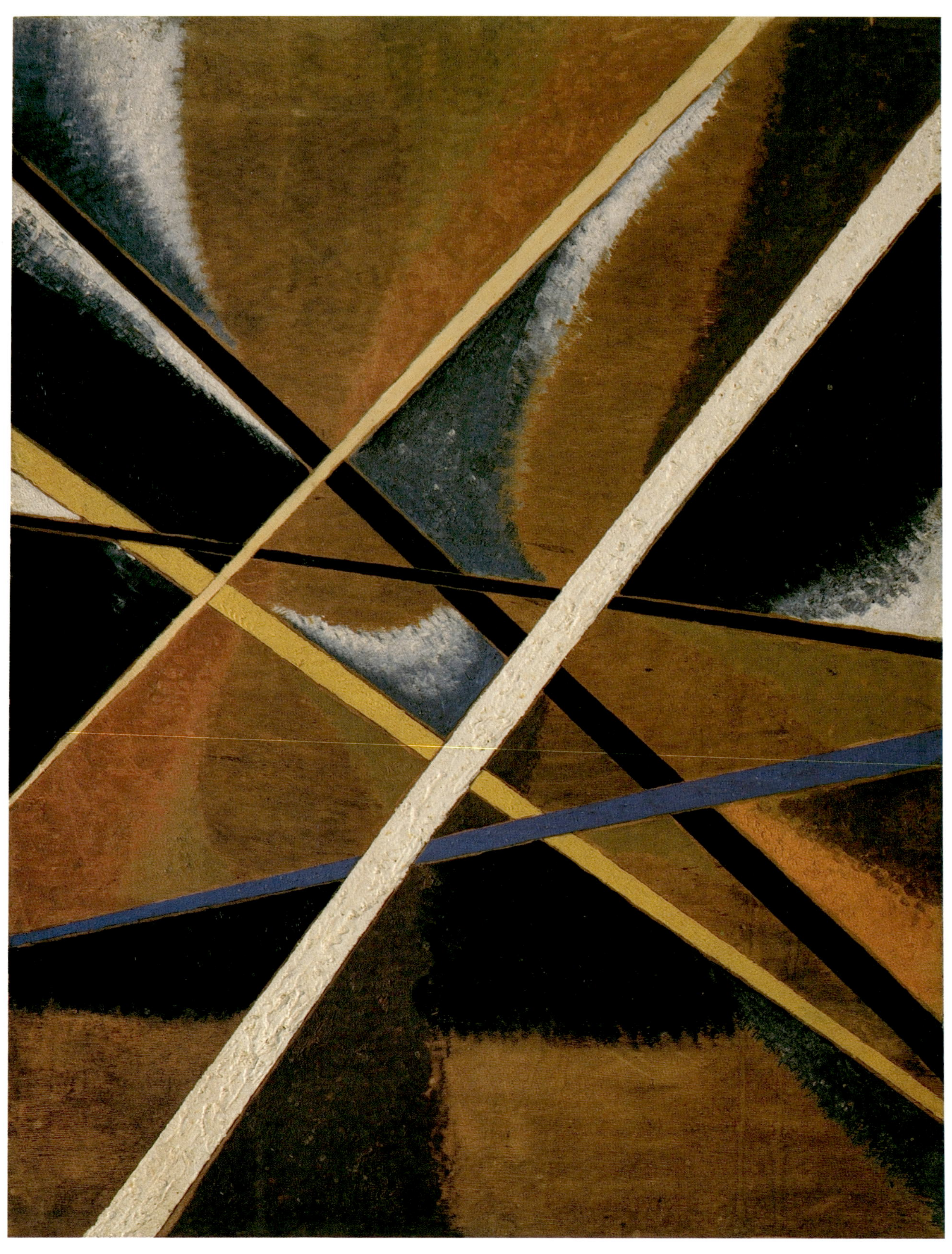

Space-Force Construction
1921
Oil on plywood
$32\frac{7}{8} \times 25\frac{3}{8}''$

Space-Force Construction
1921
Oil on plywood
$25\frac{1}{8} \times 23\frac{5}{8}$"

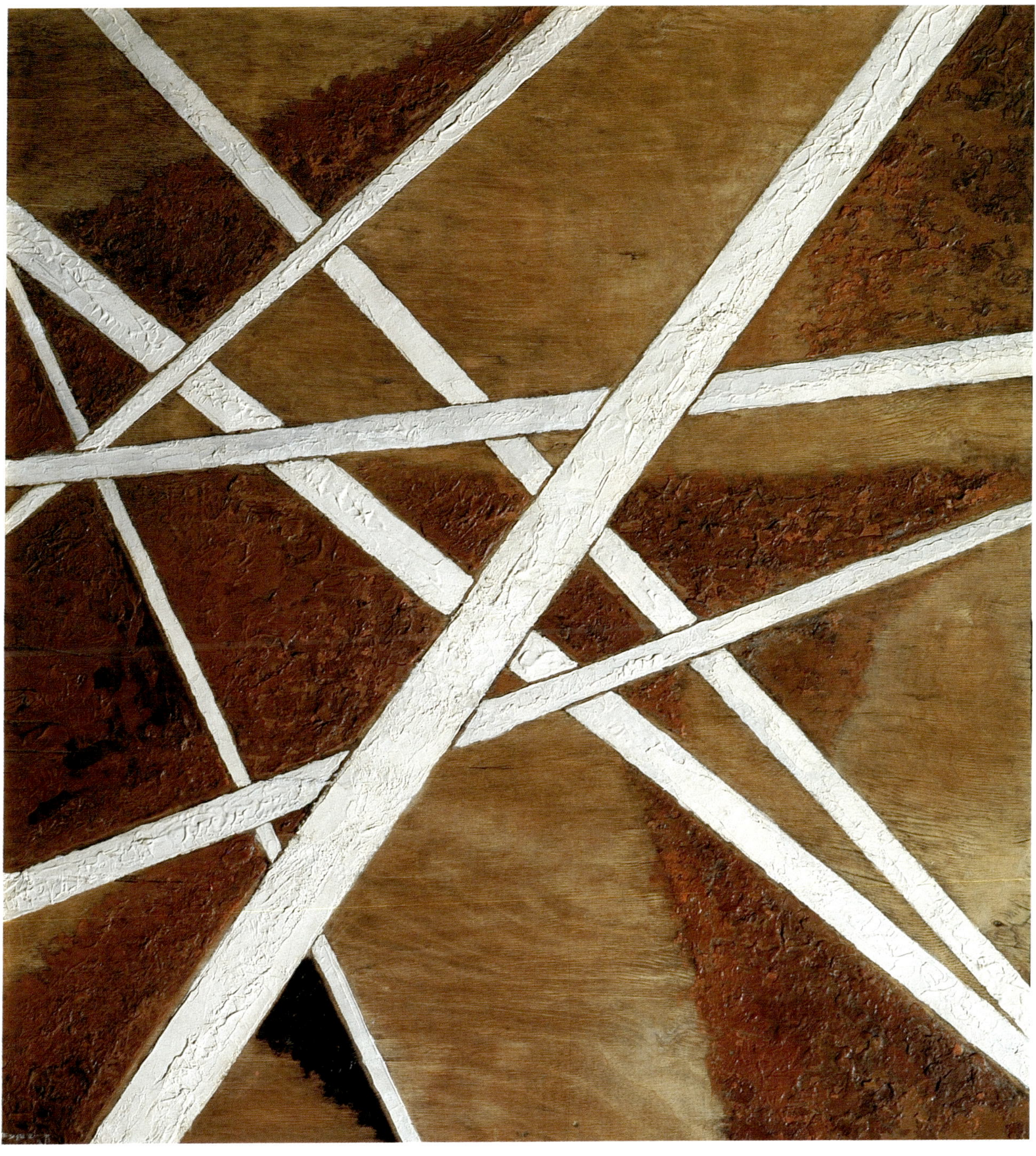

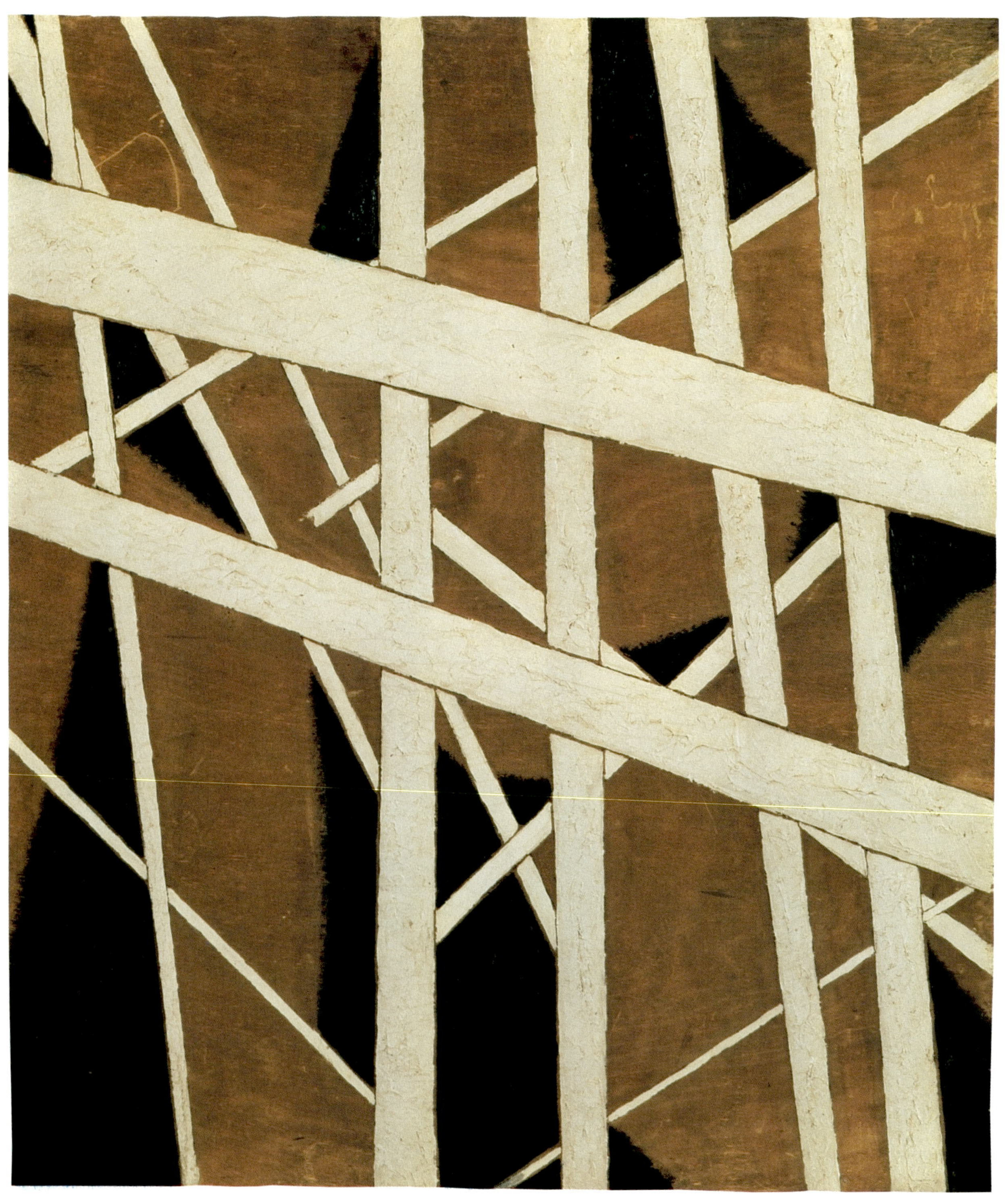

Space-Force Construction
1921
Oil with marble dust on plywood
27⅞ × 25⅛"

Space-Force Construction
1921
Oil and gouache on board
13¾ × 10¾″

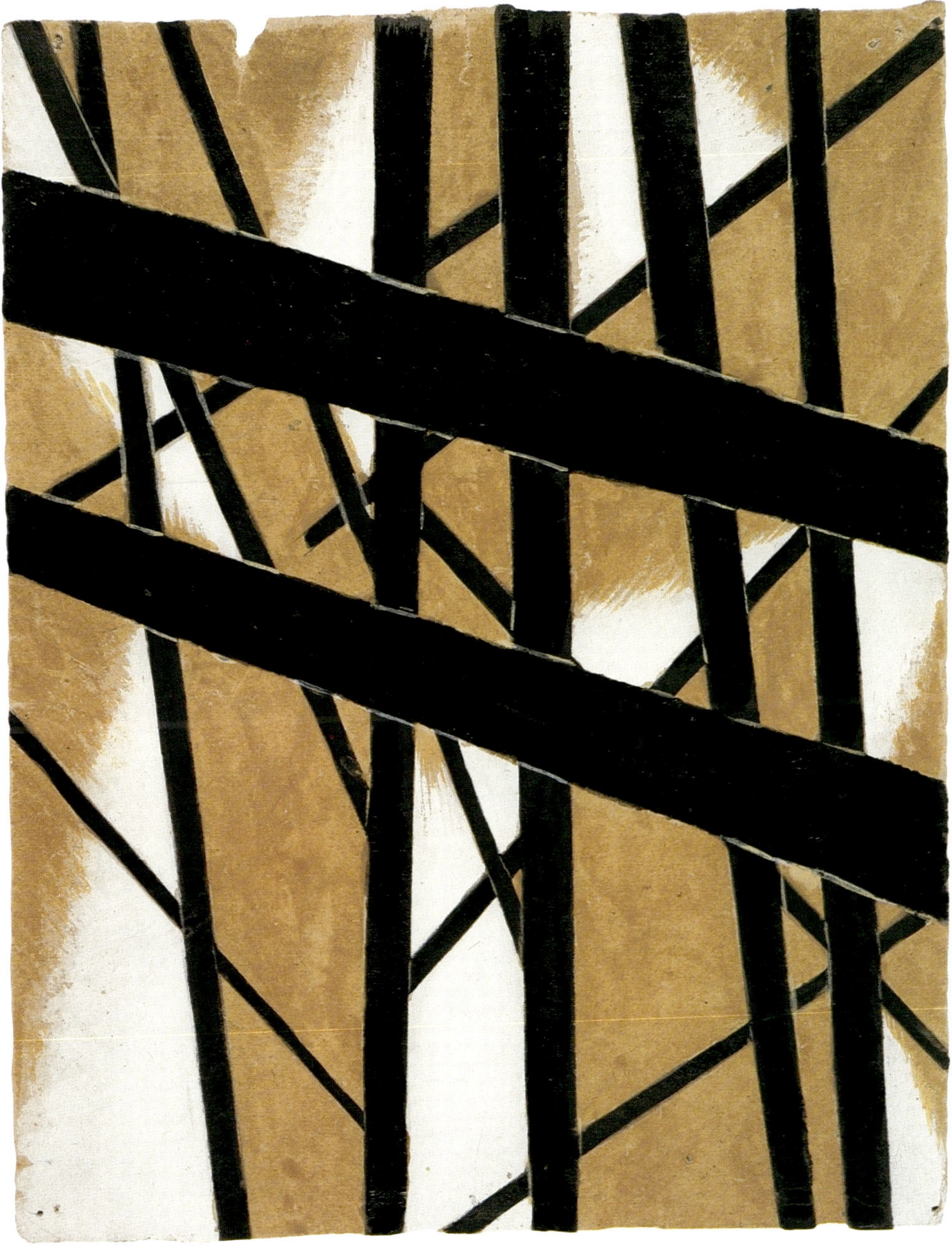

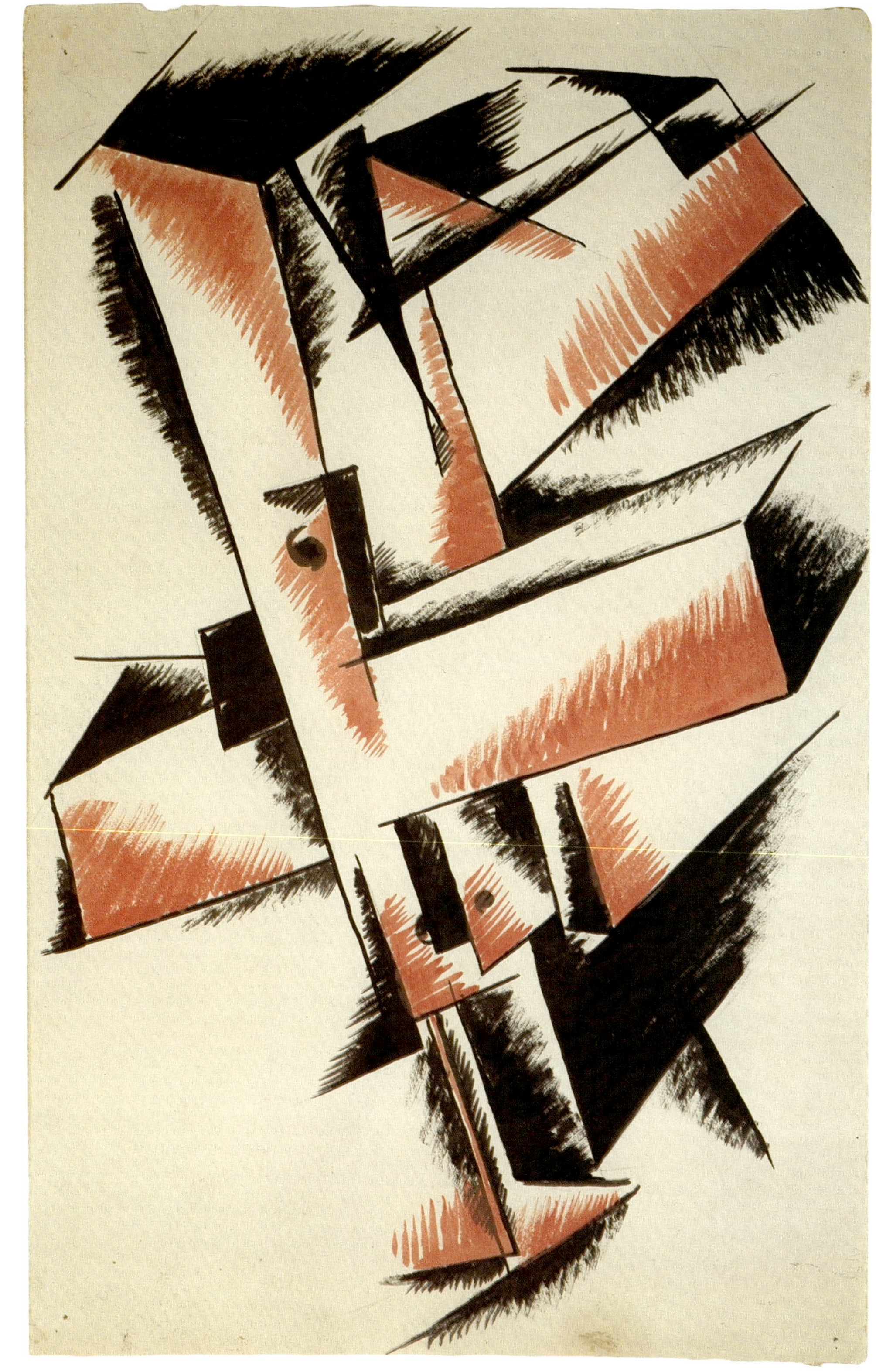

Space-Force Construction
1921
Ink on paper
17 × 10⅞″

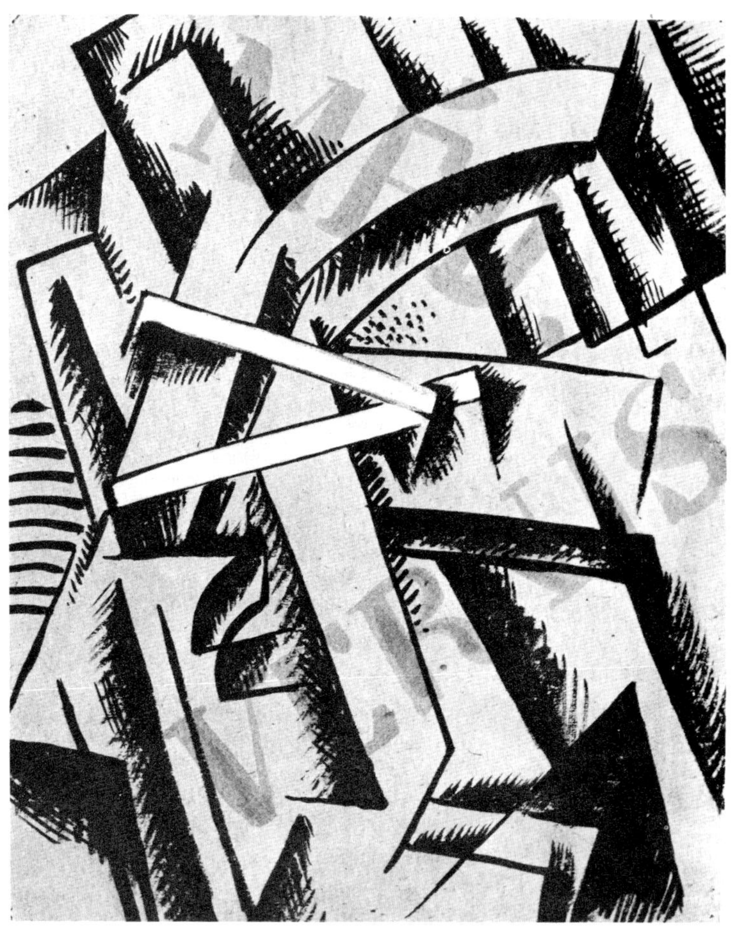

Med Vervis
c. 1921
Brush and India ink
and watercolor on paper
$13\frac{5}{8} \times 10\frac{7}{8}$"

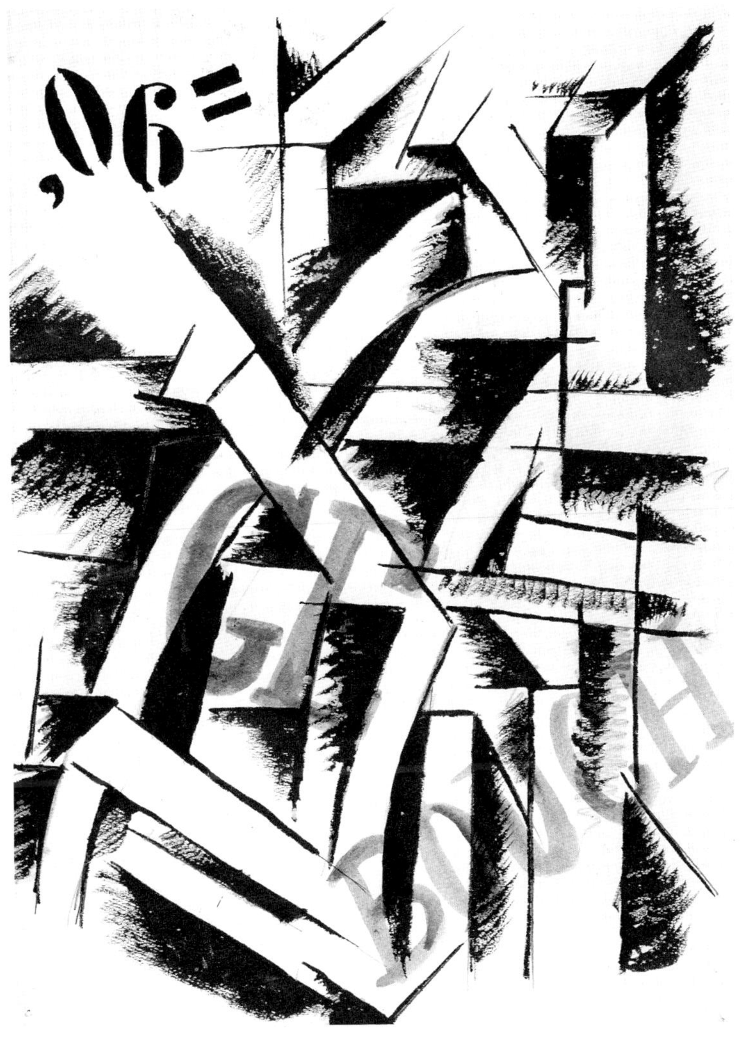

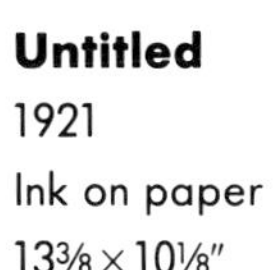

Untitled
1921
Ink on paper
$13\frac{3}{8} \times 10\frac{1}{8}$"

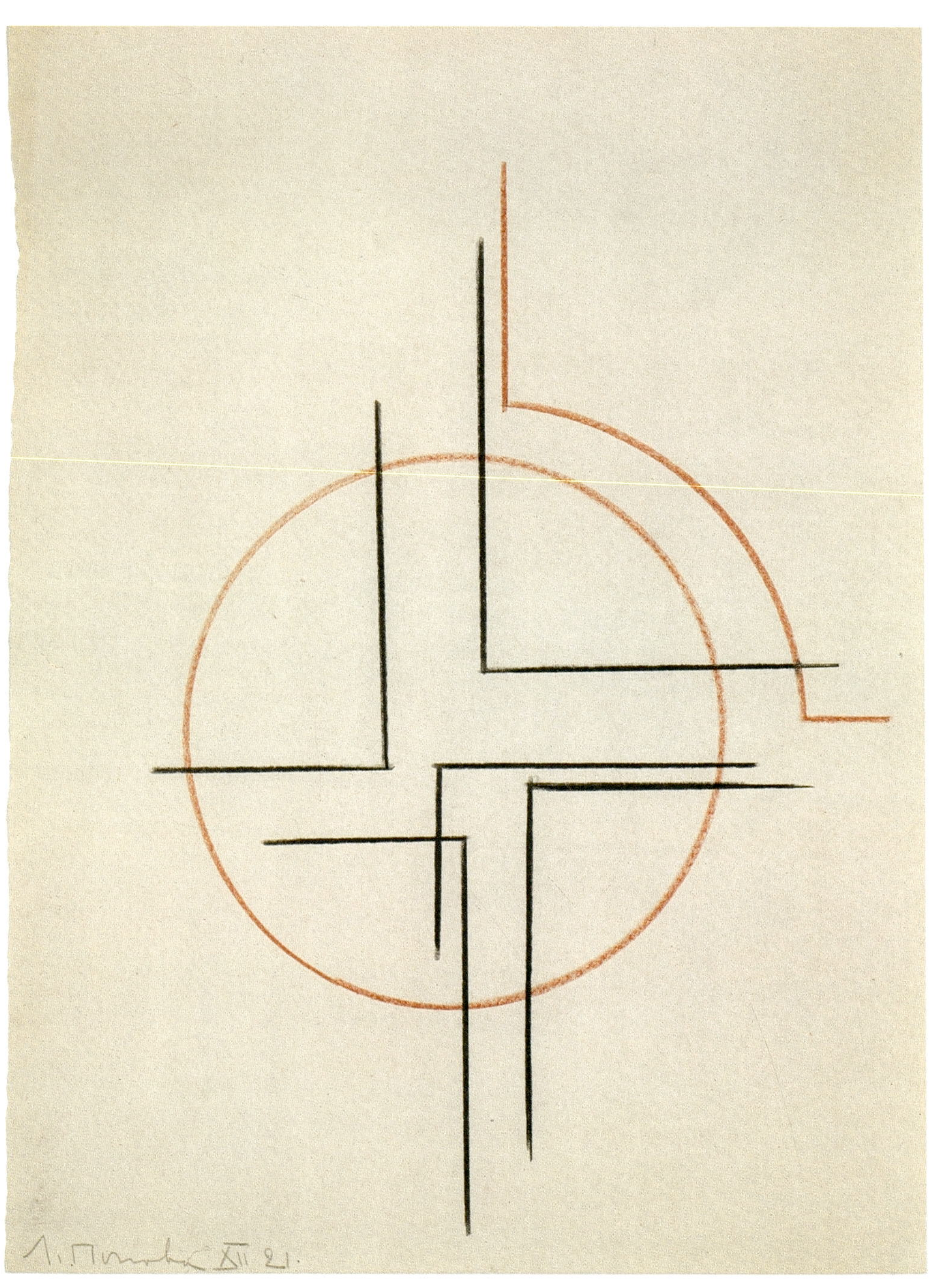

Space-Force Construction
1921
Red and black pencil on paper
10⅞ × 8⅛″

Space-Force Construction
1921–22
Watercolor on paper
18⅛ × 15¾"

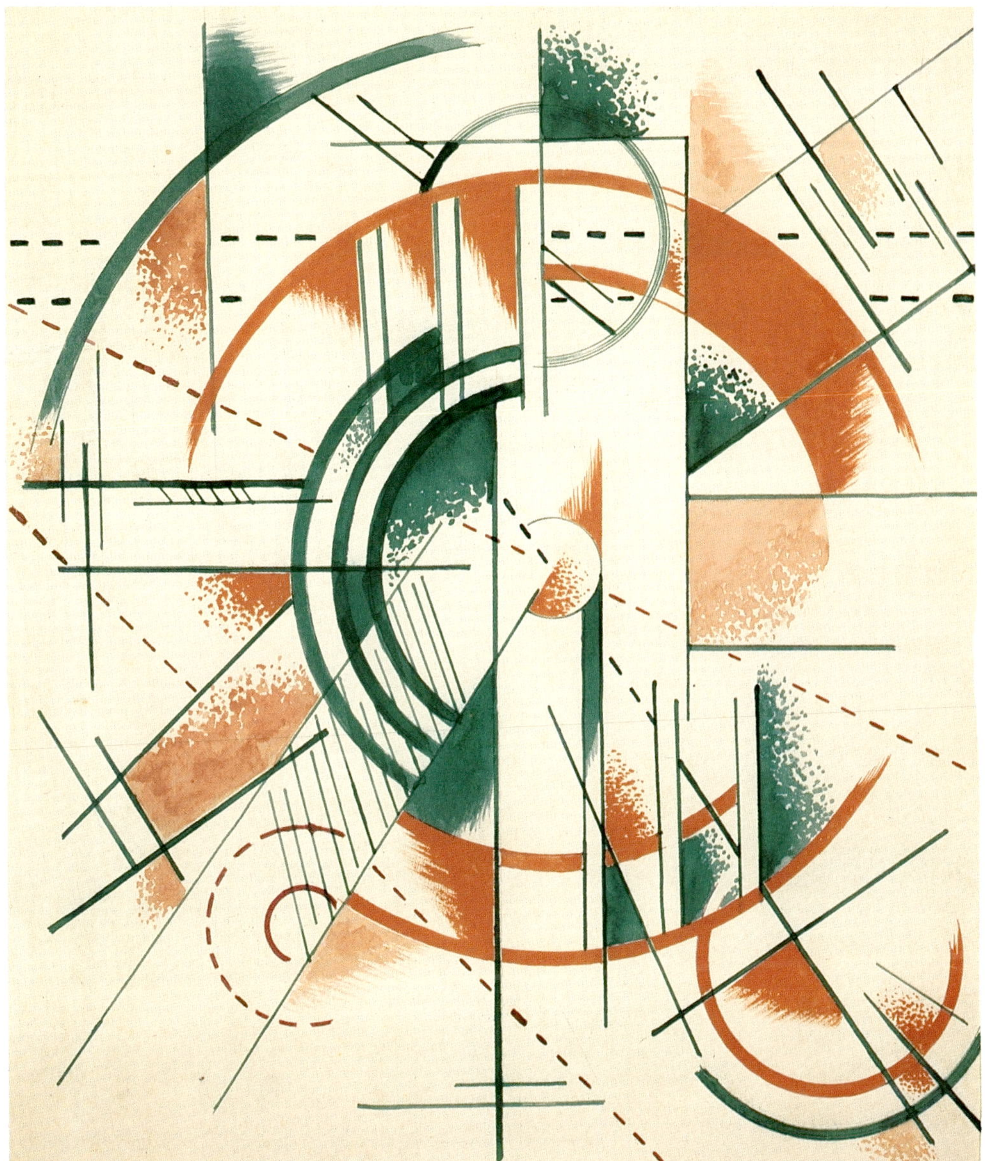

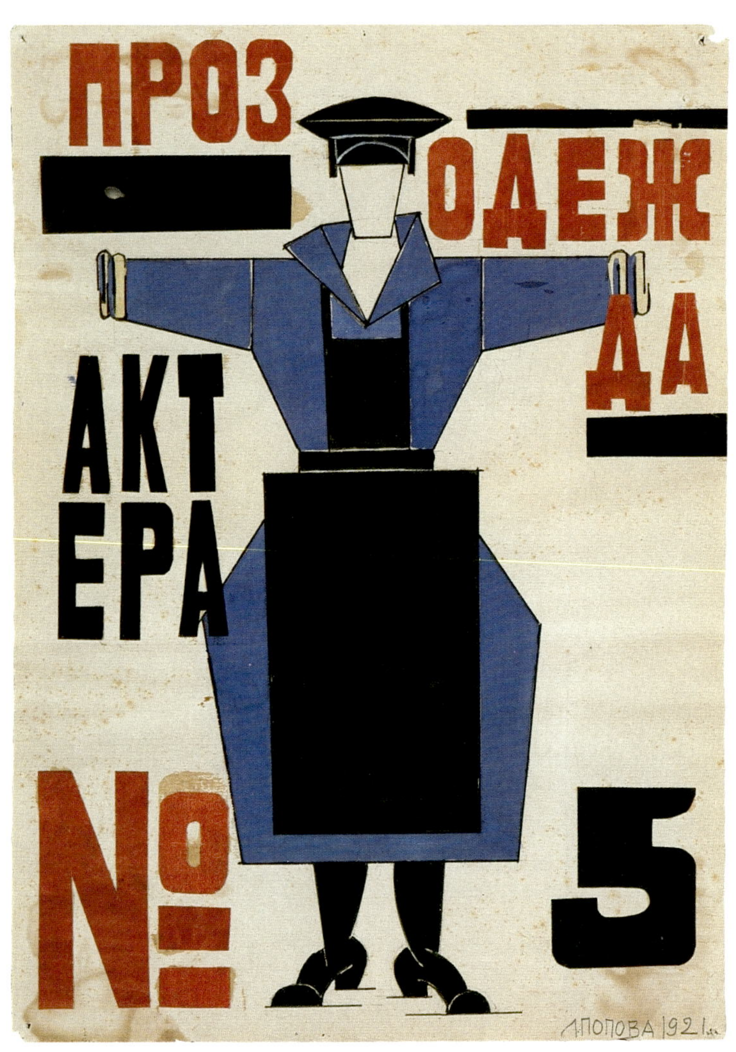

Working Clothes for Actor No. 5
1921
Gouache, India ink, and paper collage on paper
13½ × 9⅝″

Working Clothes for Actor No. 6
1921
Gouache, India ink, and paper collage on paper
12⅞ × 9⅜″

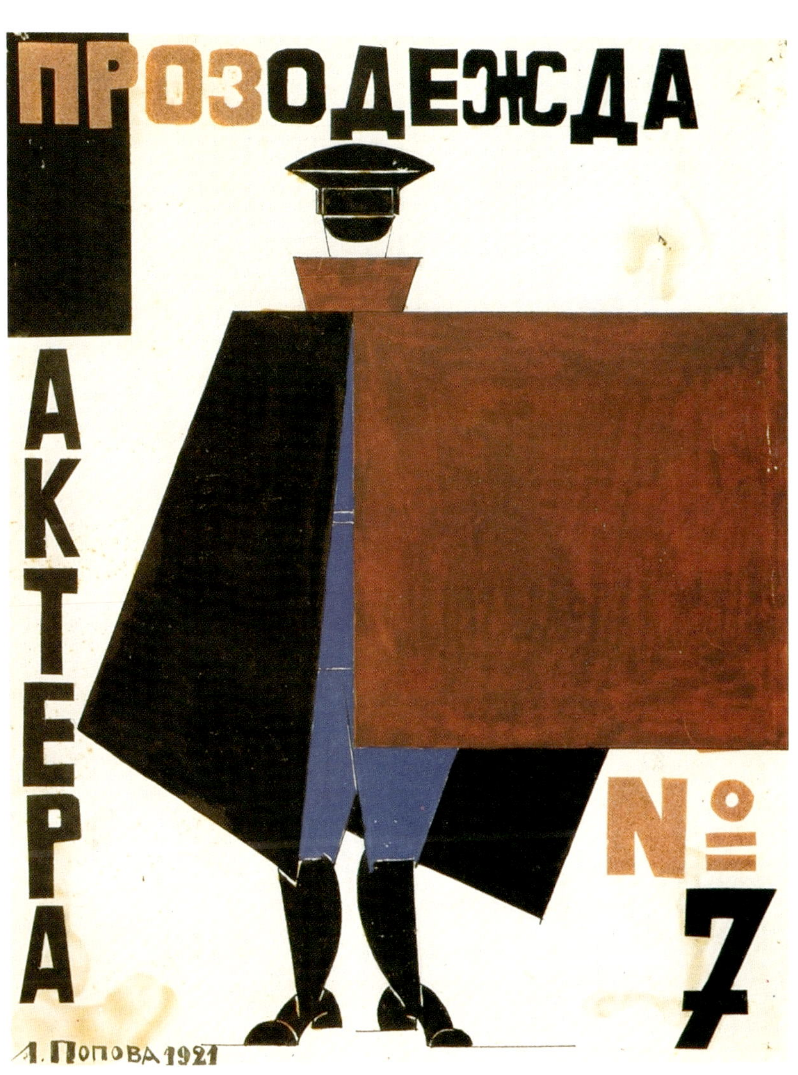

Working Clothes for Actor No. 7
1921
Gouache, India ink, varnish,
and paper collage on paper
glued to pasteboard
13⅜ × 9⅞″

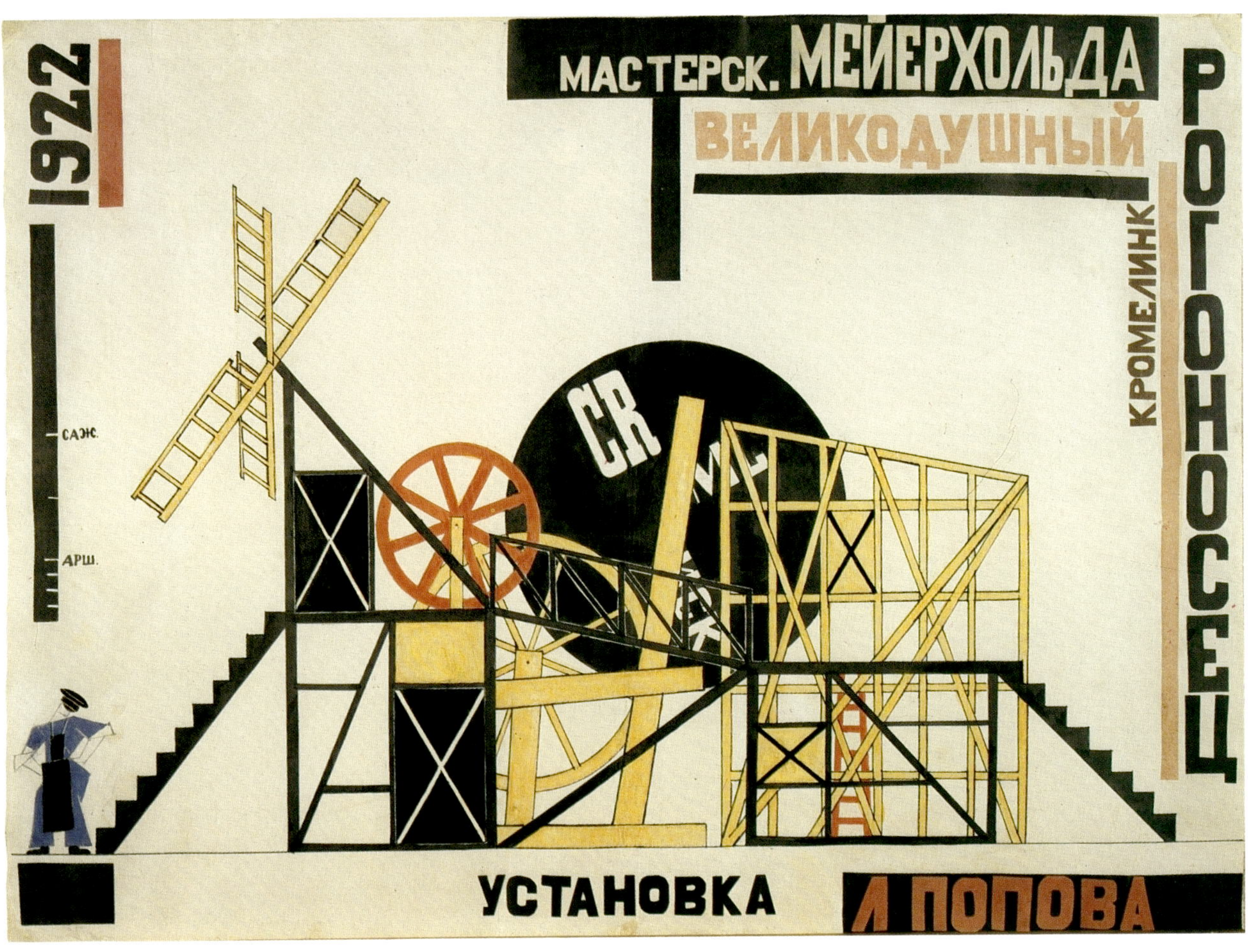

Design for Stage Set
of *The Magnanimous Cuckold*
1922
India ink, watercolor, paper collage,
and varnish on paper
19¾ × 27¼″

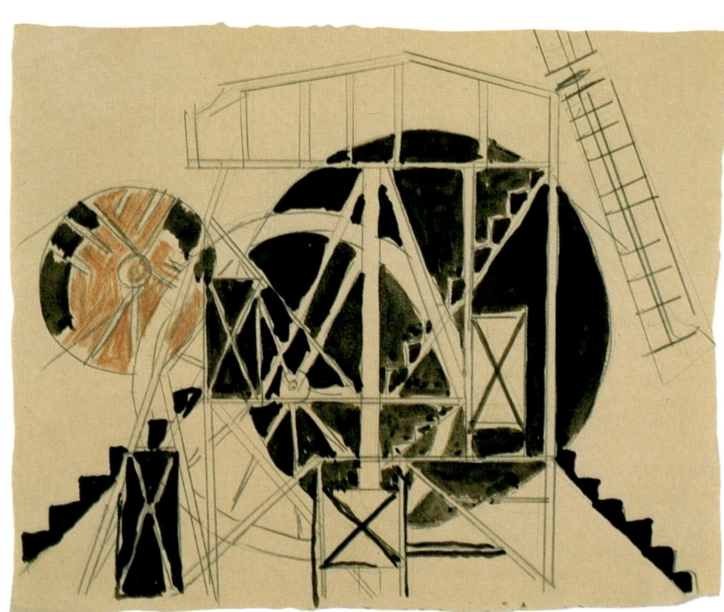

Design for Stage Set
of *The Magnanimous Cuckold*
1921–22
Watercolor and pencil on paper
8⅝ × 10¾″

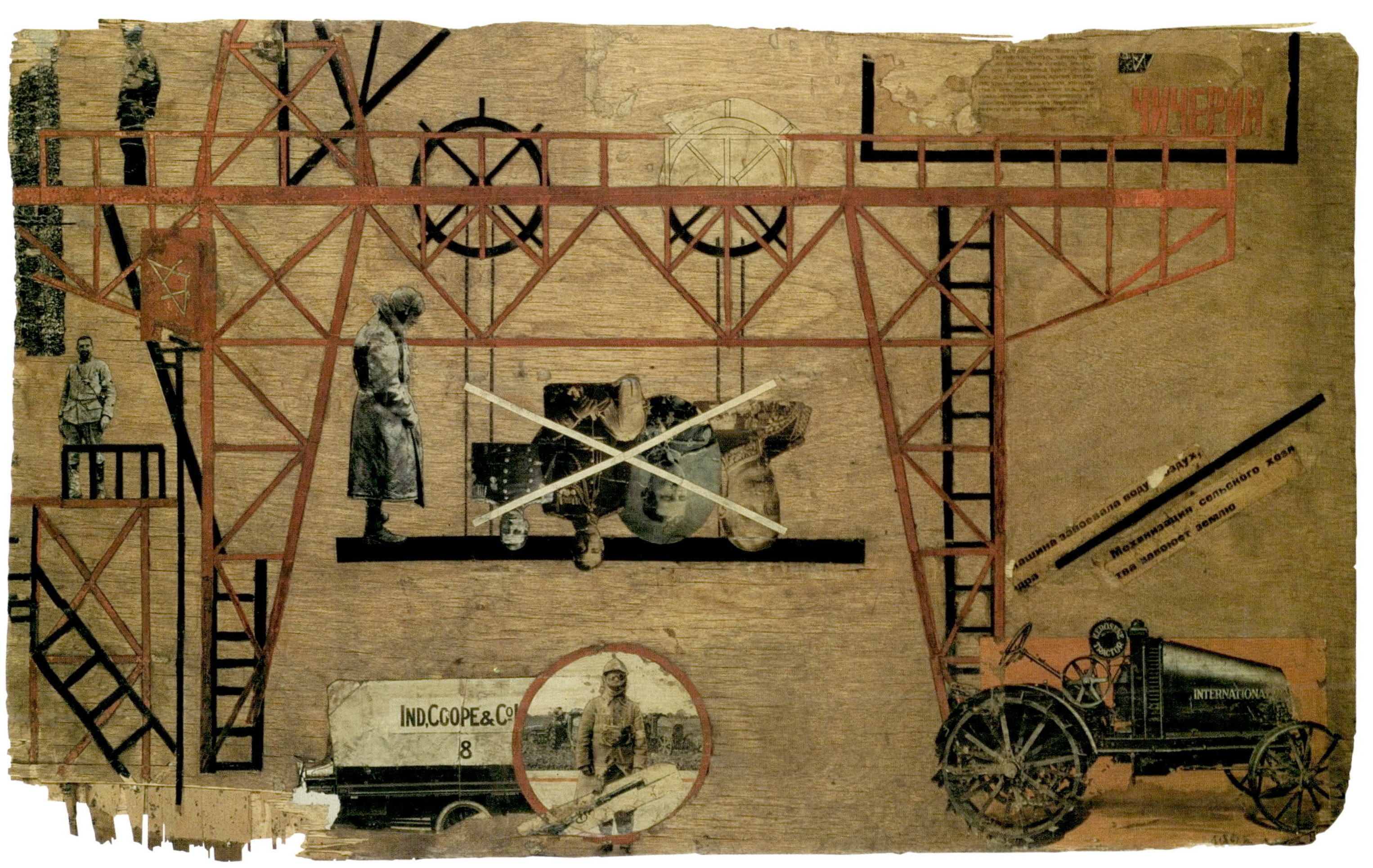

Design for Stage Set of
Zemla Dybom (Earth in Turmoil)
1923
Photomontage, gouache, newspaper, and photographic–paper collage on plywood
19⅜ × 32⅝″

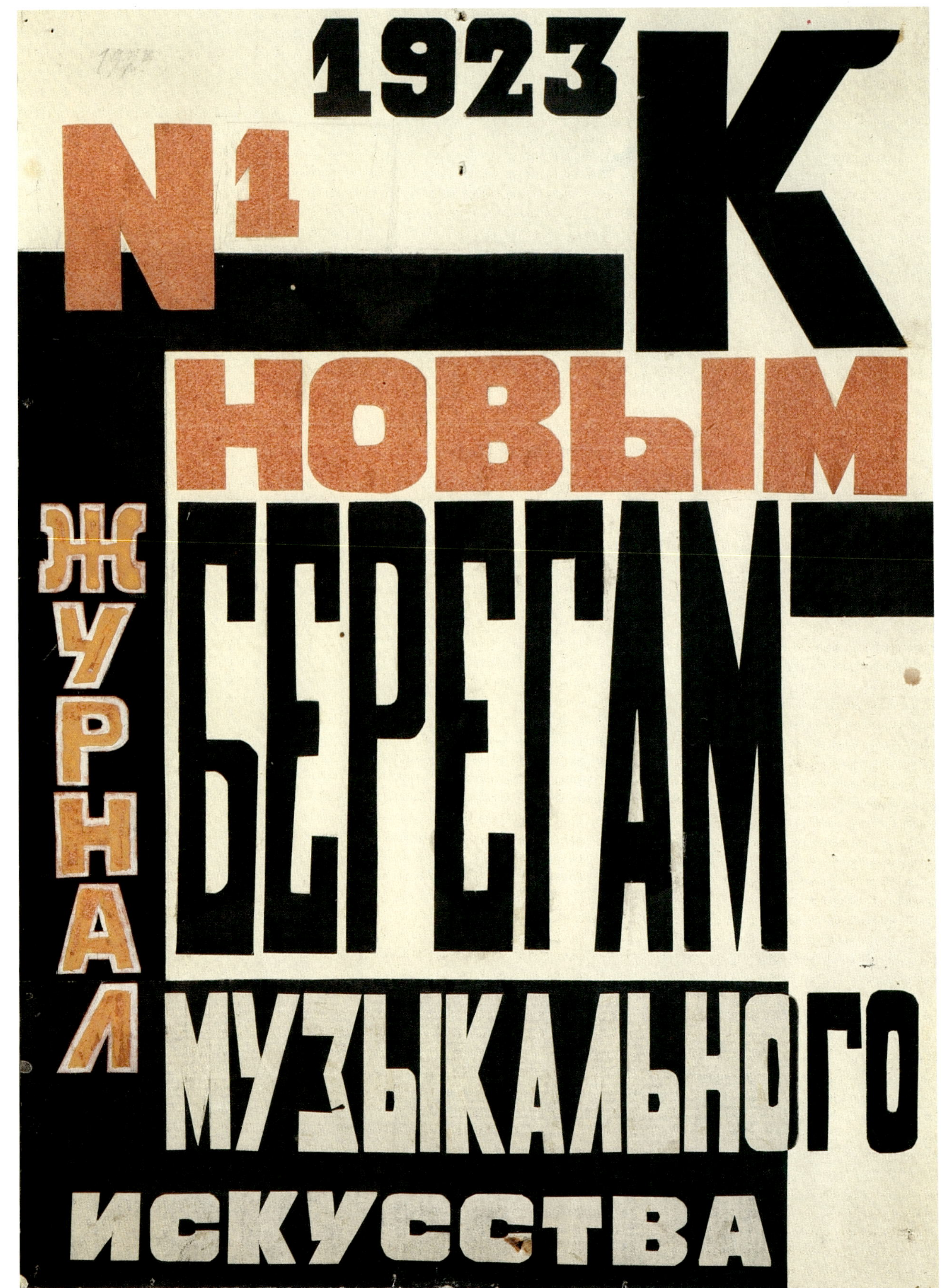

Design for Cover of Music Journal
K Novym Beregam
(*Toward New Shores*), No. 1
1923
Gouache and paper collage on paper
9⅞ × 7⅜″

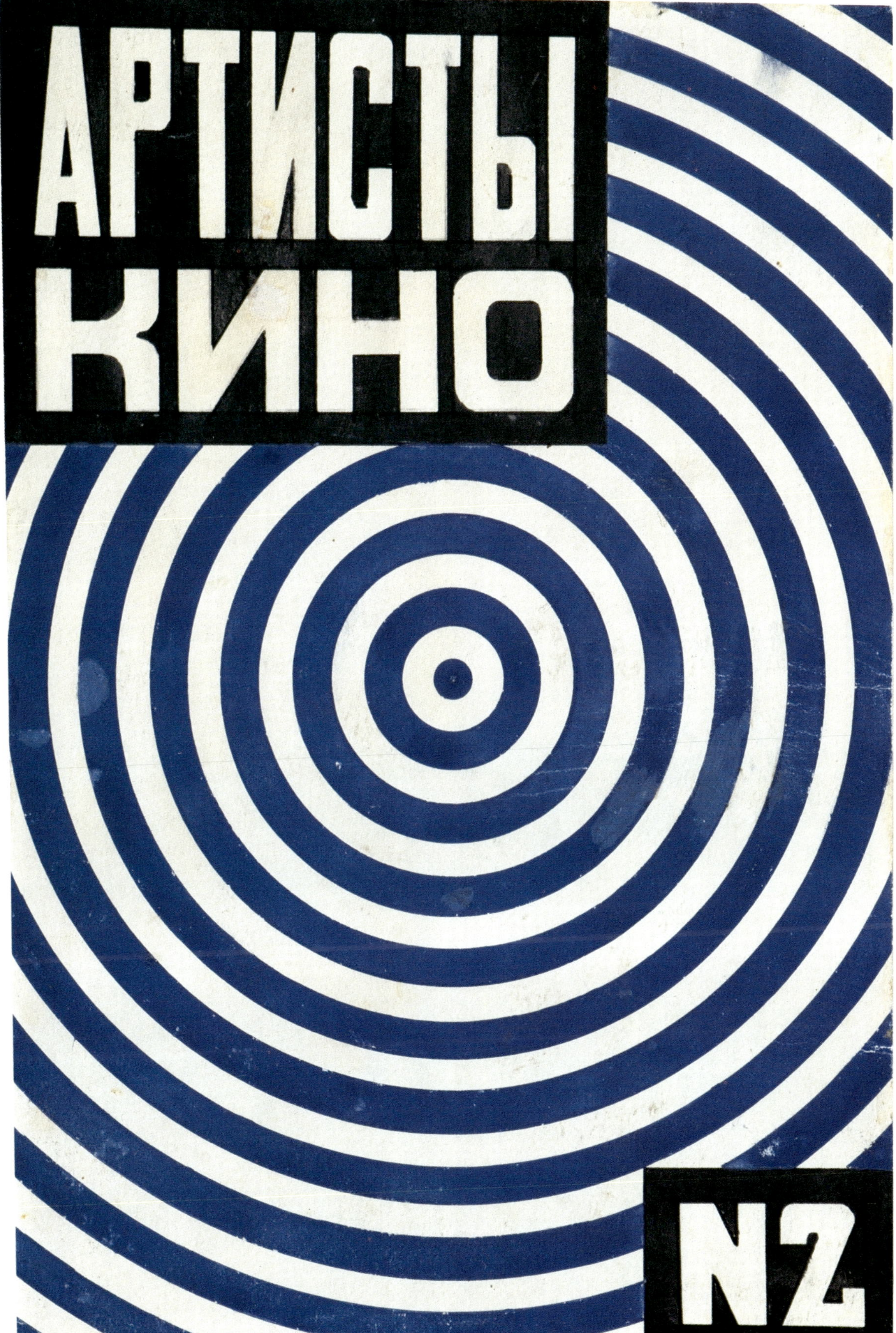

Design for Cover of Journal *Artisty Kino* (*Film Artists*), No. 2
c. 1922–24
Gouache on board
9¼ × 6¼″

Textile Design
c. 1923–24
Gouache and pencil on paper
11 × 13¾″

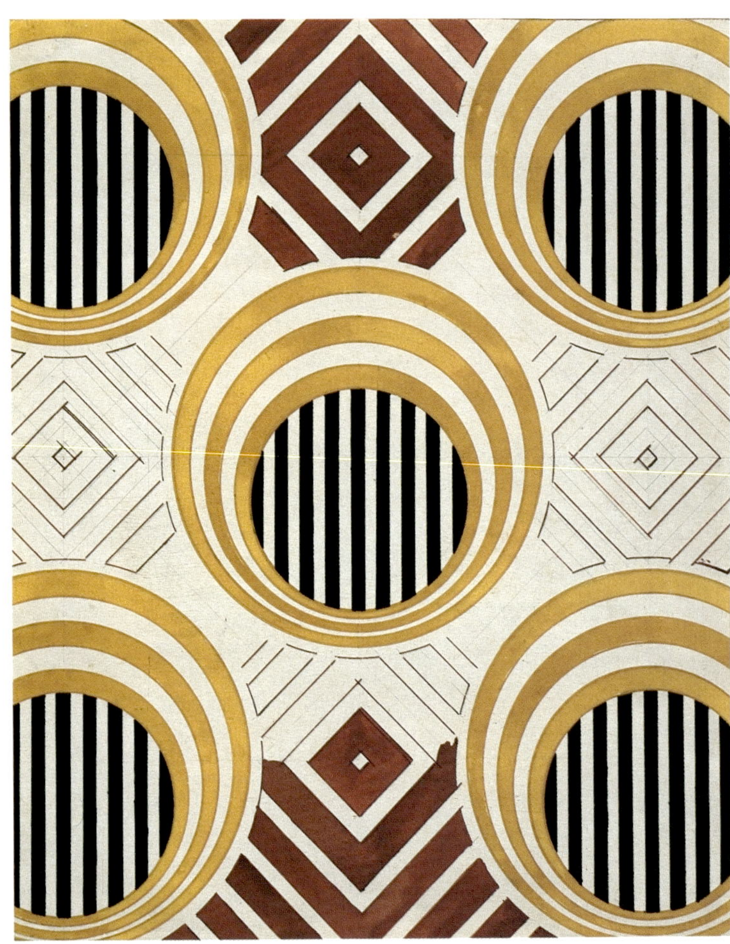

Embroidered Book Cover
c. 1923–24
Silk thread on grosgrain
17¾ × 12⅜″

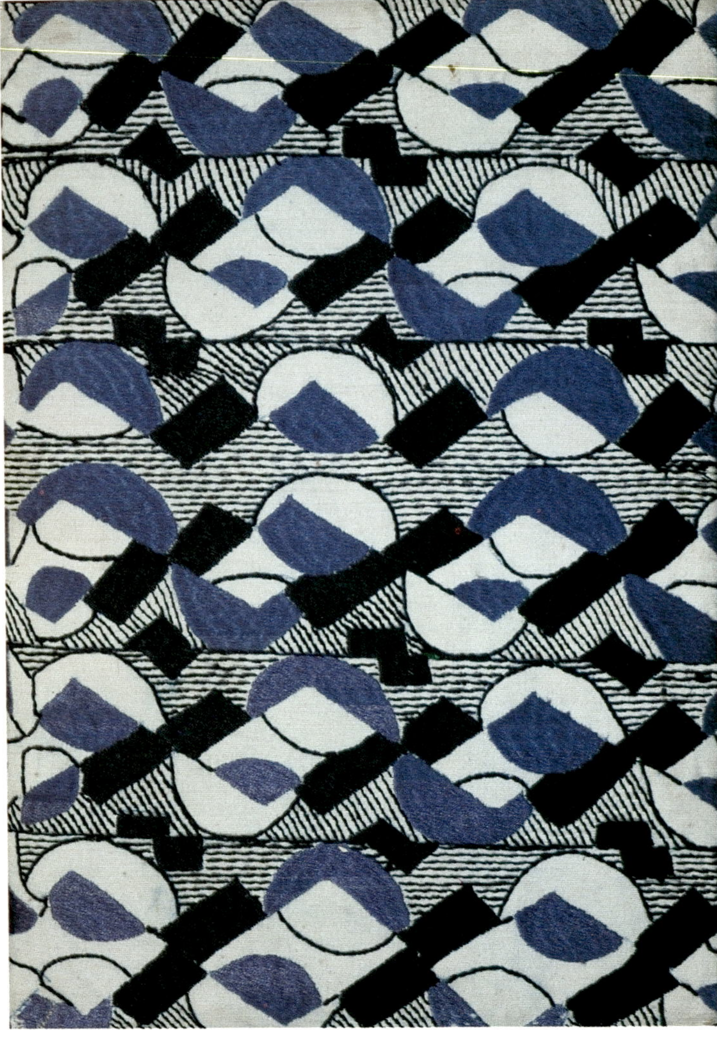

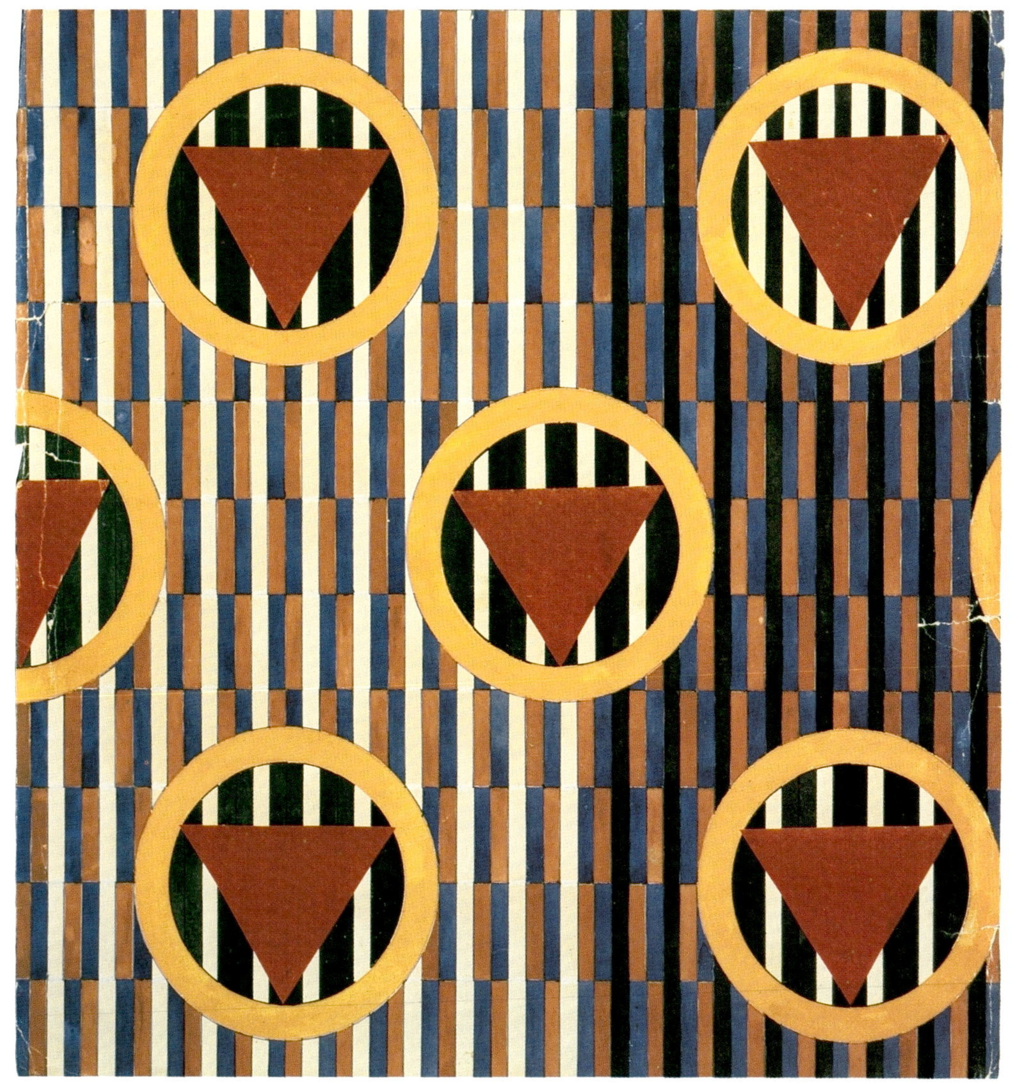

Textile Design with Red Triangle within a Circle
1923–24
Gouache and colored-paper collage on paper
15⅛ × 14⅝″

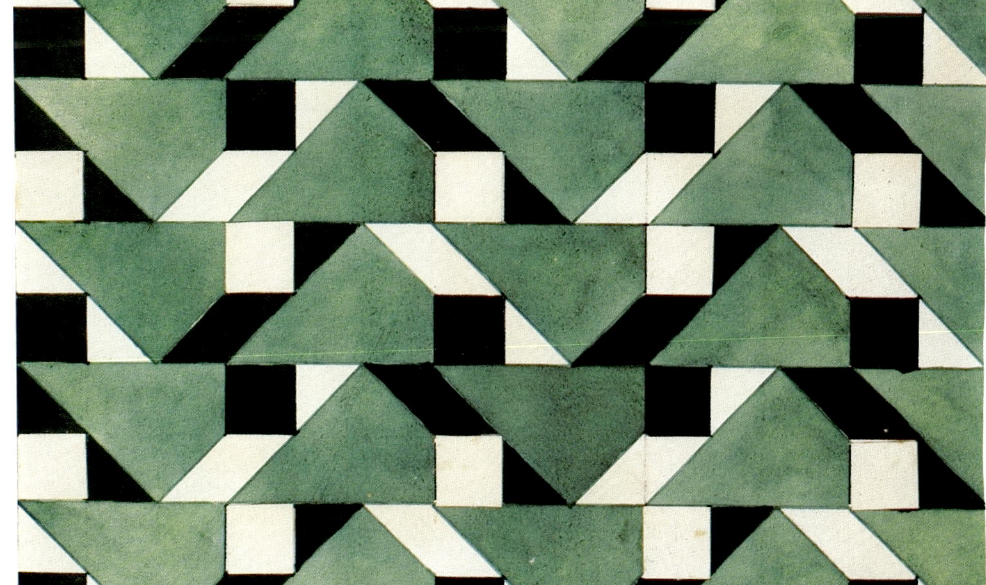

Textile Design with Truncated Triangles
1923–24
Colored and black India ink on paper
9¾ × 6¾″

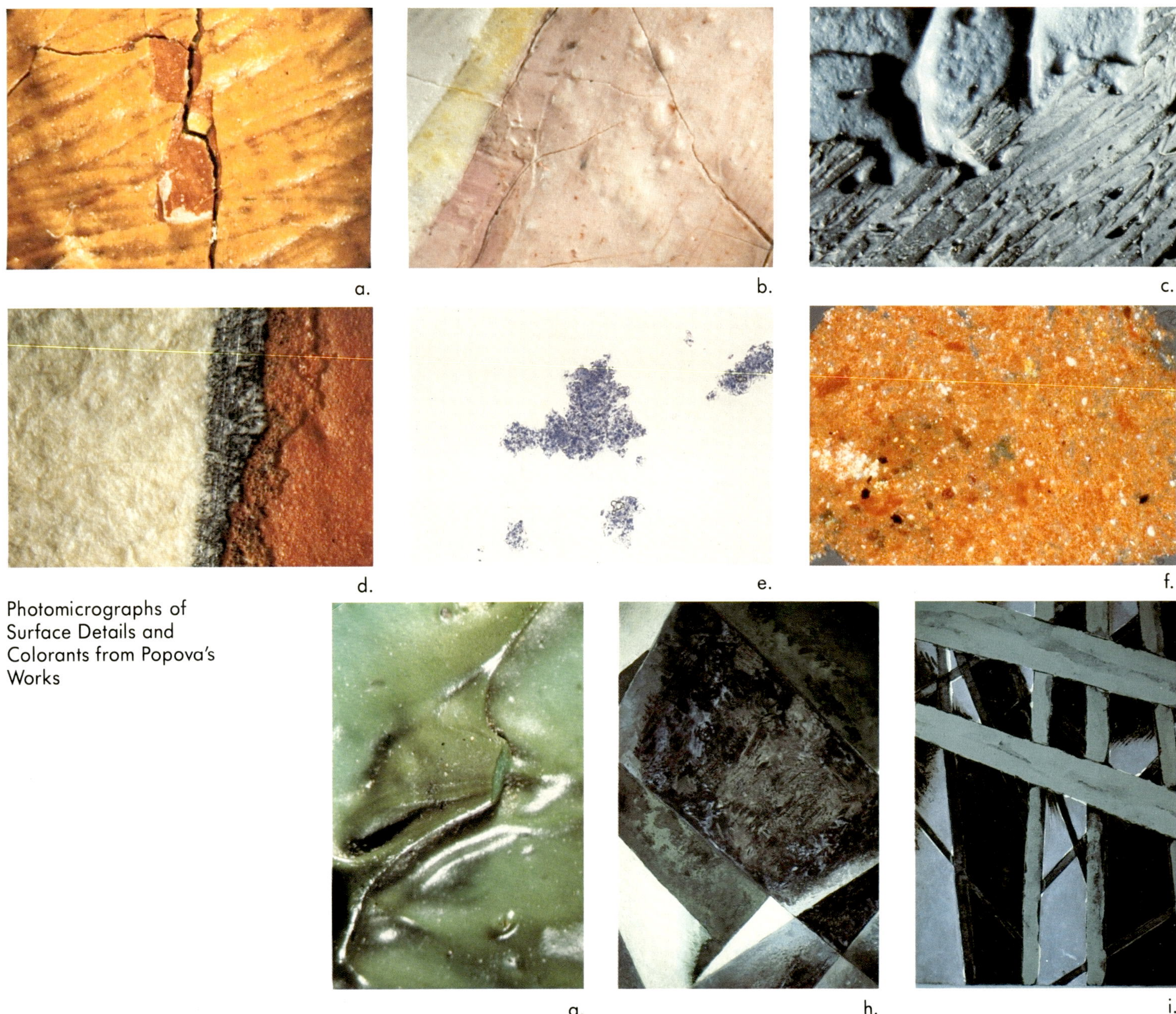
a. b. c. d. e. f. g. h. i.

Photomicrographs of Surface Details and Colorants from Popova's Works

popova's working methods and materials

Eugena Ordonez

The Russian avant-garde included many artists who created technically innovative and experimental work, often exploring a new range of materials and expanding the potential of such elements as color and texture in painting. This is particularly evident in the case of Liubov Popova, whose work shows a great interest in manipulating and further exploring the potential of her painting materials. A better understanding of her working methods and materials as well as those used by other artists has been limited, however, by the scarcity of technical research and the lack of primary documentation.

For the past five years the Conservation department at The Museum of Modern Art has attempted to help fill this void by conducting technical research on the methods and materials used by these artists—an effort greatly motivated by the Museum's extensive Russian holdings. The Popova retrospective at the Museum has provided the impetus to summarize findings from previous research on her works in the Museum and the opportunity to study some of her paintings from other collections. The specific goals directing this research were to identify the materials used by Popova, to determine how the works were constructed, and to relate this information to the artist's possible aesthetic intentions.

Three paintings and three works on paper were studied. The paintings are *Objects from the Dyer's Shop* (1914; The Museum of Modern Art; page 43), *Painterly Architectonic* (1917; The Museum of Modern Art; page 71), and *Painterly Architectonic* (1918; private collection; page 78). The works on paper are *Painterly Architectonic* (1918; Yale University Art Gallery; page 77), *Costume Design for "Romeo and Juliet"* (1920; The Museum of Modern Art), and *Space-Force Construction* (1921; private collection; page 88). The general construction of these works will be summarized here, starting with a description of the support and ending with the varnish layer.

Support and Ground

The supports for *Objects from the Dyer's Shop* and the Museum's *Painterly Architectonic* are coarsely woven fabrics. The reverse side of the former reveals that the canvas consists of two pieces of fabric hand sewn horizontally across the top about one-third of the way down. *Painterly Architectonic* (private collection) was done on a moderately thin, brown fiberboard. A study of the reverse side indicates that the fiberboard had a previous use (possibly not even art-related). The supports for the Yale *Painterly Architectonic* and for *Costume Design* are wove papers, the former an off-white color, textured to simulate laid paper, and the latter a light brown with an unusual pitted texture (evident in the unpainted areas). *Space-Force Construction* was done on a thick brown wove paper.

The ground layers for the three paintings are similiar; they are all thin and white, and appear to have been applied by the artist. They differ in the type of pigment(s) used as well as in the composition of the binders. None of the works on paper has a ground layer or an apparent surface coating.

Evidently Popova was using a variety of supports for her works, including some that may not have been produced intentionally as artists' materials. Also, she apparently did not take advantage of modern conveniences such as commercially stretched canvases with a ground layer already applied.[1] Instead she seems to have prepared the canvases herself, even making the ground material. These decisions were probably based not on financial considerations but on an artistic sensitivity to these materials or in some cases on their unavailability.[2]

Underdrawing and Paint Layers

In all six works one finds a black underdrawing as the first step in creating the image. These underdrawings are sparse linear frameworks with very little, if any,

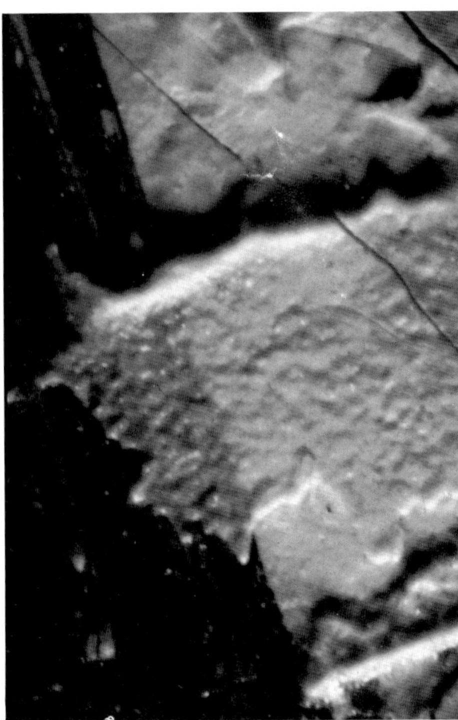

Fig. 1. A translucent white layer has been applied over an opaque white layer.

shading or development of form. Within these black borders the paint layers were carefully applied with strokes parallel or perpendicular to the edges of the form. In the paintings one can still see portions of the underdrawings between color areas. In the works on paper the underdrawing is more evident, and in *Costume Design* it plays an active role in the final image. In this work Popova first lightly sketched in the composition freehand, then redid the design with bold, forceful pencil marks, the indentations of which can easily be seen on the reverse side. The original sketch was then erased, although traces of it are still present. For example, slight changes made in the bottom portion of the helmet and in the orientation of the lance and hand are still visible.

The paint layering can be complex and reflects the numerous color changes and reworkings, as well as the diversity of Popova's brushwork and paint formulation. Color changes in *Objects from the Dyer's Shop* are seen, for example, in the crimson bell-shaped form in the upper right-hand corner, which was previously yellow; the yellow-to-green cone-shaped form toward the center, which was an olive green; and the orange-to-yellow form in the upper left corner, which evolved from numerous applications of varying shades of yellow and orange (page 112, fig. a). In *Painterly Architectonic* (private collection) the large black area in the center was originally a gradated blue, and in the Museum's *Painterly Architectonic,* the white background was originally yellow (page 112, fig. b). With the possible exception of the white background in the Museum's *Painterly Architectonic,* it should be noted that these color changes were not done as part of an indirect painting technique whereby a lower layer affects the appearance of an upper layer. The thickness and opacity of the final layer indicate a decisive change in the color relations. In the Museum's *Painterly Architectonic,* the final white layer is thin and is affected by the yellow underlayer; a distinct warming of the white occurs. But there is also another white paint layer *underneath* the yellow layer, which suggests that the artist may have painted a white background initially, changed it to yellow and then back to white, albeit a warmer white by intention or accident. The works on paper show only nominal changes in color: for example, in the Yale picture some of the black areas were originally blue. In the case of *Space-Force Construction* and *Costume Design,* this may be due partly to the simplified palette and imagery. It should be noted, however, that other versions of *Costume Design* exist in which the color of the armor has been changed. In one other work owned by the Museum, *Composition* (c. 1920), also on paper, several color changes were observed.

The brushwork varies considerably, although one can generalize that the paint is usually applied more boldly in the paintings, with more impasto and diversity, than in the works on paper. The brushwork in these paintings includes smooth passages with little hint of any brushstrokes; thick, wide, well-defined strokes; areas where the artist had manipulated the brush in order to create local areas of high impasto; and areas where a palette knife was used. Examples of all these types of brushwork can be found in *Objects from the Dyer's Shop* and to varying degrees in the other two paintings.

In all three paintings an indirect way of layering the paint was also observed. Within each form this consisted of applying an underlayer of low impasto, just enough so that fine crisp brushmarks appear. The layer might be composed of one or more colors across a form; this was perhaps indicative of a method used by Popova to lay out the general color relations. Over each color area another layer of paint was then applied, which differed in value, type of impasto, texture, and the extent to which it approached the edge of the form. The paint texture of the upper layer was changed by the generous addition of coarse particles of various extenders such as calcite (marble dust), plaster of paris, and gypsum. In oil paint (which was used on these works), the extenders also increased its translucency. Mock-ups of Popova's paint made in the conservation laboratory showed that the immediate effects of adding these extenders were a decrease in gloss of the paint and a more putty-like consistency conducive to creating various types of impasto. Examples of this type of indirect layering are the white areas in *Objects from the Dyer's Shop,* such as the gloves, where an almost frothy, translucent white layer has been applied over a smooth opaque white layer (fig. 1). In the Museum's *Painterly Architectonic,* the extenders can be seen with the naked eye in the large red-orange triangle and in a magnified detail (fig. 2; see also page 112, fig. b, for a similar layering of the pink). In *Painterly Architectonic* (private collection), a coarser-textured impastoed blue has been layered over a blue-gray lower layer (page 112, fig. c).

These blue areas also exemplify Popova's continuous evolution of the fine details of color relations. One can see from a small loss in the upper right-hand corner of the painting that the lower layer is light blue here, whereas in the blue areas in the lower left corner the lower layer is quite dark. These lower layers affect the final image because they are not entirely covered over. Another example of how Popova evolved a color would be the red bar in the upper right corner of the Museum's *Painterly Architectonic.* To the naked eye, the color appears to consist of one thick red layer. A cross-section taken from this area and viewed with ultraviolet light shows that the color consists of at least three layers of different red paints.

The brushwork in the works on paper tends to be less varied and more delicate; the strokes can be very fine and feathery, wash-like, or relatively thick. The artist built up the paint film in three ways: by adding extenders as mentioned above, by applying an unextended paint thickly, or by applying several layers of a basically thin paint. An example of layering can be seen in the white areas of the Yale *Painterly Architectonic.* As many as three layers of white were applied, each slightly glossier than the one preceding because each time less binder was absorbed by the paper support. In *Space-Force Construction,* unextended black paint was applied thickly in the large bars.

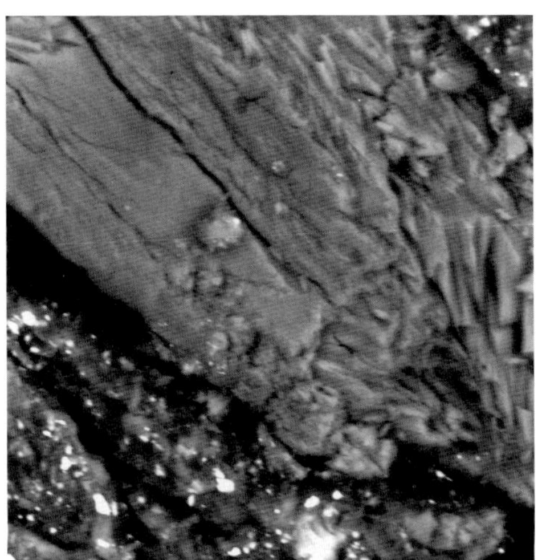

Fig. 2. The small, roundish, white specks in the lower left corner represent red pigment particles. The large gray area occupying most of the image is the extender (backscatter electron image).

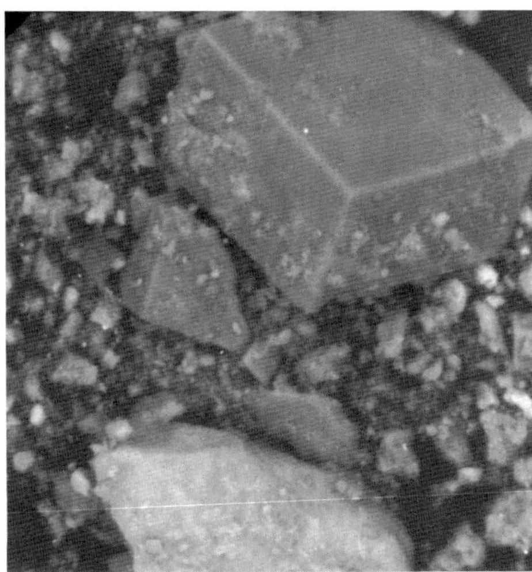

Fig. 3. The numerous small particles are typical-sized calcite particles. The large form in the upper right is also calcite (backscatter electron image).

Although the indirect layering technique mentioned above was not found in the works on paper, it was noted that Popova did texture the paint by the addition of extenders. For example, in *Space-Force Construction,* large particles of calcite were added (fig. 3), and in *Costume Design,* gypsum was added to thicken the red paint (page 112, fig. d).

Popova's technique as observed in these six works indicates that the linear framework of the image was more clearly fixed in her mind than were the color relations. This is noteworthy in that there seem to be no preparatory drawings for any of these works and there is very little compositional change between the underdrawing and the final image. The colors, on the other hand, were worked out and refined as the painting progressed. Popova used color to create harmony in the work as well as to change the energetics of the image. These changes in color relations demonstrate how the artist evolved the optimum color-form combinations and their harmonic interrelation,[3] as well as how she altered the energetics of the image by changing the "weight" of the color.[4] Her sensitivity to color is also evident in her methods of combining pigments. Popova appears to have had a preference for the color of certain pigments (for example, some blues are consistently made from one pigment; see page 112, fig. e), whereas other pigments are usually combined in complex mixtures (for example, up to eight different pigments are used in the orange-red colors; page 112, fig. f). Popova's characteristic manipulation of the paint materials (the pigments, extenders, and binders) and her awareness of each pigment's nuance of color suggest that she was also very involved with the raw materials from which the formal element of color was created.

The variety of brushwork, the direct and indirect layering techniques, and the introduction of extenders to change the consistency of paint all indicate that the paint's texture, that is, its three-dimensional quality, was another major consideration for Popova. Although texture is more pronounced in her later works, *Objects from the Dyer's Shop,* done in 1914, attests to the fact that Popova was concerned with texture all along.

Glazes and Varnishes

Only one area of glazing was observed, namely over portions of the green of *Painterly Architectonic* (private collection). Here a brown glaze was applied over the intense green upper layer (page 112, fig. g), thus toning it down and reinforcing the layering of the planes.

Of the three paintings studied, it appears that only *Painterly Architectonic* (private collection) may still have the original varnish. The varnish is localized within portions of the black form, and with ultraviolet light one can see that there are actually two varnishes—one fluorescing a warm brown color, the other a bright cool white (page 112, fig. h). These varnished areas serve to emphasize the layering of the blacks by contrasting the slightly mat lower layer with the glossy varnished upper layer. Both *Objects from the Dyer's Shop* and the Museum's *Painterly Architectonic* have modern synthetic varnishes on the surface, so one can no longer be sure of what the artist intended as a surface coating. With ultraviolet light one can still see a thin, discontinuous layer fluorescing a light green color over the black form in the Museum's *Painterly Architectonic.* This may represent the residue of an original localized varnish.

In *Space-Force Construction,* the artist applied a varnish over most of the black bars. With ultraviolet light one can see that a wide brush was used to apply this light green fluorescing varnish thickly (page 112, fig. i). It is important to point out that the varnish is integrated into the paint layers in this work. That is, the varnish was applied after just the black-and-white areas had been painted in. The yellow-brown areas were painted after varnishing and slightly overlap the varnish. The yellow-and-white linear highlights, which were used to clarify the relative positions of the bars, also overlap the varnish. The artist applied localized varnishes in *Composition* (c. 1920), in The Museum of Modern Art, and may have also applied them in the Yale *Painterly Architectonic.*

Localized varnishes enhance contrast in

the image by changing the surface texture and gloss as well as the color, which is typically darker where it has been varnished. Popova appears to have been aware of the visual impact and used localized varnishes, as did other Russian artists such as Lissitzky and Rodchenko. She may also have changed binding-medium formulations in order to produce a different gloss in certain areas.

In these works it is clear that Popova consistently acknowledged the paint itself as a vehicle for the expression of artistic content. Throughout her explorations of form, movement, color, abstraction, and construction she maintained an appreciation of the visual and dynamic impact that paint texture, gloss, and color could produce. The results are images filled with a unique painterly vocabulary through which Popova defined and energized her forms.

Methods and Conclusions

This essay is intended as a general introduction to Popova's materials and methods. The analytical methodologies or instrumentation are not described fully, data are not presented, and general conclusions are only outlined below.

Briefly, each sample was analyzed by at least two of the following methods: polarized light-transmitted microscopy, scanning electron microscopy with backscatter electron imaging and x-ray microanalysis, x-ray diffraction, fluorescent dyes/histochemical stains with reflected light microscopy, and Fourier transform-infrared spectroscopy (FT-IR). The works of art were studied with stereo-microscopy, infrared reflectography, and ultraviolet illumination. Fiber analysis of paper supports was done by W. Rantanen of Integrated Paper Services, Appleton, Wisconsin.

Objects from the Dyer's Shop:

Support: bast fiber canvas mounted on a four-member keyable wooden (original) stretcher

Ground: zinc white and kaolin in oil-and-glue emulsion

Pigments and Binder: lead white, zinc white, calcite, barite, bone black, vermilion, red lead, cadmium orange (CdS) and cadmium red (CdS[Se]), zinc yellow, chrome yellow, iron oxides, synthetic ultramarine, viridian, unidentified organic reds, green, yellow, and blue. Pigment bound in oil

Varnish: synthetic (not applied by artist)

Painterly Architectonic
(The Museum of Modern Art):

Support: bast fiber canvas (painting is wax-resin lined, original stretcher removed)

Ground: zinc white in oil (estimate)

Pigments and Binder: zinc white, plaster of Paris (calcium sulfate hemihydrate), blanc fixe, chrome yellow, zinc yellow, vermilion, red lead, organic red(s), synthetic ultramarine, bone black. Pigment bound in oil, except in red area in upper right, where FT-IR indicated that the binder was not quite an oil or a wax but some related material

Varnish: remnants of a natural varnish over black form

Painterly Architectonic (private collection):

Support: .3-cm-thick fiberboard made of grass fiber, probably a cereal straw or reed

Ground: lead white in oil

Pigments and Binder: zinc white, calcite, carbon black, Prussian blue, emerald green, iron oxides. Pigment bound in oil

Varnishes: not fully identified yet; one varnish appears to be oil-based

Painterly Architectonic (Yale):

Support: no fiber or media analysis was done on this work.

Pigments: lead white, bone black, cadmium yellow, zinc yellow, organic red, unidentified iron-based pigment, unidentified blue

Costume Design for "Romeo and Juliet":

Support: softwood and hardwood bleached sulfite, trace of grass fiber

Pigments and Binder: gypsum, vermilion, red lead, organic red, synthetic ultramarine, bone black, aluminum silicates. Pigment bound in gum

Space-Force Construction:

Support: softwood groundwood (75%), softwood unbleached sulfite (25%), traces of flax bast fibers and grass fibers

Pigments: lead white, calcite, bone black, iron oxides mixed with silicates

Varnish: natural resin, probably mastic

notes

I would like to thank Antoinette King, Director of Conservation at The Museum of Modern Art, for her constant encouragement and support; Dr. Alan Pooley of Yale University for generously sharing his expertise in scanning electron microscopy; Dr. Dusan Stulik of the Getty Conservation Institute for providing the opportunity to do media analysis; Michele Derrick, also of the Getty Conservation Institute, for her tremendous help in FT-IR media analysis; Dr. John Reffner and W. T. Wihlborg of Spectra-Tech, Stamford, Connecticut, for analyzing samples; Aneta Zabela of Los Angeles for her help in researching archival information; and Magdalena Dabrowski for sharing her thoughts on the artists of the Russian avant-garde and providing the opportunity to present this contribution to a fascinating area of research.

1. Commercially prepared supports had been available in standard sizes in France since the early nineteenth century. It is likely that these supports were available in other countries, including Russia.

2. There is very little primary information about the materials used by Popova. One reference notes that owing to the shortage of paint she had to use shoe polish and rouge for the set construction of *The Magnanimous Cuckold* (see Angelica Z. Rudenstine, ed., *The George Costakis Collection: Russian Avant-Garde Art* [New York: Harry N. Abrams, 1981]). There are also a few general references on the unavailability of basic art necessities such as pencils (see, e.g., Henry Petroski, *The Pencil* [New York: Alfred A. Knopf, 1990]). A thorough understanding of Popova's selection of materials would entail knowing the basis of her choices (aesthetic, social, practical, etc.).

3. See Dimitri Sarabianov, "Space in Painting and Design," in Krystyna Rubinger, ed., *From Painting to Design: Russian Constructivist Art of the Twenties* (Cologne: Galerie Gmurzynska, 1981).

4. See Magdalena Dabrowski, "The Plastic Revolution: New Concepts of Form, Content, Space, and Materials in the Russian Avant-Garde," in Stephanie Barron and Maurice Tuchman, eds., *The Avant-Garde in Russia, 1910–1930: New Perspectives* (Los Angeles: Los Angeles County Museum of Art, 1980).

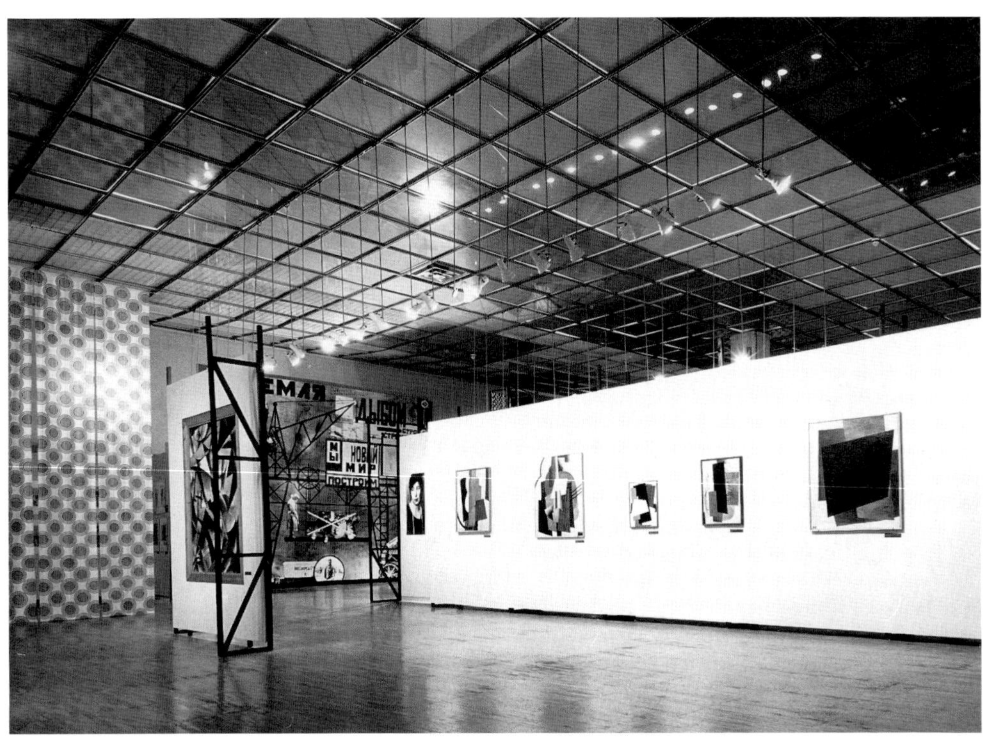

Installation view of the Liubov Popova Centennial Exhibition,
State Tretyakov Gallery, Moscow, 1989–90

popova at the tretyakov gallery

Irina Pronina

Note: We are fortunate to have been able to include in this volume a scholarly note on the first important Popova exhibition in the Soviet Union since the artist's posthumous exhibition of 1924–25. The exhibition was organized by and shown at the State Tretyakov Gallery in Moscow in celebration of the 100th anniversary of the birth of the artist. As few Western viewers have seen the centennial exhibition, the references to the works mentioned in this essay have been correlated with the catalogue numbers of the present Popova exhibition for ease of identification. Irina Pronina is Senior Research Curator in the Department of Soviet Painting of the Tretyakov Gallery.

—M.D.

In 1989, in honor of the 100th anniversary of the birth of Liubov Sergeevna Popova, the State Tretyakov Gallery in Moscow organized an exhibition that consisted of works from museums and private collections in the Soviet Union. On view were forty-eight paintings and approximately three hundred works on paper, including many related to Popova's production art and designs for the theater. Contributing to an understanding of Popova's artistic aspirations were her fabric designs as well as the only remaining examples of original fabrics made in the 1920s.

A separate section of the exhibition was devoted to manuscripts and archival materials dating from the 1920s, which represented Popova's pedagogical experience at the Vkhutemas and Gvytm and her activities at Inkhuk. Also exhibited were original photographs from the family albums of Popova's maternal relatives the Zoubovs, letters to Alexander Vesnin, and rare editions of typewritten catalogues for the "5 x 5 = 25" exhibition.

The repository of the largest public Popova collection in the world, consisting of twenty paintings and 176 works on paper, the Tretyakov Gallery wished to organize an exhibition—the first since the artist's posthumous exhibition in 1924–25—that would be deemed a worthy representation of Popova's brief but distinguished career. Her art has always been an integral part of any major survey of the Russian avant-garde, but she has consistently been represented by the same limited group of works. As a result, her creative evolution as an original master whose work developed under the influence of her older contemporaries Kazimir Malevich and Vladimir Tatlin, had never been clearly demonstrated.

In 1972, the two "discoverers" of Liubov Popova—George D. Costakis and Dimitri V. Sarabianov—acquainted Muscovites with their personal collections in an exhibition at the Palace of Culture of the Kurchatov Institute of Atomic Energy. Owing to the limited space and accessibility, however, the exhibition made no attempt at scholarly documentation. This task, the first comprehensive study of the artist's legacy, was therefore undertaken in conjunction with the Tretyakov's centennial exhibition. Just as the exhibition catalogue was being prepared, a large monograph on Popova's work was completed (although not yet published) by Natalia A. Adaskina and Dimitri V. Sarabianov. The authors kindly agreed to participate in our project, allowing us to augment our documentation with their invaluable suggestions and advice.

As Popova's works arrived at the Gallery from museums and private collections, they were catalogued by the Tretyakov staff using two primary sources: a list from 1921 written by the artist and a more comprehensive posthumous document of 1924. We were able to find the numbers corresponding to the 1921 list on the backs of several works.[1] We had learned of the existence of the 1921 list from "A Listing of the Works of L. S. Popova," the second document, which was compiled in the artist's studio after her death in 1924 by a committee of the Institute of Artistic Culture, whose members included her close friends Vesnin, Ivan Aksyonov, V. Shamshin, and her brother Pavel Popov.[2] The committee also numbered the works themselves while compiling the 1924 list, and it is still possible to locate some of these numbers on the works, not only on the reverse side but occasionally on the front.[3]

The dates of the works found in the studio that appear on the 1921 list were recorded in a separate column of the "Listing." At the end of that document the following explanation appears: "All listed works have been located in the studio of Liubov Sergeevna Popova or in her apartment, Novinski Boulevard, d. 117, apt. 4. In the absence of a notation on a particular work, the date was reconstructed according to the list compiled by Liubov Sergeevna in 1921. In the case of works created prior to 1913 [which do not appear on the artist's list] the dating is done from memory or on the basis of explanations received from Liubov Sergeevna during her lifetime. 22 July 1924. Moscow."[4]

In any discussion of the Tretyakov Gallery's Popova exhibition, one must emphasize the role of the Costakis collection in perpetuating the artist's legacy. It was Costakis who located and carefully restored these masterpieces of Russian art. Furthermore, it was his gift to the Tretyakov Gallery that provided the foundation not only of its Popova collection but of the centennial exhibition as well. Prior to this gift, the Tretyakov's Popova collection consisted of a small number of her works acquired in the late 1920s from the State Museum holdings. These included *Italian Still Life* (1914; cat. 24), *Violin* (1915; cat. 29), *Painterly Architectonic* (1917), *Painterly Architectonic* (1918; cat. 74), *Construction* (1920; cat. 81), *Space-Force Construction* (1921; cat. 88), as well as three works on paper.

Then in 1977 the Tretyakov Gallery received the generous gift of major Russian avant-garde works that had been amassed by George Costakis. With this gift the representation of Liubov Popova in the Tretyakov Gallery attained a rare depth and distinction. Included in the gift were key works by Popova; the centerpiece of the collection is the large double-sided work, *Painterly Architectonic* (1916–17; cat. 56a) and *Painterly Construction* (1920; cat. 56b). Early works displaying the artist's vision of nature characteristic of that period were also acquired: *Portrait of a Girl by a Stove* (1909) and *Male Model* (c. 1910; cat. 9). Completing the representation of Popova's Cubist period are *Study of a Model* (c. 1913; cat. 10) and *Composition with Figures* (1913; cat. 11). The sole example of Popova's "plastic painting," *The Jug on the Table* (1915; cat. 41), reflects her attraction to the counter-reliefs of Vladimir Tatlin, which are now also in the Tretyakov's collection.

The pride of any collection is the work that hints at the formation of an artist's individual style. One of the first of Popova's works to be dubbed an "architectonic" is *Painterly Architectonic with Yellow Board* (1916; cat. 49). *Painterly Architectonic: Black, Red, Gray* (1916; cat. 53) differs from other "architectonic" works in its consistent adaptation of Malevich's principles of Suprematism. The composition for this Costakis gift can be traced back to her drawing of the logo for Malevich's Supremus group (1916–17; cat. 57), shown in the exhibition along with other works from various sources. Her paintings of 1918 bear witness to her changing views on the interaction of form and space. By 1921 her series of Space-Force Constructions represents easel painting at its highest. The cycle of five works on plywood from the Tretyakov collection was augmented at the centennial exhibition by the previously unexhibited *Space-Force Construction* (1921) from the collection of the Maritime Art Gallery in Vladivostok.

Throughout her life, from her early Cubo-Futurist period to her fully developed mature style, Popova tirelessly reworked her compositions to achieve a level of perfection in her Space-Force Constructions. In the creation of her expressive "architectonics" she drew inspiration from her careful study of Italian Renaissance art and her immersion in the images of ancient Russian art. In her drawings perhaps even more clearly than in her paintings, the exploratory atmosphere of Popova's work is captured. The drawings created before 1922 are very similar stylistically to paintings of that period. The thematic content, however, is much richer, as may be seen in the marvelous series of trees (1911–12; similar to cats. 4–6), the portrait drawings (1911–12), and the embroidery sketches for Verbovka (1917; cats. 66a–k).

An abundance of material—works on paper and cardboard—has been preserved from the years 1922–24 when Popova was engaged in production art. Space limitations do not allow a detailed analysis of this part of the collection, but it should be noted that many of Popova's theatrical sketches possess all the immediacy of the completed works. Among the best-known examples are the drawings for the Meyerkhold production of *The Magnanimous Cuckold* (1921–22; cats. 107–110) and the sketches for actors' working clothes for the Meyerkhold Free Studio at Gvytm (1921; cats. 104–106).

The last of Popova's major works was the set design for *Earth in Turmoil* in 1923 (cat. 111). Every conceivable form of technical equipment was included in the original staging, both inside the theater and in the open air where performances sometimes took place. This equipment included bicycles, motorcycles, agricultural implements, even airplanes and balloons, all of which expressed the spirit of the time and introduced a "real" dynamism into the set. Nevertheless, all these practical items, used here in an artistic framework, lost part of their utilitarian meaning and became distinctive "objects."

In an effort to provide a fuller appreciation of Popova's theatrical designs, the organizers of the centennial exhibition displayed a group of reconstructed works side by side with original pieces. For example, a 1927 scale model of the set design for *The Magnanimous Cuckold* was shown, as were dresses made in 1979 for an exhibition at the Galerie Gmurzynska, Cologne, based on Popova's original sketches.

The inclusion of such reconstructions owes a debt to the creative judgment and understanding of the Constructivist character of Popova's late works by Yuri Avvakumov, the young Muscovite designer and architect who installed the show. The original concept for the staging of *Earth in Turmoil* was one of the greatest theatrical projects in the history of the Soviet theater and a good example of Popova's creativity. The photomontage she used for the set of that innovative production was the focal point of the Tretyakov installation. Enlarged to enormous proportions, and viewable from every point of the centennial exhibition, it was the key element used by Avvakumov to unite all of Popova's works: the fabricated constructions on which the works were displayed, the above-mentioned reconstructions, fabrics, display cases with archival materials, enlarged documentary photographs, explanatory panels, and even the staircase of the hall itself. In other words, all elements of this exhibition in honor of Liubov Popova followed Constructivist logic in the celebration and presentation of her work.[5]

notes

1. These are noted in the entries to the catalogue of the centennial exhibition: *L. S. Popova: 1889–1924. Exhibition of Works from the Centennial Exhibition* (Moscow: State Tretyakov Gallery/ARS Publications Limited, 1990).

2. The "Listing," nine typed pages, is in a private archive in Moscow.

3. This resulted in two sets of numbers, and occasionally a single work is inscribed with two different numerals.

4. Because the two lists provided a new basis for dating the works, the information in the Tretyakov catalogue often differs from that in the Popova monograph by Adaskina and Sarabianov as well as from the catalogue raisonné of the Costakis collection, both of which are listed in the bibliography of this volume.

5. Translated from the Russian by Andrew Stivelman.

chronology

1889
April 24: born Liubov Sergeevna Popova in Ivanovskoe, near Moscow, the second of four children of Sergei Maximovich Popov and Liubov Vassilievna Zoubova. Her father, a philanthropist and patron of music and the theater, is a wealthy textile merchant. Early years spent on the family estate Krasnovidovo.

1902
Family moves to Yalta in the Crimea. Attends Yaltinskaya Women's Gymnasium.

1906
Family moves to Moscow.

Attends Arsenieva Gymnasium, then studies for two years at A. S. Alfierov's school, where she receives a degree in literature.

1907
Studies in the private studio of the Impressionist painter Stanislav Zhukovski.

1908
Enters private studios of Konstantin Yuon and Ivan O. Dudin. At that time meets Alexander Vesnin, Liudmila Prudkovskaya (Nadezhda Udaltsova's sister), and Vera Mukhina.

1909
Travels to Kiev and visits the Church of St. Cyril, where the religious works of the Symbolist painter Mikhail Vrubel have enormous psychological impact on her.

1910
Spring: travels to Italy and is greatly impressed by Early Renaissance artists, particularly Giotto and Pinturicchio.

June: visits ancient Russian cities Novgorod and Pskov; discovers icon painting and is influenced by medieval Church art and architecture.

1911
Summer: travels to St. Petersburg and sees collection at Hermitage Museum.

Fall: continues trips to Russian cities: Rostov Veliki, Suzdal, Yurev Polski, Pereyaslavl, and Kiev.

In Moscow, shares studio with Prudkovskaya.

1912
Summer: travels to Yaroslavl with Prudkovskaya.

Works in The Tower, a studio on Kuznetski Most, with Viktor Bart, Kirill Zdanevich, Anna Troyanovskaya, Vladimir Tatlin, Ivan Axionov, and Alexei Grishchenko.

Becomes close friend of Nadezhda Udaltsova.

Visits Sergei Shchukin's private collection (which opened to the public in the spring of 1909) and sees the paintings of Georges Braque and Pablo Picasso for the first time.

Fall–winter 1913: lives in Paris with Udaltsova. Both study under Jean Metzinger and Henri Le Fauconnier at one of the teaching studios within the Académie "La Palette."

October: Metzinger and Albert Gleizes publish *Du Cubisme,* regarded by Russian avant-garde artists as the authoritative source on Cubism.

1913
Visits studios of Ossip Zadkine and Alexander Archipenko.

June 20–July 16: probably sees Boccioni's sculpture exhibition at Galerie La Boëtie. The show includes *Development of a Bottle in Space, Unique Forms of Continuity in Space,* and *Head + House + Light.*

Fall–winter: returns to Russia and works through 1916 in Tatlin's studio at Ostozhenka 37 with Udaltsova, Vesnin, and Alexei Morgunov.

1914
January–February: exhibits for the first time with the Jack of Diamonds group, Moscow. Shows two Cubist paintings alongside works by Udaltsova, Alexandra Exter, Kazimir Malevich, Le Fauconnier, Braque, Picasso, André Derain, and Maurice Vlaminck.

March: returns to Paris with Vera Mukhina.

April: with Mukhina, travels extensively in Italy for two months.

Summer: returns to Russia at the outbreak of World War I and resumes work in Tatlin's studio.

Winter: conducts meetings in her Moscow apartment with the aim of uniting left-wing avant-garde artists. Udaltsova, Vesnin, Grishchenko, the art historians B. P. Vipner and Boris von Eding, and the philosopher P. A. Florenskii are among the participants.

Continues studying medieval Russian art.

Her paintings of this period such as *Seated Female Nude* and *Italian Still Life* reveal influence of both Cubism and Futurism.

1915
March 3: participates in "Tramway V: The First Futurist Exhibition of Paintings," Petrograd, with Tatlin, Malevich, Udaltsova, Exter, Ivan Kliun, Ivan Puni, Olga Rozanova, and others. Tatlin exhibits seven of his counter-reliefs.

Becomes involved with the Cubo-Futurist group surrounding Malevich (including Udaltsova, Kliun, and Rozanova) and their examples of volumetric art. Creates her first Cubist collages and three-dimensional reliefs, which she terms "plastic paintings."

December 19, 1915–January 19, 1916: exhibits in "The Last Futurist Exhibition of Paintings: 0.10," Petrograd. Here Malevich unveils his new Suprematist style and Tatlin exhibits his reliefs. First exhibition of Popova's Cubist reliefs.

Late 1915 or early 1916: begins to paint in non-objective style.

1916
Travels to Samarkand; influenced by Islamic architecture.

March: participates in "The Store," Moscow, a group exhibition organized by Tatlin in a rented empty shop, with Tatlin, Kliun, Pestel, Lev Bruni, and Alexander Rodchenko.

November: participates in "Jack of Diamonds" exhibition, Moscow, with Malevich, Marc Chagall, Kliun, Puni, Rozanova, and Udaltsova. Shows her first non-objective paintings, six Painterly Architectonics. Stylistically, the early non-representational compositions, with their superimposed layering of flat, brightly colored planes suspended in the center of the canvas, display a clear debt to Suprematism.

December 10, 1916–January 14, 1917: two paintings included in the "Modern Russian Painting" exhibition at Nadezhda Dobychina's gallery, Petrograd.

Winter 1916–17: joins Supremus, Malevich's Suprematist artists' association, which includes Natalya Davydova, Exter, Kliun, Alexei Kruchenykh, Mikhail Menkov, Vera Pestel, Rozanova, and Udaltsova. Designs logo for journal of same name, which is never published.

1917
In response to the Revolution, in company with other avant-garde artists, paints public buildings and designs propaganda posters.

Creates collages for embroidered fabric to be produced by the Verbovka company.

1918
Becomes faculty member of Svomas (Free State Art Studios), the post-revolutionary Moscow art schools.

March: marries Boris von Eding, an art historian specializing in ancient Russian architecture.

April: collaborates with Vesnin on creating decorations for the Mossoviet May Day celebration.

Late May–June: exhibits in the "First Exhibition of Paintings of the Professional Association of Artists," Moscow.

November: son born. She virtually stops painting until November 1919.

Her work included in the "Fifth State Exhibition: From Impressionism to Non-objective Art," Moscow.

Her series of Painterly Architectonics of 1918 employs interpenetrating planes and gradations of color in a dynamic articulation of space that applies Constructivist sculptural ideas to the two-dimensional medium.

1919
January: exhibits in "The Tenth State Exhibition: Non-objective Creation and Suprematism," Moscow, with Malevich, Kliun, Rodchenko, Stepanova, and Vesnin.

Summer: travels to Rostov on the Don River with husband and son. Her husband is stricken with typhus and dies. Popova also becomes seriously ill but recovers.

November: returns to Moscow.

December: formation of the Soviet Masterov, or Council of Masters—a direct forerunner of Inkhuk (Institute of Artistic Culture)—by several artists including Vasily Kandinsky, Rodchenko, Stepanova, and Popova.

1920
Begins designing sets and costumes for the theater: Alexander Tairov's production of *Romeo and Juliet* (Popova's sets, deemed too impractical, are rejected in favor of those designed by Exter); Alexander Pushkin's *The Tale of the Priest and His Workman Balda,* for Moscow Children's Theater; Anatoli Lunacharsky's *The Locksmith and the Chancellor* at the Korsh Theater.

Creates maquettes for book covers.

May: Inkhuk is formally established under leadership of Kandinsky. Popova joins and remains active member through 1923.

November 23: first meeting of the General Working Group of Objective Analysis at Inkhuk, during which Kandinsky resigns. On December 25, Alexei Babichev rewrites administrative program to embrace "theoretical" and "laboratory" (or group-oriented) investigations of artistic concepts.

November 29: Svomas reorganized as Vkhutemas (Higher State Artistic and Technical Studios) with the goal of training artists for industrial production. Within the basic course, an introductory program on the fundamentals of design, Popova directs the section on color. In 1921 or 1922 she and Vesnin initiate changes in the class, subsequently called "Color Construction," in which they approach "color as an independent organizational element." She also teaches printing and designing for the theater and mass spectacles.

1921
January–April: at Inkhuk, participates in series of debates on distinction between "composition" and "construction" in order to formulate definition of Constructivism. Discussions lead to splintering of artists into groups; Popova allies herself with Vesnin, Udaltsova, and Alexander Drevin in the Working Group of Objectivists, which holds its first meeting on April 15.

May: collaborates with Vesnin on proposal for mass military spectacle to be directed by Vsevolod Meyerkhold, in celebration of the Spring 1921 meeting of the Third World Congress of the Communist International, Moscow; project is canceled because of financial difficulties.

September–October: "5 × 5 = 25" group exhibition in Moscow consists of five works by five painters: Popova, Rodchenko, Stepanova, Exter, and Vesnin. First exhibition of Popova's Space-Force Constructions. Creates (until 1922) many such paintings on wood and corresponding works on paper, which are characterized by a strong linearity and a limited color range of black, white, and reddish orange. In some, the composition is structured entirely by thin lines intersecting at angles, with heavier lines crossing over them to produce tension between foreground and background space. Others introduce circular and arc shapes.

November: as a result of third restructuring of Inkhuk, signs proclamation with twenty-five fellow artists rejecting easel painting in favor of utilitarian art forms.

December: writes article in support of production art ("Concerning New Methods in Our Art Schools") at request of Inkhuk governing board.

Meyerkhold admires her work in "5 × 5 = 25" and invites her to teach course in set design, "Analysis of the Elements of Material Design," at his State Higher Theatrical Studios, Gvytm (later renamed State Institute of Theatrical Art, Gtis). Sergei Eisenstein is one of her students.

1922

April 25 and 26: premiere of Meyerkhold's production of Fernand Crommelynck's *The Magnanimous Cuckold,* designed by Popova. Her mobile Constructivist sets and "production clothing" costumes emphasizing functionalism are a great success.

April 27: lectures at Inkhuk about her innovations in theater design.

Fall: exhibits several works in the "First Russian Art Exhibition," at the Galerie van Diemen, Berlin. Of four works on paper in the show, two are purchased from the gallery by Katherine Dreier. Both are now in the collection of the Yale University Art Gallery.

1923

March 4: premiere of Meyerkhold's production of *Earth in Turmoil,* Sergei Tretyakov's version of Marcel Martinet's *La Nuit.* Popova composes sets that make use of industrial objects, screened projection of political slogans and photographs, leaflets dropped from a model airplane, and automobile fumes pumped into the theater.

Through 1924, works with Stepanova at the First State Textile Print Factory (formerly the Emil Tsindel Factory), Moscow, creating textile and dress designs for mass production. Focuses on adaptability of fashion to movement of the body. Also executes designs for posters, book covers, and porcelain.

1924

Contracts scarlet fever from her son, who dies.

May 25: dies of scarlet fever, Moscow.

December 21, 1924–January 1925: posthumous retrospective, Stroganov Institute, Moscow, includes seventy-seven paintings, as well as book, poster, and textile designs, and line engravings.

bibliography

Books

Adaskina, Natalia A., and Dimitri V. Sarabianov. *Lioubov Popova.* Paris: Philippe Sers, 1989; New York: Harry N. Abrams, 1990.

Carandente, Giovanni, ed. *Arte Russa e Sovietica.* Milan: Fabbri Editori, 1989.

Gray, Camilla. *The Great Experiment: Russian Art 1863–1922.* New York: Harry N. Abrams, 1962.

Lodder, Christina. *Russian Constructivism.* New Haven: Yale University Press, 1983.

Rudenstine, Angelica Z., ed. *The George Costakis Collection: Russian Avant-Garde Art.* New York: Harry N. Abrams, 1981.

Yablonskaya, M. N. *Women Artists of Russia's New Age: 1900–1935.* New York: Rizzoli International Publications, 1990.

Exhibition Catalogues

Art and Revolution. Essays by A. A. Strigalev and Y. Nakahara. Tokyo: The Seibu Museum of Art, 1982.

Art into Life. Introduction by Richard Andrews and Milena Kalinovska. Essays by J. Andel, S. Bann, H. Foster, S. O. Khan-Magomedov, C. Lodder, A. Senkevitch, Jr., and A. Strigalev. Artist biographies by Owen Smith. Seattle: Henry Art Gallery, University of Washington, 1990.

Bakos, Katalin, ed. *Art and Revolution: Russian and Soviet Art 1910–1932.* Vienna: Austrian Museum of Applied Arts, 1988.

Douglas, Charlotte. *Liubov Popova: Spatial Force Constructions, 1921–22.* New York: Rachel Adler Gallery, 1985.

Kersting, Hannelore, and Bernd Vogelsang. *Raumkonzepte: Konstruktivistische Tendenzen in Bühnen- und Bildkunst 1910–1930.* Frankfurt: Städtische Galerie im Städelschen Kunstinstitut, 1986.

Marcadé, Jean-Claude, and Valentine Marcadé. *L'Avant-Garde au Feminin: Moscou—Saint-Petersbourg—Paris 1907–1930.* Paris: Artcurial, Centre d'Art Plastique Contemporain, 1983.

Nakov, Andréi B. *Russian Pioneers: At the Origins of Non-objective Art.* London: Annely Juda Fine Art, 1976.

L. S. Popova, 1889–1924: Katalog posmertnoy vystavki khuidozhnika konstruktora L. S. Popovoy (Catalogue of the Posthumous Exhibition of the Artist-Constructor L. S. Popova). Moscow, 1924.

Rakitin, Vasilii. "Ljubow Popowa." In Krystyna Rubinger, ed. *Women Artists of the Russian Avant-Garde: 1910–1930.* Cologne: Galerie Gmurzynska, 1980. Artist's biography by John E. Bowlt, p. 174. Excerpts from the artist's manuscripts and notes, pp. 211–14.

Rowell, Margit, and Angelica Zander Rudenstine. *Art of the Avant-Garde in Russia: Selections from the George Costakis Collection.* New York: Solomon R. Guggenheim Museum, 1981.

Sarabianov, Dimitri. "The Painting of Liubov Popova." In Stephanie Barron and Maurice Tuchman, eds. *The Avant-Garde in Russia, 1910–1930: New Perspectives.* Los Angeles: Los Angeles County Museum of Art, 1980.

Sarabianov, Dimitri. "Space in Painting and Design." In Krystyna Rubinger, ed. *From Painting to Design: Russian Constructivist Art of the Twenties.* Cologne: Galerie Gmurzynska, 1981.

Starr, S. Frederick. "Foreword." In *Russian Avant-Garde 1908–1922.* Essay by John E. Bowlt. New York: Leonard Hutton Galleries, 1971.

Weiss, Evelyn. *Avantguarda Russa 1910–1930. Museu i Col.lecció Ludwig.* Barcelona: Fundació Joan Miró, 1985.

Articles

Bowlt, John E. "From Surface to Space: The Art of Liubov Popova," *The Structurist* (Saskatoon, Saskatchewan, Canada), nos. 15–16 (1975–76), pp. 80–88.

Peck, George, and Lilly Wei. "Liubov Popova: Interpretation of Space," *Art in America,* October 1982, pp. 94–104.

catalogue of the exhibition

In the following entries, the works of art are listed by catalogue number within a chronological framework. The title or description of each work is given in boldface type and followed by the date of the work, its medium, and dimensions. The latter are given in inches and centimeters, height preceding width. This information is followed by the name of the present owner of the work. A page reference in italics at the end of the entry indicates a plate illustration.

1. Still Life
1907–08
Oil on canvas
27¾ × 21⅛" (70.6 × 53.7 cm)
George Costakis Collection (Art Co. Ltd.)
Page 33

2. Untitled
c. 1908
Ink and wash on paper
17⅝ × 13¾" (45 × 34.9 cm)
George Costakis Collection (Art Co. Ltd.)
Page 34

3. Untitled
c. 1908
Ink and wash on paper
14 × 8⅞" (35.6 × 22.5 cm)
George Costakis Collection (Art Co. Ltd.)
Page 34

4. Untitled (Tree)
c. 1911–12
India ink and wash on paper
14 × 8⅞" (35.6 × 22.5 cm)
Private collection, courtesy Leonard Hutton Galleries, New York
Page 34

5. Untitled (Blooming Tree)
c. 1911–12
India ink and wash on paper
14 × 8¾" (35.6 × 22.2 cm)
Private collection, courtesy Leonard Hutton Galleries, New York
Page 34

6. Trees
1911–12
Oil on canvas
23⅞ × 18¾" (60.5 × 47.5 cm)
Private collection, Moscow
Page 35

7. Female Model
early 1910s
Pencil on paper
10½ × 8½" (26.7 × 21.6 cm)
State Tretyakov Gallery, Moscow

8. Female Model
early 1910s
Pencil on paper
10½ × 8½" (26.7 × 21.6 cm)
State Tretyakov Gallery, Moscow

9. Male Model
c. 1910
Oil on canvas
39 × 30" (99 × 76 cm)
State Tretyakov Gallery, Moscow
Gift of George Costakis
Page 35

10. Study of a Model
c. 1913
Oil on canvas
41¾ × 27¾" (106 × 70.6 cm)
State Tretyakov Gallery, Moscow
Gift of George Costakis
Page 36

11. Composition with Figures
1913
Oil on canvas
63⅜ × 48⅜" (161 × 123 cm)
State Tretyakov Gallery, Moscow
Gift of George Costakis
Page 36

12. Seated Woman
1913–14
Oil on canvas
24 × 19⅝" (61 × 50 cm)
Galerie Gmurzynska, Cologne
Page 37

13. Seated Figure
c. 1913–14
Pencil on paper
10½ × 8¼" (26.7 × 21 cm)
George Costakis Collection (Art Co. Ltd.)
Page 38

14. Seated Female Nude
c. 1913–14
Oil on canvas
41¾ × 34¼" (106 × 87 cm)
Museum Ludwig, Cologne
Page 38

15. Figure + House + Space
1913–14
Oil on canvas
49¼ × 42⅛" (125 × 107 cm)
State Russian Museum, Leningrad
Page 39

16. Man's Head
1913–14
Pencil on paper
10½ × 8½" (26.7 × 21.6 cm)
State Tretyakov Gallery, Moscow

17. Anatomical Study
c. 1913–14
Pencil on paper
10½ × 8⅛" (26.7 × 20.6 cm)
George Costakis Collection (Art Co. Ltd.)
Page 40

18. Standing Figure
c. 1913–14
Pencil on paper
10½ × 8⅛" (26.7 × 20.6 cm)
George Costakis Collection (Art Co. Ltd.)
Page 40

19. Anatomical Study
c. 1914
Pencil on paper
10½ × 8⅛" (26.7 × 21.6 cm)
George Costakis Collection (Art Co. Ltd.)
Page 41

20. Seated Figure
c. 1914
Pencil on paper
8½ × 6⅝" (21.6 × 16.8 cm)
George Costakis Collection (Art Co. Ltd.)
Page 41

21. Female Model
1914
Pencil on paper
10½ × 8½" (26.7 × 21.6 cm)
State Tretyakov Gallery, Moscow
Page 10

22. Cubist Cityscape
1914
Oil on canvas
41 × 34" (104 × 86.5 cm)
Private collection, Switzerland
Page 42

23. Objects from the Dyer's Shop (Early Morning)
1914
Oil on canvas
28 × 35" (71 × 89 cm)
The Museum of Modern Art, New York
The Riklis Collection of McCrory Corporation (fractional gift)
Page 43

24. Italian Still Life
1914
Oil, plaster, and paper collage on canvas
24¼ × 19" (61.5 × 48 cm)
State Tretyakov Gallery, Moscow
Page 44

25. Still Life
1914
Oil on canvas
34⅝ × 22⅝" (88 × 57.5 cm)
Museum Ludwig, Cologne
Page 45

26. Still Life with Guitar
1914–15
Oil on canvas
26 × 18⅛" (66 × 46 cm)
Galerie Gmurzynska, Cologne
Page 46

27. The Pianist
1915
Oil on canvas
41⅞ × 34⅞" (106.5 × 88.7 cm)
National Gallery of Canada, Ottawa
Page 47

28. Lady with a Guitar
1915
Oil on canvas
42⅛ × 28⅛" (107 × 71.5 cm)
State Museum of History, Architecture, and Fine Arts, Smolensk
Page 48

29. Violin
1915
Oil on canvas
34⅞ × 27¾" (88.7 × 70.6 cm)
State Tretyakov Gallery, Moscow
Page 48

30. Objects
1915
Oil on canvas
24 × 17½" (61 × 44.5 cm)
State Russian Museum, Leningrad
Page 49

31. Sketch for a Portrait
1915
Pencil on paper
14⅛ × 8½" (35.9 × 21.6 cm)
Private collection, Moscow

32. Study for a Portrait
1915
Oil and marble dust on canvas
27¾ × 18½" (70.6 × 47 cm)
Private collection, Moscow
Page 50

33. Portrait
1915
Oil on paperboard
23½ × 16⅜" (59.5 × 41.6 cm)
George Costakis Collection (Art Co. Ltd.)
Page 51

34. Study for Portrait of a Philosopher
1915
Black gouache on pasteboard
20½ × 14⅞" (52 × 37.8 cm)
State Tretyakov Gallery, Moscow
Page 52

35. Portrait of a Philosopher
1915
Oil on canvas
35 × 24¾" (89 × 63 cm)
State Russian Museum, Leningrad
Page 53

36. Traveling Woman
1915
Oil on canvas
56 × 41½" (142.2 × 105.5 cm)
Norton Simon Art Foundation
Page 54 (not in the exhibition)

37. Traveling Woman
1915
Oil on canvas
62⅜ × 48½" (158.5 × 123 cm)
George Costakis Collection (Art Co. Ltd.)
Page 55

38. Study for a Two-Figure Composition
1915
Charcoal on paper
17½ × 13⅞" (44.5 × 35.2 cm)
Private collection, Moscow
Page 52

39. Study
1915
Pencil on paper
10½ × 8⅛" (26.7 × 20.6 cm)
George Costakis Collection (Art Co. Ltd.)
Page 52

40. Portrait of a Lady (Plastic Drawing)
1915
Oil on paper and cardboard on wood
26⅛ × 19⅛" (66.3 × 48.5 cm)
Museum Ludwig, Cologne
Page 56

41. The Jug on the Table (Plastic Painting)
1915
Oil on cardboard mounted on wood
23¼ × 17⅞" (59.1 × 45.3 cm)
State Tretyakov Gallery, Moscow
Gift of George Costakis
Page 57

42. The Grocery Store
1916
Oil on canvas
21¼ × 16⅞" (54 × 42.9 cm)
State Russian Museum, Leningrad
Page 58

43. Box Factory
1916
Gouache on paper mounted on board
16½ × 12¼" (41.9 × 31.1 cm)
Collection Ruth and Marvin Sackner
Page 59

44. Birsk
1916
Oil on canvas
41¾ × 27⅜" (106 × 69.5 cm)
Solomon R. Guggenheim Museum, New York
Gift of George Costakis
Page 59

45. Study for Painterly Architectonic
1916
Watercolor, gouache, and pencil on paper
13⅜ × 8½" (34 × 21.6 cm)
Private collection, Moscow

46. Painterly Architectonic (Still Life: Instruments)
1916
Oil on canvas
41½ × 27¼" (105.5 × 69.2 cm)
Thyssen-Bornemisza Collection, Lugano, Switzerland
Page 60

47. Painterly Architectonic with Three Stripes
1916
Oil on canvas
42⅛ × 35" (107 × 89 cm)
Private collection, Moscow
Page 62

48. Painterly Architectonic
1916
Oil on canvas
20⅛ × 13" (51 × 33 cm)
State Russian Museum, Leningrad
Page 63

49. Painterly Architectonic with Yellow Board
1916
Oil on canvas
34½ × 30⅝" (87.5 × 78 cm)
State Tretyakov Gallery, Moscow
Gift of George Costakis
Page 63

50. Painterly Architectonic
1916
Gouache, India ink, and pencil on paper
13⅛ × 9⅝" (33.3 × 24.4 cm)
Private collection, Moscow

51. Painterly Architectonic
1916
Watercolor, gouache, and pencil on paper
7½ × 5⅜" (19 × 13.5 cm)
Private collection, Moscow

52. Study for Painterly Architectonic
1916
India ink and gouache on paper
7 × 4¾" (17.8 × 12.1 cm)
Private collection, Moscow

53. Painterly Architectonic: Black, Red, Gray
1916
Oil on canvas
35⅛ × 27⅞" (89 × 71 cm)
State Tretyakov Gallery, Moscow
Gift of George Costakis
Page 64

54. Painterly Architectonic
1916
Gouache and pencil on paper glued to pasteboard
7 × 4¾" (17.8 × 12.1 cm)
Private collection, Moscow

55. Painterly Architectonic
1916
Oil on board
23½ × 15½" (59.5 × 39.4 cm)
Scottish National Gallery of Modern Art, Edinburgh
Page 65

56a. (recto)
Painterly Architectonic
1916–17
Oil on canvas
62½ × 49⅛" (159 × 124.8 cm)
State Tretyakov Gallery, Moscow
Gift of George Costakis
Page 66

56b. (verso)
Painterly Construction
1920
Oil on canvas
62½ × 49⅛" (159 × 124.8 cm)
State Tretyakov Gallery, Moscow
Gift of George Costakis
Page 67

57. Cover Design for the Society of Painters Supremus
1916–17
Ink on paper
3½ × 3⅛" (8.9 × 7.9 cm)
George Costakis Collection (Art Co. Ltd.)
Page 68

58. Untitled
c. 1916–17
Gouache on cardboard
19½ × 15½" (49.5 × 39.4 cm)
The Museum of Modern Art, New York
The Riklis Collection of McCrory Corporation (fractional gift)
Page 68

59. Painterly Architectonic
1916–17
Oil on canvas
17⅛ × 17¼" (43.5 × 43.9 cm)
George Costakis Collection (Art Co. Ltd.)
Page 69

60. Pictorial Architectonic
1916–17
Oil on canvas
41½ × 27¾" (105.5 × 70.6 cm)
Private collection, Switzerland
Page 70

61. Painterly Architectonic
1917
Oil on canvas
31½ × 38⅝" (80 × 98 cm)
The Museum of Modern Art, New York
Philip Johnson Fund
Page 71

62. Study for Painterly Architectonic
c. 1917
Gouache and pencil on paper
6⅞ × 4¾" (17.5 × 12.1 cm)
Private collection, Moscow

63. Untitled
1917
Cut-and-pasted paper mounted on paper
9⅜ × 6⅛" (23.8 × 15.6 cm)
The Museum of Modern Art, New York
Gift of Mr. and Mrs. Richard Deutsch
Page 72

64. Composition
1917
Gouache on paper
13⅛ × 9⅝" (33.3 × 24.4 cm)
Private collection
Page 72

65. Composition
1917
Gouache on paper
13⅝ × 10¾" (34.6 × 27.3 cm)
Private collection
Page 73

66a–k. Embroidery designs for Verbovka
1917
a. colored paper collage on gray cardboard
3⅜ × 6½" (8.6 × 16.5 cm)
b. colored paper collage on gray cardboard
2¾ × 6" (7 × 15.2 cm)
c. colored paper collage on gray cardboard
2⅞ × 7⅞" (7.3 × 20 cm)
d. colored paper collage on paper
4½ × 9⅛" (11.4 × 23.2 cm)
e. colored paper collage on paper
6 × 4⅜" (15.2 × 11.1 cm)
f. colored paper collage on gray cardboard
2 × 2⅛" (5.1 × 5.4 cm) and
colored paper collage on gray cardboard
2 × 2⅛" (5.1 × 5.4 cm)
g. colored paper collage on paper
5½ × 5" (13.9 × 12.7 cm)
h. colored paper collage on paper
7⅜ × 6⅛" (18.7 × 15.6 cm)
i. colored paper collage on paper
6⅞ × 6⅛" (17.5 × 15.6 cm)
j. colored paper collage on paper
5⅜ × 3⅜" (13.7 × 8.6 cm)
k. colored paper collage on paper
6⅛ × 9¼" (15.6 × 23.5 cm)
Private collection, Moscow

67. Untitled
1917
Pencil and colored pencil on paper
13⅛ × 9⅝" (33.3 × 24.4 cm)
Private collection, courtesy Leonard Hutton Galleries, New York
Page 74

68. Untitled
c. 1917–19
Gouache, watercolor, and pencil on paper
12⅞ × 9⅝" (32.7 × 24.4 cm)
Private collection, courtesy Leonard Hutton Galleries, New York
Page 74

69. Untitled
c. 1917–19
Watercolor, pencil, and ink on paper
13⅞ × 8¾" (35.2 × 22.2 cm)
George Costakis Collection (Art Co. Ltd.)

70a–g. Portfolio: *Six Prints*
c. 1917–19
Seven linoleum cuts, printed in color
a. (cover)
16⅜ × 11¾″ (41.6 × 29.8 cm)
b. 13¾ × 10⅛″ (34.9 × 25.7 cm)
c. 13½ × 10¼″ (34.3 × 26 cm)
d. 13½ × 10¼″ (34.3 × 26 cm)
e. 12⅞ × 9½″ (32.7 × 24.1 cm)
f. 13½ × 10¼″ (34.3 × 26 cm)
g. 13⅜ × 10¼″ (34 × 26 cm)
George Costakis Collection (Art Co. Ltd.)
Pages 75–76

71. Painterly Architectonic
1918
Gouache and watercolor with touches of varnish on paper
11½ × 9¼″ (29.3 × 23.5 cm)
Yale University Art Gallery
Gift from the Estate of Katherine S. Dreier
Page 77

72. Painterly Architectonic
1918
Oil on board
23⅜ × 15½″ (59.2 × 39.4 cm)
Private collection, courtesy Leonard Hutton Galleries, New York
Page 78

73. Painterly Architectonic
1918
Oil on canvas
17¾ × 20⅞″ (45 × 53 cm)
Thyssen-Bornemisza Collection, Lugano, Switzerland
Page 61 (not in the exhibition)

74. Painterly Architectonic
1918
Oil on canvas
24½ × 17½″ (62.2 × 44.5 cm)
State Tretyakov Gallery, Moscow
Page 79

75. Painterly Architectonic
1918
Oil on canvas
22⅞ × 20⅞″ (58 × 53 cm)
State Museum of Fine Arts, Gorky
Page 80

76. Painterly Architectonic
1918
Oil on board
20½ × 17½″ (52 × 44.5 cm)
Private collection
Page 81

77. Painterly Architectonic
1918–19
Oil on canvas
27⅞ × 22⅞″ (71 × 58.1 cm)
George Costakis Collection (Art Co. Ltd.)
Page 82

78. Painterly Architectonic
1918–19
Oil on canvas
28¾ × 18⅞″ (73.1 × 48.1 cm)
George Costakis Collection (Art Co. Ltd.)
Page 83

79. Composition
1920
Gouache and paper collage on paper
11¾ × 9⅛″ (29.8 × 23.2 cm)
Private collection, courtesy Leonard Hutton Galleries, New York
Page 84

80. Composition
1920
Gouache and paper collage on paper
17½ × 11¾″ (44.5 × 29.8 cm)
Private collection, courtesy Leonard Hutton Galleries, New York
Page 85

81. Construction
1920
Oil on canvas
42 × 34⅞″ (106.8 × 88.7 cm)
State Tretyakov Gallery, Moscow
Page 86

82. Construction with White Crescent
1920–21
Gouache on cardboard
13⅛ × 10⅝″ (33.3 × 27 cm)
State Tretyakov Gallery, Moscow
Gift of George Costakis
Page 87

83. Construction with White Crescent
1921
Gouache on board
13¼ × 10¼″ (33.7 × 26 cm)
Collection Thomas P. Whitney
Page 87

84. Composition
1921
Gouache on paper
13½ × 10⅞″ (34.3 × 27.6 cm)
George Costakis Collection (Art Co. Ltd.)
Page 88

85. Space-Force Construction
1921
Colored crayons on paper
10⅞ × 8⅛″ (27.6 × 20.6 cm)
Private collection, courtesy Leonard Hutton Galleries, New York
Page 88

86. Space-Force Construction
1921
Oil with marble dust on plywood
44⅜ × 44⅜″ (112.7 × 112.7 cm)
George Costakis Collection (Art Co. Ltd.)
Page 89

87. Space-Force Construction
1921
Colored pencil on paper
13⅞ × 8½″ (35.2 × 21.6 cm)
George Costakis Collection (Art Co. Ltd.)
Page 90

88. Space-Force Construction
1921
Oil with bronze powder and marble dust on plywood
27⅝ × 20⅜″ (70 × 51.6 cm)
State Tretyakov Gallery, Moscow
Page 90

89. Space-Force Construction
1921
Oil over pencil on plywood
48⅞ × 32¼" (124 × 82 cm)
State Tretyakov Gallery, Moscow
Gift of George Costakis
Page 91

90. Constructivist Composition
1921
Oil on board
36⅝ × 24¼" (93 × 61.5 cm)
Private collection
Page 92

91. Composition No. 47
1921
Gouache, watercolor, India ink,
and pencil on paper
20 × 13¾" (50.7 × 34.9 cm)
Private collection, Stockholm
Page 93

92. Design for Cover of Exhibition Catalogue *5 × 5 = 25*
1921
Collage, India ink, and colored crayons
on gray paper
8½ × 6¾" (21.6 × 17.1 cm)
Private collection, courtesy Leonard Hutton
Galleries, New York
Page 95

93. Vern 34
c. 1921
Watercolor and gouache on paper
13¾ × 10¾" (34.9 × 27.3 cm)
George Costakis Collection (Art Co. Ltd.)
Page 94

94. Space-Force Construction
1921
Oil on plywood
32⅞ × 25⅜" (83.5 × 64.5 cm)
State Tretyakov Gallery, Moscow
Gift of George Costakis
Page 96

95. Space-Force Construction
1921
Oil on plywood
25⅛ × 23⅝" (64 × 60 cm)
State Tretyakov Gallery, Moscow
Gift of George Costakis
Page 97

96. Space-Force Construction
1921
Oil with marble dust on plywood
27⅞ × 25⅛" (71 × 64 cm)
George Costakis Collection (Art Co. Ltd.)
Page 98

97. Space-Force Construction
1921
Oil and gouache on board
13¾ × 10¾" (34.9 × 27.3 cm)
Private collection, courtesy Leonard Hutton
Galleries, New York
Page 99

98a–e. The City
1921
Five linoleum cuts, printed in color
a. 4⅝ × 3¼" (11.7 × 8.3 cm)
b. 10⅞ × 6¾" (27.6 × 17.1 cm) and
6½ × 5½" (16.5 × 13.9 cm)
c. 6½ × 5½" (16.5 × 13.9 cm)
d. 6½ × 2¾" (16.5 × 7 cm)
e. 6½ × 2½" (16.5 × 6.4 cm)
State Tretyakov Gallery, Moscow

99. Space-Force Construction
1921
Ink on paper
17 × 10⅞" (43.2 × 27.6 cm)
George Costakis Collection (Art Co. Ltd.)
Page 100

100. Untitled
1921
Ink on paper
13⅜ × 10⅛" (34 × 25.7 cm)
George Costakis Collection (Art Co. Ltd.)
Page 101

101. Med Vervis
c. 1921
Brush and India ink and watercolor on paper
13⅝ × 10⅞" (34.6 × 27.6 cm)
Collection Robert and Maurine Rothschild
Page 101

102. Space-Force Construction
1921
Red and black pencil on paper
10⅞ × 8⅛" (27.6 × 20.6 cm)
State Tretyakov Gallery, Moscow
Page 102

103. Space-Force Construction
1921–22
Watercolor on paper
18⅛ × 15¾" (46 × 40 cm)
State Tretyakov Gallery, Moscow
Gift of George Costakis
Page 103

104. Working Clothes for Actor No. 5
1921
Gouache, India ink, and paper collage
on paper
13½ × 9⅝" (34.3 × 24.4 cm)
Private collection, Moscow
Page 104

105. Working Clothes for Actor No. 6
1921
Gouache, India ink, and paper collage
on paper
12⅞ × 9⅜" (32.7 × 23.8 cm)
George Costakis Collection (Art Co. Ltd.)
Page 104

106. Working Clothes for Actor No. 7
1921
Gouache, India ink, varnish, and paper collage
on paper glued to pasteboard
13⅜ × 9⅞" (34 × 25.1 cm)
Private collection, Moscow
Page 105

107. Design for Stage Set of *The Magnanimous Cuckold*
1921–22
Pencil on paper
10⅝ × 8⅛" (27 × 20.6 cm)
State Tretyakov Gallery, Moscow

108. Design for Stage Set of *The Magnanimous Cuckold*
1921–22
Pencil on paper
10⅜ × 8⅛" (26.4 × 20.6 cm)
State Tretyakov Gallery, Moscow

109. Design for Stage Set of *The Magnanimous Cuckold*
1921–22
Watercolor and pencil on paper
8⅝ × 10¾" (21.9 × 27.3 cm)
State Tretyakov Gallery, Moscow
Page 106 (not in the exhibition)

110. Design for Stage Set of *The Magnanimous Cuckold*
1922
India ink, watercolor, paper collage, and varnish on paper
19¾ × 27¼" (50 × 69.2 cm)
State Tretyakov Gallery, Moscow
Page 106

111. Design for Stage Set of *Zemla Dybom (Earth in Turmoil)*
1923
Photomontage, gouache, newspaper, and photographic-paper collage on plywood
19⅜ × 32⅝" (49 × 82.7 cm)
George Costakis Collection (Art Co. Ltd.)
Page 107

112. Design for Cover of Music Journal *K Novym Beregam (Toward New Shores)*, No. 1
1923
Gouache and paper collage on paper
9⅞ × 7⅜" (25.1 × 18.7 cm)
George Costakis Collection (Art Co. Ltd.)
Page 108

113. Design for Cover of Music Journal *K Novym Beregam (Toward New Shores)*, No. 1
1923
India ink and gouache on paper
9⅝ × 7⅜" (24.4 × 18.7 cm)
Private collection, Moscow

114. Design for Cover of *Muzyka (Music)*, No. 1
1923
Black and colored paper collage and India ink on paper
9½ × 7¼" (24.1 × 18.4 cm)
State Tretyakov Gallery, Moscow

115. Design for Cover of Journal *Artisty Kino (Film Artists)*, No. 2
c. 1922–24
Gouache on board
9¼ × 6¼" (23.5 × 15.9 cm)
George Costakis Collection (Art Co. Ltd.)
Page 109

116. Textile Design
c. 1923–24
Gouache and pencil on paper
11 × 13¾" (27.9 × 34.9 cm)
George Costakis Collection (Art Co. Ltd.)
Page 110

117. Embroidered Book Cover
c. 1923–24
Silk thread on grosgrain
17¾ × 12⅜" (45 × 31.4 cm)
George Costakis Collection (Art Co. Ltd.)
Page 110

118. Textile Design with Red Triangle within a Circle
1923–24
Gouache and colored-paper collage on paper
15⅛ × 14⅝" (38.4 × 37.1 cm)
Private collection, Moscow
Page 111

119. Textile Design with Black and Blue Striped Diamonds
1923–24
Colored India ink on paper
9⅝ × 6⅜" (24.4 × 16.2 cm)
State Museum of Decorative and Applied Art of the People of the U.S.S.R., Tsaritsino

120. Textile Design with Concentric Circles
1923–24
India ink and gouache on paper
12⅜ × 10" (31.4 × 25.4 cm)
State Museum of Decorative and Applied Art of the People of the U.S.S.R., Tsaritsino

121. Textile Design with Triangles
1923–24
Colored India ink and paper collage on paper
7⅝ × 5⅜" (19.4 × 13.7 cm)
State Museum of Decorative and Applied Art of the People of the U.S.S.R., Tsaritsino

122. Textile Design with Truncated Triangles
1923–24
Colored and black India ink on paper
9¾ × 6¾" (24.8 × 17.1 cm)
State Museum of Decorative and Applied Art of the People of the U.S.S.R., Tsaritsino
Page 111

lenders to the exhibition

Solomon R. Guggenheim Museum, New York
Museum Ludwig, Cologne
The Museum of Modern Art, New York
National Gallery of Canada, Ottawa
Scottish National Gallery of Modern Art, Edinburgh
State Museum of Decorative and Applied Art of the People of the U.S.S.R., Tsaritsino
State Museum of Fine Arts, Gorky
State Museum of History, Architecture, and Fine Arts, Smolensk
State Russian Museum, Leningrad
State Tretyakov Gallery, Moscow
Yale University Art Gallery

George Costakis Collection (Art Co. Ltd.)
Gaby and Werner Merzbacher
Robert and Maurine Rothschild
Ruth and Marvin Sackner
Thyssen-Bornemisza Collection, Lugano, Switzerland
Thomas P. Whitney
Four anonymous lenders

Galerie Gmurzynska, Cologne
Leonard Hutton Galleries, New York

trustees of the museum of modern art

photograph credits

The photographers and sources of the illustrations are listed alphabetically below, followed by the number of the page on which each illustration appears.

© George Costakis Collection (Art Co. Ltd.): 33, 38 left, 40 left and right, 41 left and right, 51, 52 top right, 55, 57, 63 right, 68 top, 69, 75, 76, 82, 83, 87 left, 88 left, 89, 90, 94, 97, 98, 100, 101, 104 right, 107, 108, 109, 110 left and right.

Antoni E. Dolinski, Norton Simon Art Foundation: 54.

Pierre Dupuy: 87 right.

Galerie Gmurzynska, Cologne: 37, 46, 93.

© 1990 The Solomon R. Guggenheim Foundation: David Heald, 59 left; Robert E. Mates, 14 bottom.

Private collection, courtesy Leonard Hutton Galleries, New York: 78, 84, 85, 88 right, 91.

Geraldine T. Mancini, Yale University Art Gallery: 77.

The Museum of Modern Art: 12 top and bottom, 13 bottom, 15 top and bottom, 16 top and bottom, 17 bottom, 18, 22 bottom, 101 right; Kate Keller, 22 top, 24, 34 top left and right, 71, 72 left; Mali Olatunji, 43; Sandak, Inc., 68 bottom; Soichi Sunami, 14 top.

Eugena Ordonez: 112, 114, 115.

Philadelphia Museum of Art: 13 top.

Courtesy private collection: 72 right, 73, 81, 92, 95.

Courtesy private collection, Switzerland: 70.

Rheinisches Bildarchiv, Cologne: 38 right, 45, 56.

Earl Ripling: 34 bottom left and right, 74 left and right.

Courtesy Ruth and Marvin Sackner: 59 right.

John Sargent, National Gallery of Canada, Ottawa: 47.

Scottish National Gallery of Modern Art, Edinburgh: cover, 65.

Philippe Sers: 17 top.

State Russian Museum, Leningrad: 39, 49, 53, 58, 63 left.

State Tretyakov Gallery, Moscow, courtesy ARS Publications Limited: 10, 35 left and right, 36 left and right, 39, 44, 48 left and right, 50, 52 left and bottom right, 53, 58, 62, 63 left, 64, 66, 67, 79, 80, 86, 90 right, 91, 96, 102, 103, 104 left, 105, 106 top and bottom, 111 top and bottom, 118.

Thyssen-Bornemisza Collection, Lugano, Switzerland: 60, 61.